T0329489

IN SEARCH OF HARMONY

In Search of Harmony
in a Disharmonious World

Leadership Manual for
Change Agents and Dreamers

Velimir Srića

Algora Publishing
New York

Library of Congress Cataloging-in-Publication Data —

Srica, Velimir.
    In search of harmony in a disharmonious world / Velimir Srica.
        pages cm
    Includes bibliographical references and index.
    ISBN 978-1-62894-090-9 (soft cover: alk. paper) — ISBN 978-1-62894-091-6 (hard
cover: alk. paper) — ISBN 978-1-62894-092-3 (ebook) 1. Leadership. I. Title.
    HD57.7.S69953 2014
    658.4'092—dc23

                        2014025805

Printed in the United States

Table of Contents

PREFACE

This book owes its existence to a few proverbs. The first says that mistakes are the doorways to discovery. I have done many different things in life and managed to learn a lot by trial and error. You may think OK, wise men learn from others' mistakes; the fools from their own; but that's just another proverb. My trials, errors and successes have been painful and rewarding, foolish and clever, sour and sweet, and, above all, enlightening; enough to encourage me to write this book.

My CV might give the impression of a *Jack of all trades, master of none*. Or, if you are a kind person, you might prefer *the more, the merrier*. I have been fortunate enough to live, lead, consult, engage in politics, learn and teach in the exciting environments of the developed West, the emerging East and the transitional Central Europe. This has enabled me to fully enjoy a variety of challenges, positions, responsibilities and areas of work, providing me with a rather unique insight, and it is all reflected in this book. I hope you will enjoy reading it as much as I enjoyed writing it.

It is an unusual book because, like my biography, it tries to build bridges and discover synergies among different topics and approaches. It deals with philosophy, sociology, futurology, the economy, politics, and technology at the same time. It draws on management consulting, civil service, political practice, scientific research, teaching, novel writing and journalism. However, there is a common denominator. According to Abraham Maslow, if the only tool you have is a hammer, you tend to see every problem as a nail. I guess my hammers are leadership and organizational culture, and to me everything looks like an opportunity to "hammer out" a solution aiming for harmony.

As a teenager, I played in a rock band and music is still my favorite hobby.

According to dictionaries, harmony is such state of a system in which all the components are pleasingly, or appropriately, combined in agreement or accord. Or, simply stated, it all sounds right. In this sense, the book is dedicated to the search for harmony in a disharmonious world. If you want me to push the musical analogy further, leadership is the key, the leader is the player, values are the score, and the whole globe and all its organizational units are the instruments. Along this line, the book is meant to lift us above the noise and teach us how to replace the growing cacophony with sounds of music which please the ear and the soul.

Finally, it is a book intended to build your appetite for change and provide you with a few ideas where to start. If you are satisfied with your life, your job and the world as is, don't waste your time on this text; buy a musical instrument, a novel or a book of poetry instead. But if you are a change agent, a dreamer, or a dormant revolutionary, join me and, maybe together we can, at least a little, improve the world's harmony. However, if we want our dream come true, we must learn to be leaders. If we don't, those who foster disharmony will lead us into a nightmare!

PART 1 — SETTING THE STAGE FOR REFOLUTION

> A good horse has many faults; a bad one has only one—it's a
> lemon.
>
> Croatian proverb

1.1. How Do Aliens See Us?

Imagine an alien spy on a mission to study Earth over the last ten years. All he has to do is analyze the headline news. Choosing at random, what would he find? In 2008, the first truly global economic crisis started. Six years later, the recession is still here and most analysts wonder for how long. Another couple of years? A whole decade? Or maybe a whole generation? Is it just a long downturn in market fluctuation, or are we witnessing the last twitches of an obsolete growth economic model? As always, the experts disagree.

Not only is the economy in trouble. In the last several years, Europe as well as the Arab world has been shattered by international wars, the Facebook revolution, "color revolutions" and coups. One by one, rulers have been forced from power in Iraq, Tunisia, Egypt (twice), Libya, and Yemen; major protests occur in Algeria, Bahrain, Jordan, Kuwait, Morocco, Turkey and Sudan; and protests and riots also take place all across the United States and in Canada, France and other developed Western nations as well as in Lebanon, Mauritania, Oman, Saudi Arabia, Djibouti, and Western Sahara, and elsewhere around the world.

In July 2005, the British Prime Minister Tony Blair was forced to dramatically pronounce: *We want to protect our way of life and our values.* On that day, the city of London was severely shattered by terrorist bombs. Almost the same words were used by Norwegian Prime Minister after one Anders Breivik, in July 2011, killed 76 young political enthusiasts on Utoya Island. George W. Bush had hit the same note in September 2001 atop the debris of the World Trade Center, and, of course, Vladimir Putin made a similar point in the aftermath of the terrorist attacks in Russia that threatened the safety of the 2014 Winter Olympics in Sochi.

In April 2011 an earthquake in Japan caused huge damage to the Fukushima nuclear power plant. Investigations reveal that it was human error and slow response that made the situation catastrophic. In the fall of 2005, two hurricanes, Katrina and Wilma, caused panic and damage to the US south, mainly due to poor preparation stemming from lack of leadership and bad decision making at the city, state and national levels. Almost the same month, a mob of underprivileged immigrants looted Paris, burning 800 cars. A couple of months later, there was a Titanic-size disaster involving an Egyptian ferry. A few weeks later, a Danish newspaper made fun of the prophet Mohammed, causing the Moslem world rise in a global protest. Almost the same month, the Palestinian elections were won by Hamas, until then considered a terrorist organization. That autumn, the polar ice decreased by 7% ; still another pandemic bird flu was announced, followed by an expected mutation of the traditional flu virus. Good news only for the pharmaceutical industry.

For over a decade, the Hague tribunal has been busy trying and sentencing dozens of Balkan leaders for crimes against humanity, including the former Serbian president. In the meantime, in the aftermath of wars in Iraq and Afghanistan, both countries are close to civil war. In 2007 Paul Wolfowitz,, a former U.S. Ambassador to Indonesia and Deputy Secretary of Defense,, resigned as the President of the World Bank due to a series of scandals. His colleague, Dominique Strauss-Kahn, had to leave the position of Managing Director of the International Monetary Fund in 2011, after a personal scandal of his own. The richest man in Russia, Mr. Khodorkovsky, as well as other Russian tycoons worth tens of billions of dollars, are in and out of jail. One of them, Boris Berezovsky, was found dead in his huge London apartment a year ago.

In September 2008, Lehman Brothers went down, in the largest bankruptcy filing in U.S. history, worth $600 billion. A month later, the WorldCom CEO was sentenced to 25 years for business fraud, which reminded the public of quite a few Enron executives who met the same fate a few years before. The collapse of both companies started in 2001, and caught most agonized investors by surprise. Enron took down its close associate, Arthur Andersen — the world's largest auditing company. The bankruptcy of Parmalat in Italy took place in 2004 and has been a front page topic for years, just like numerous affairs associated with Mr. Berlusconi, former Italian Prime Minister. In 2013, he was finally sentenced. That year saw a growing number of former presidents and prime ministers on trial for corruption or abuse of power, from Jacques Chirac in France to Ivo Sanader in Croatia; from Thaxin Shinawatra in Thailand to Bo Xilai in China.

In the fall of 2012, Sandy, the most destructive hurricane of the season, caused $50 billion in damage, of which the insurers were expected to pay out $20 billion. The 2013 Istanbul uprising at Gezi Park and the adjacent Taksim Square grew into the biggest riot in years, and, almost at the same time, nearby in the Mediterranean neighborhood, the banks of Cyprus suddenly declared bankruptcy, leaving the population without their hard-earned savings. Next door, the chronically ill Greece was again rocked by waves of bloody protests against the EU and the local government. Up north, the color revolution in Ukraine was followed by a coup d'état and the burning of central Kiev; the long-term effects are still unfolding.

It is not hard to imagine what our alien spy would report to his headquarters, based on randomly selected "breaking news" events from the last decade or so. The alien should be quite convinced that Earth is overwhelmed with turmoil, scandals, disasters, economic, political and moral crisis; each year, the most visible trends are negative, and no one has announced a viable vision or plan for reversing them. In conclusion, the alien would probably state that, due to poor leadership, and the value system of global capitalism, the troubled planet seems to be heading towards a disaster.

Maybe you disagree? In that case, help me by answering the following questions: Why are some of the most successful companies making headlines as colossal failures? Why are a growing number of most respectable politicians and business executives becoming prime suspects and convicts? Why are we still witnessing bloody revolutions, wars and unrest? Why are 824 million people worldwide starving, while 630 million are homeless, and 40 million people are infected with the HIV virus? Despite all the technological innovation, why haven't we managed to deal with the burning issues of political instability, suspended economic growth, poverty, injustice, international terrorism, global warming, or mass murders committed by frustrated individuals?

Of course, the problem is not that we cannot do it, but that we don't try hard enough. And why is that? Some cynics would say that people are nothing but selfish animals. Is that right?

Suppose there are five monkeys in a cage. You hang a bunch of bananas at the cage top and place a ladder nearby. Soon, a monkey climbs the ladder, trying to get some bananas. The moment he touches the ladder, you sprinkle all the animals with ice-cold water and they quickly back off. Soon, another monkey goes for the ladder, just to find out that the ice-cold-water situation is still there. From that moment on, you don't need the sprinkler any more. If a monkey even tries to get close to the ladder, other monkeys are sure to knock him flat.

Now, you remove one monkey from the cage and replace him with a newcomer. Seeing the bananas, he tries to reach for the ladder, only to find his ass kicked by all others. You replace another monkey with a new one. If he tries to reach for the ladder, he is severely beaten by all, including the former newcomer. Repeat the procedure until the initial five are removed from the cage. Regardless of the fact that none of the remaining monkeys has ever been sprinkled with ice-cold water, none of them ever tries to get the bananas because, if he did, he would immediately be stopped by all the others. Why? They have learned the way things are done here. And who are they to question the common practice?

Yes, this is how any organizational culture works. You may be offended by the comparison, but the monkey cage perfectly describes the behavior of nations, tribes, employees, politicians or citizens, who accept the prevailing norms and values. Remember the Germans under Hitler? The Founding Fathers of the USA, many of whom were slave owners? And the tale of the Emperor who had no clothes? We know what happens when people accept the existing paradigm and don't question its inherent contradictions, limitations and shortcomings.

Of course, we also know that the worst world problems have not come about by sheer chance. There are strong forces behind the cold-water sprinklers that train various groups of people to stomp each other from time to time. These forces are a clear reflection of the global power structure of modern capitalism, and they are more often than not designed and supported by politicians serving corrupt interests, whether the super-wealthy, the super-corporations, powerful bureaucracies, controlled media and other tools of plutocracy and ideological manipulation.

Just take a look at the present world from the common people's point of view. Aren't we all, to a certain extent, trapped in the monkey cage of an old economic, social and political paradigm? Strange, crazy, even outrageous things are constantly taking place around us, but we treat them as normal. That's why we don't try hard enough! If something is not perceived as a problem, nobody seeks solutions. If we don't question the illogical, irrational and problematic behavior and situations we encounter, they can go on from now to eternity.

So, is our world really heading towards a catastrophe? Most politicians, especially those in power, try to persuade us it's not. But what if the world is doomed and we don't notice, or have learned to live with it. Like the monkeys in that cage. Or like a joke about a guy, falling from an eighty storey building. As he passes by the fiftieth floor, his mobile phone rings, and a friend asks him: How are you doing today? So far, so good, replies the guy.

I guess, dear readers, some of you still say OK, we do have problems, but are they really that big? The word *catastrophe* is too strong. Is human history anything but a series of catastrophes? We managed to survive and even develop and grow.

On the other hand, if the wars, terrorist attacks, bankruptcies and riots are all just the tip of an iceberg, the growing tensions cannot be resolved using the existing paradigm.

We all read that there is a growing gulf between the rich and the poor, and wars break out all over the world. Tensions between the developed and the underdeveloped, the successful and the less successful, create a divide that is unprecedented in any period of human history. There are a growing number of political discrepancies, from interest-driven wars to corrupt government officials, from inefficient bureaucracies to inadequate protection of human rights. All that makes the average person lose faith in democratic institutions. There are growing ecological issues, from the greenhouse effect to water pollution, which make the future look bleak. There are burning moral and ethical dilemmas associated with changing roles of family, religion and nation, cutting deeply into the bedrock of the meaning of existence, freedom, wealth, justice, fairness and legacy...

I believe that while most people actually wish for essentially similar things, humanity is confronted with a lack of common vision, distorted value systems, unsuccessful models of government, a poorly educated and misguided population and, above all, bad leadership. Faced with challenges and threats of reason, meaning, ethics, conflict and survival, we seem to be losing the battle for the future. What should we do to reverse the trends?

1.2. Where Is the World Going?

Old wisdom teaches that, if you don't know where to go, any road will lead you there. Where are we going? Do we know the destination? Are we still on track, or should we alter the course? Some 2500-year-old advice from Sun Tzu, in a book on Tao warfare[1], says: "You must plan what is complicated while it is still simple. Try to do big things while they are still small. The most difficult things must be done while they are still easy." Are today's political and business leaders up to the growing challenges? Can we prepare for the future, and initiate needed political and business reforms while they are still "small," like the wise men who never have to perform mighty feats in order to achieve greatness?

---

1 http://suntzusaid.com/

We are living in interesting times. Our medicine is so advanced that practically no man is completely healthy. Go to a doctor and he will find some problem that should be treated. By analogy, our world is so advanced that a growing number of countries, and individuals, live in a state of constant trouble.

According to our alien spy's observations, the 2008 recession has evolved into a chronic disease. Greece is faced with bankruptcy; Spanish banks have been saved, for the moment, with €100 billion in monetary injections from the EU, and Italy, Portugal, even France are teetering. The Occupy Wall Street movement popped up all across America and the government cracked down. Mass shootings in US schools continue to shock us. Swiss bankers are still afraid to travel abroad, and a British parliament member attracted media attention by stating that it is better to admit child abuse than say one works for a financial institution. Niall Ferguson, a historian from Harvard, says: "There will be bloodshed, political and economic unrest will destabilize countries, governments will fall, and civil wars will break out." [1]

In 2013, President Obama's financial mastermind, Timothy Geithner, resigned as US Treasury Secretary. Four years ago, Nobel-prize winner Joseph Stiglitz had lambasted the "Geithner plan" to save the American banking system, saying it "will rob American taxpayers." A team of UN experts, headed by Stiglitz, anticipates a global tide of 30 to 50 million people losing their jobs each year. Columbia University professor Jeffrey Sachs, who predicted the global demise of socialism, thinks that the present recession could last a whole generation and not just five years, as posited by most politicians. According to Nassim Nicholas Taleb, author of *The Black Swan*,[2] "humanity has never faced such deep social and economic problems, and, at the same time, was equipped with such a low level of understanding of the scope and reach of these problems." Sustainable growth is not likely until a change of values takes place.

The world we live in is full of paradoxes. One of the best golfers is black, and the best rapper is white. The most opulent .01% control 90% of private wealth. In the US alone, every six hours a million plastic glasses are used on domestic flights; every five minutes 2 million plastic bottles are thrown in garbage cans; every hour a million paper bags are spent in supermarkets, and every two minutes, 28,000 gallons of fuel are burned. Pessimists say that if we survive the recession, we are going to die in revolutions caused by a growing gap between the rich and the poor, or by the greenhouse effect and

---

1 He made this remark in a lecture in my hometown Zagreb in 2011 (http://www.velikabritanija.net/2011/07/07/niall-ferguson-u-zagrebu/ (in Croatian) and has made similar observations in various articles and books: http://www.theguardian.com/books/niall-ferguson

2 http://www.amazon.com/Nassim-Nicholas-Taleb/e/B000APVZ7W

its consequences on the climate change, or by the ozone hole, or by terrorists using weapons of mass destruction, or, we are simply going to drown in oceans of plastic waste and garbage.

Is it just another cyclical recession, after which we should expect economic growth again? Or is it a fatal disease of the present model of capitalism, so that we are faced with quick agony before a certain death?

Twenty five years ago, the collapse of the socialist economic system was proclaimed; is it capitalism's turn now? If so, when, and what's next? And who is to be blamed, the politicians, governments, democratic institutions?

Are we living in a true democracy or is it just a travesty, a system carefully designed to protect the interests of the rich and powerful? And is democracy any better than other political systems? Is the market economy better than socialism? Looking from that angle, how do we explain the problems in the newly "opened up" Ukraine, Iraq, Afghanistan or Egypt, and the indisputable success of the absolutist China, Singapore, Saudi Arabia, Qatar, or Dubai?

Do we have the right answers to these and similar questions? Or any answers at all?

1.3. Ideological Deceptions

I come from a former "socialist" country. The two and half decades of our "transition" can teach the rest of the world a few interesting lessons. Remember Warren Buffett's quip that finance and debt pyramids are financial weapons of mass destruction? Today they go hand in hand with mass deception.

One good example is Western capitalism's ideological conquest of the former socialist countries. The Soviet Union's main goal in replacing communism with a free market was to enable Russia get out of the arms race and devote more resources to producing consumer goods and adequate housing. The aim was long-term stability, peace (that is, less pressure from nations espousing different political/economic systems) and to use a price feedback system (supply and demand) that would raise industrial productivity and living standards. Disillusioned with bureaucratic collectivism, the former "socialist" countries hurriedly adopted the neoliberal economic model and Western democracy, but the ultimate outcome was kleptocracy and debt slavery. And as in most cases of mass deception, it all happened voluntarily, quite like the Stockholm syndrome, when victims of kidnapping look to their kidnappers for protection. Basically, the more a country is pushed into poverty and debt, the more the weak identify their interests with those of their oppressors. They somehow start to believe that the rich will save them from the problems they created in the first place. The effect is a demoralized and fearful population, dependent on their oppressors, the rich and the powerful.

In such an environment, Western advisors managed to persuade the "transitional" political structures to give away valuable public assets and property to individuals, preferably to plant managers and political insiders. The notion was that it did not really matter who got them, because private initiative in itself would lead the new owners to re-organize production along the most profitable lines.

Of course, the former communist leaders, now newly fledged nationalists and "democrats", became very enthusiastic about gaining control over natural resources, real estate, public utilities and public transportation infrastructure and factories. Together with the politicians and consultants from the West, they persuaded the public that property has its own logic of self-interest which serves the social good of the population at large.

However, in practice the free market became a vehicle for ruthless looting. The ownership of public goods and natural resources was given to the chosen few who made personal fortunes by selling these to foreign investors. Western banks helped the local tycoons and oligarchs keep the proceeds from these sales abroad so that they didn't have to reinvest the wealth at home or pay taxes. Instead, the tax burden was placed on labor and consumers, and not on the unearned gains, like natural resource rents, land rent or monopoly rent.

Instead of creating industrial capitalism with subsidized technology and protected agriculture, the process led to de-industrialization of most post-Soviet economies. Ironically, as Michael Hudson points out,[1] kleptocracy became the final stage of Stalinism. In his book *My Fellow Prisoners* Mikhail Khodorkovsky described the Russian transition like this: "Decent people get out of the system, leaving 'idiots and lowlifes' — great material for building up the machinery of state."[2] Most socialist countries like my Croatia fit perfectly into that framework.

The described transition teaches us that finance can become war by non-military means. There is no longer need for a military conquest. Appropriation of wealth can be done through debt service and privatization. Selling the family farm and leasing it back at a rate that is harder and harder to pay is, obviously, a short road to ruin. It's easy to subdue economies by indebting their governments to other nations and using high debt as a tool to seize public goods at outrageously low prices. Some authors call it the New Cold War;[3] backed by the IMF and European Central Bank as the

---

1 http://michael-hudson.com/books/the-bubble-and-beyond/
2 http://www.amazon.com/My-Fellow-Prisoners-Mikhail-Khodorkovsky/dp/014197981X
3 http://m.strategic-culture.org/news/2014/05/21/the-new-cold-war-ukraine-gambit.html

---

knee-breakers, the Western investors are provided with a macroeconomic environment that allows them to gain control over the most valuable assets in the post-Soviet economies. The tycoons and oligarchs in these countries are eventually forced to sell major ownership shares in their companies to foreign investors. This gives the West a stake in protecting the assets (but not the citizens), pressuring governments to tax working people rather than the wealthy, and helping them cash out and keep their takings to finance Western economies instead of their own countries. And, of course, instead of building a more successful and harmonious "transitional" economy and society, the process leads to growing inequalities, tensions, instabilities and long-term problems.

1.4. Where Does the Crisis Come From?

We clearly see the effects, but what are the causes? Let's take a look at Dani Rodrik's research[1] on the impact of individual and group interest on global changes. According to the well-known Harvard professor, the current crisis is definitely caused by politicians and interest groups. They have created an environment in which the rich and powerful get what they want, and everybody else suffers the consequences. Financial legislation is tailored to the interests of the banks; health policy is tailored to the interests of insurance companies; taxation favors the rich; labor laws favor employers. Governments are just transmissions; everything is decided elsewhere. American politicians have long believed that what is good for the Wall Street must be good for the economy, politics and the society. The leaders of what we like to think of as the Free World have blindly followed the idea all along. And now it's coming back like a boomerang and hitting us all in the head.

The 2008 crisis was the first real global phenomenon of its kind, affecting every part of the world. According to some analysts, its impact seems to be similar to the fall of the Berlin Wall, which was then described by Vaclav Havel[2] as "the end of life in lies." He naively believed that the grass was greener on the other side of the Iron Curtain. Overwhelmed by the Czechs' soft revolution, he could not foresee that soon we would live in a world of even bigger lies.

Contemporary politicians use a language similar to George Orwell's "Newspeak." In his political science-fiction novel *Nineteen Eighty-Four*[3], the term describes an artificial language used to denounce individualism and independent thinking as *thoughtcrimes*. It is invented by the regime to help eradicate "suspicious" ideas like freedom and rebellion. Has the fiction

---

1 http://www.hks.harvard.edu/fs/drodrik/Bio_CV.html
2 http://www.brainyquote.com/quotes/authors/v/vaclav_havel.html
3 http://en.wikipedia.org/wiki/Nineteen_Eighty-Four

turned into reality? Every day we are bombarded with terms like patriotism, protection of human rights, fight for democracy and our way of life, used to justify political and economic decisions undertaken to protect the interests of the power elites.

In the past, strong political figures like Churchill, Tito, Stalin, Roosevelt, De Gaulle and Truman used simple, straightforward language everyone could understand. Current and mainly faceless political leaders have become sophisticated seducers of the masses, well equipped with all the tricks of the trade. Trained by communication experts, they often stand for nothing but are unscrupulous lobbyists, protecting the interests of finance and business giants who helped them seize power and position in the first place. The best recent example was the justification of the Iraq war using a fabricated story of weapons of mass destruction.

Allow me a little hyperbole, taking into account that there is often a touch of truth in speculation. The two Bushes, both former US presidents, were also the guardians of the Texas oil and weapons industries. Soon after being elected or re-elected, each initiated a war, in or around the Persian Gulf. Why? Was it to protect American freedoms, to remove a tyrant from power, or to save the world from terrorism? Suppose, for example, that the production cost of a barrel of Texas crude oil is $30. If there is no war in the Gulf, oil production and distribution are stable, the price stays low and there are no extra profits to be made. With a war, crude oil prices fly above $100 per barrel and the (Texan) oil companies rake it in. Meanwhile, the US government and the Congress are forced to increase the war budget, which is spent in part on weapons produced in Texas. Hasn't history repeated itself several times? Politicians use lies to start wars, the media engage in creating mass hysteria, people get frightened, angry and supportive of the war effort; soldiers fight and die, thousands of miles away from home, while the elites count the profits.

Who should be blamed for the actual crisis, then? Bad and deceitful politicians, selfish interest-driven power structures, corporations? For most analysts, the primary suspect is the world financial infrastructure, and a lack of public control and regulation thereof. Instead of servicing the economy, it has become its master, a tail waving the dog. Instead of an artless and austere infrastructure, providing money to business, it has been turned into an elaborate gambling machine, a sick combination of Wall Street and Las Vegas. As if, when you want to withdraw $100 from an ATM, the payoff is delayed by an offer: *Double or nothing!* The system, originally intended to provide individuals, industry and the economy with a flow of necessary money and credits, evolved into a sophisticated playground for gamblers, speculators and profiteers. Continuously inventing options, funds, derivatives and other "innovations" to play irresponsibly with risk, financial institutions have created a morbid world of instant, often undeserved, gain and loss. As an outcome, speculation (not prudence) was proclaimed a virtue and greed (instead of living within one's means) have become the norms of life.

This all happened with full government support and was fueled by unconstrained consumerism, something John Steinbeck, the American author, used to call the *Domino effect of materialism*[1]: "The more things I possess, the more things I want, until I become their prisoner." The spirit of consumerism turned the rich into filthy rich and exposed the rest of us to potential borrowers' slavery. The concept of the "free market" has become a tool to carry out a coup against individuals and society as a whole. For decades, politicians and bankers have managed to gamble away the government budget. At whose expense? Who won, and who lost?

Let's take a look at the numbers. In 2007, Wall Street paid $39 billion in bonuses to managers. A year later its recovery cost, paid by taxpayers, amounted to a trillion dollars. What happened next? Wall Street managers' bonuses climbed to $117 billion by the end of that year.

All the wealth is sucked up by the ultra-rich, and the "free market" creates unprecedented monopolies. A two-income family in the USA is 15% poorer than a one-income family 40 years ago. Last year the 500,000 richest people in the world (less than one tenth of a tenth of a percent, .001% of the global population) controlled 90% of all private wealth. The world's leading 1,318 corporations control 60% of the world market, monopolizing the global economy. As an example, just in the past year, *Oracle* has spent $50 billion to buy 752 former startups. In 1960, the ratio between the salary of an average CEO and the President of the United States was 2:1; fifty years later it is 20:1. In 1980, the ratio between the salary of a CEO and an average worker was 40:1; fifty years later it had sky-rocketed to 360:1. In 1950, movie stars, the most successful entertainers and the top sport stars often earned just a decent living. In 2013, they could earn a thousand times more than the average salary. Doesn't such inequality remind you of the days of slavery, or the early years of feudalism? How long can the world survive without a revolution?

1.5. We Do What We Believe In

The state of the world economy and society is based on the prevailing values; we always try to do what is considered right, good, useful, correct, and acceptable. People behave according to their beliefs. That's why a multinational company, faced with a decline in profits, may decide to

---

[1] http://www.brainyquote.com/quotes/authors/j/john_steinbeck.html

downsize and lay off workers, moving its production lines to countries with cheap labor; or it may adopt a strategy to invest in work force training in order to increase their loyalty and competence, which, in turn means more innovation, lower costs and higher quality. It all depends on the beliefs shared by the owner and the top management. Likewise, political leaders could decide to increase their impact by honoring a selected bunch of obedient followers, or by promoting reforms and democratic changes. Again, it all depends on what the politicians believe in.

In order to solve its economic problems, a country can try to build up its export capabilities (like China), or develop a despotic system relying on repression and strong army (like the Middle East). Again, it entirely depends on the ruling ideology, norms, perceptions and beliefs. For example, we could jokingly say that socialism never took root in North America because the poor saw themselves not as an exploited proletariat but as temporarily embarrassed millionaires[1]. Simply stated, if we want to change the behavior, we must first change the perceptions, norms, beliefs and values.

As usual, the depth and length of the existing crisis bring around a growing number of prophets who know exactly what needs to be done. The only problem is that they are in mutual disagreement. Should we increase savings or stimulate consumption? Should the monetary surplus be directed to public investment or used to lend wings to private sector and entrepreneurship? Should we refine, or abandon, the concept of liberal capitalism? Is the expected economic turning point going to be a result of stronger or weaker government regulation? Is a more rigid monetary policy needed, or we should advocate controlled inflation? Some think that monetary policy is the key; others rely on the fiscal policy magic. While some stress the importance of subsidies for entrepreneurs, others are against any subsidy because it interferes with free initiative.

There are economists who believe in market forces like in a fairytale. The only problem is the pressure of powerful interest groups, trying to impose their goals (e.g., oil and military industry, banks, insurance companies, the multinationals). If we somehow manage to get rid of the villains, we are going to live happily ever after. Less naïve economists predict and wish for the end of the free market, and still others think that only globalization can enable it to operate to its full potential. No wonder the public is totally confused!

In the meantime, it has become politically correct to blame the media because they create public opinion and have a strong impact on the public's beliefs and behavior. The spiritual father of the New Deal, John Maynard Keynes[2], used to point out that we are all victims of delusions by some long

---

1 http://www.goodreads.com/quotes/328134-socialism-never-took-root-in-america-because-the-poor-see
2 http://www.econlib.org/library/Enc/bios/Keynes.html

deceased economist. Why? Because the media and the politicians often put their faith in the wrong individual! Unfortunately, a stupid idea is not going to become smart just because millions believe it. In a globalized world, there could be billions sharing (erroneous) ideas which, in turn, heavily influence all decisions made by politicians, governments, democratic institutions, banks, corporations and managers. And history teaches us that ideas can kill faster than guns!

Almost two hundred and fifty years ago, Adam Smith[1] pointed out that, when the level of unjust profit rises high, countries enter economic crisis, then slowly or rapidly regress and finally perish. It was equally true for the Ancient Rome and the demise and fall of feudal states in Europe, and might soon come true for the present day USA and the EU economy and society. Shouldn't we, then, start paying full attention to our value system, the norms and beliefs on which we base our behavior, decisions and actions?

The main originator of all the global economic and political problems is the present "culture" characterized by lack of morality, abundance of consumerism and greed, obsession with profit and growth, resulting in a huge gap between the rich and the poor.

Or maybe not? Haven't we always been victims of double morality; we are accustomed to believe in dreams and live in harsh reality; we keep preaching heaven and go on practicing hell. As John Steinbeck[2] pointed out, "it has always seemed strange that the things we admire in men, kindness and generosity, openness, honesty, understanding and feeling, are the concomitants of failure in our system. And those traits we detest, sharpness, greed, acquisitiveness, meanness, egotism and self-interest, are the traits of success. And while men admire the quality of the first, they love the produce of the second."

I guess the time has come to end these double standards and start building a new global "culture," based on positive values. The modest task of this book is to help you shake your head, maybe rearrange its content a little bit, and join the process of paradigm change.

1.6. Can Market and Economy Be Ethical?

But is the new morality a simple answer to all the complex problems? Let us try to dig deeper into the asphalts of the actual crisis. As already pointed out, there is a growing public concern about an erosion of ethical behavior, a lack of mutual confidence, trust and search for truth in both political and business environments. For example, just one in five (18%) Britons trust politicians to tell the truth, compared to 21% trusting journalists and

1 http://www.adamsmith.org/wealth-of-nations
2 http://en.wikiquote.org/wiki/John_Steinbeck

bankers[1]. Free market ideology has reduced all relationships to transactions based on selfish interest. All values have been broken down to customer's choice and the resulting price. Oscar Wilde[2] used to say that cynical people know the price of everything but the value of nothing. Have we all become cynical? We own more things than ever, but somehow, we managed to lower the value of all our belongings, and the same happened to the meaning of life.

In times of amoral behavior, the free market of goods, labor, and ideas might become a source of total lack of freedom. Everything gets measured by the law of supply and demand; hence, everything is for sale and can be bought. If you have enough money, you can buy position, power, job, love, justice, health, youth, sport result or verdict. Money can get you out of any trouble. Everything has become an object of trade, and the resulting corruption shows what happens when people start losing dignity, when her majesty Money, the lord of consumption, becomes the absolute ruler. In such an environment, it is quite normal that the best entertainer, athlete, or movie star makes a thousand times more money than the best teacher, educator, doctor or scientist, simply because such ratio is an outcome of the free market, in other words, it reflects the supply-demand relationship.

How did it all happen? Free market and democracy assume morality of all people involved, and the system is, in principle, incapable of controlling the bad individuals. At the same time, the politicians who should be taking care about the bad guys, more often than not get connected and networked with them, openly or covertly promoting their interests. As we all know, without financial support from the *bad guys*, it is virtually impossible to get elected to any important political position. That's why, as already pointed out, the majority of the world's population tends to distrust politicians and authorities. But people need leaders and role models. In search of the lost values they either become cynical, or start to incline to the spiritual leadership of strong individuals like the Pope, Sai Baba or Dalai Lama. Again, it reflects the distorted value system.

Ten times a day one can wonder what happened to the good old fair-play, solidarity, concern for the weak, honesty, humility, modesty, honor and integrity. As pointed out by William Shakespeare,[3] "if I lose my honor, I have lost myself." Have we managed to lose ourselves without even noticing?

We must remember that the value systems come with the official ideology and mindset; they are simply the concepts and truths accepted by the majority of people in a given space and time. The paradigm we have implicitly accepted says that we are living in capitalism and democracy, the

1 http://www.ipsos-mori.com/researchpublications/researcharchive/3133/Politicians-trusted-less-than-estate-agents-bankers-and-journalists.aspx
2 http://www.brainyquote.com/quotes/authors/o/oscar_wilde.html
3 http://www.shakespeare-online.com/

best of all possible worlds. Is it really still the best?

Even though the free world is fully dedicated to the concept of democracy, there is a growing discontent with bureaucratized and corrupt political elites and parties. We seem to witness a crisis of democratic institutions as well. More and more people start questioning the mantra that our democracy is perfect — the only problem is its occasionally imperfect functioning. Ask yourself; is any system really good if it does not function properly? As far as the critics are concerned, our democracy looks more and more like a travesty, spoiled by populism, group interest, political lies, and manipulation with and by the media. A lot of empty words used to create strong emotions! Whenever there are no solutions to burning problems, the politicians initiate a witch hunt. The left-wing radicals blame capital owners, managers and employers. The right-wing radicals accuse immigrants and vulnerable ethnic groups. Even the moderate political parties try to find their place in the sun by initiating a dispute between the unions and the employers, or by creating tensions between the public and the private sector. Some blame the government for inefficiency and corruption, or public enterprises for monopolist position and lack of effectiveness. The others think that the sources of all problems are irresponsible corporations.

The intellectual elites are united only in the idea that the greatest responsibility lies on the shoulders of politically illiterate voters. They are to be blamed for the politicians they elected. As ironically stressed by George Bernard Shaw,[1] democracy guarantees only one thing; we are never ruled better than we deserve. Or, more drastically, democracy is when many incompetent vote for a few corrupt. Do we want to continue living in such an environment, or should we opt for better leaders and bore balanced values?

1.7. Crisis of Economics as Science

Democracy assumes that the majority is always right. However, we know that all progressive changes in human history have been initiated by minorities. The existing paradigm first gets questioned by the better educated, informed and skilled minorities. They come up with new ideas and innovation, and they are the first to advocate necessary changes. For a while, the conservative majority resists, trying to keep the status quo. Eventually, they get persuaded by arguments, or simply lose the ability to oppose. Only then, the change takes place and we start living a new, better and more progressive paradigm.

Are we witnessing one of those historic moments of growing awareness that the new bottles can no longer hold the old wine? How can we recognize

---

1 http://www.brainyquote.com/quotes/authors/g/george_bernard_shaw. html

the final years of an existing paradigm?

Day by day we get little signs and hints, telling us that change is unstoppable. At first, we notice a growing number of angry individuals followed by unrest, strikes, street fights. Eventually, it all grows and takes a shape of coups, big protests, frequent regime changes, falling governments, global revolutions... Ugh, we all hope it doesn't happen that way. Revolutions? No! God forbid!

But is the paradigm shift really needed here and now? Why can't we simply revive the old concepts and breathe them a new life?

It would be hard, their potential is used up. The old fashioned ideas like socialism, communism, and even traditional capitalism have become meaningless; the ideologies have failed and betrayed us. We need a system able to focus on individual well-being and pursuit of happiness. A struggle to preserve capitalism must become an opportunity to search and find better, more adequate economic and political models. However, we lack proper visions. The actual political, cultural and business elites don't have a clear picture of what the future should look like. There are neither goal nor directions.

But there are exceptions, signs that the new paradigm is on its way. For example, Lula da Silva[1], former president of Brazil during whose mandate the country managed to reach the eighth place on the world's list of economic success (climbing up eight steps), sees the end of the crisis associated with a set of value changes. According to him, we need a society dedicated to production, and not speculative activities; we need responsible financial sector, supervised by politics and the whole society, able to support entrepreneurs and startups. We need a new global governance, focusing on clean energy and ecology. We need reforms to restrain consumerism, and question the paradigm in which free consumers' choice dictates all business policies and structures. The world economy is too serious and too important to rely solely on a distorted logic of the consumers' society.

All these problems show that, maybe, we witness a global demise of the science of economics. Even though there are more than one million professional economists in the world, the global economy has never been sicker, and there is an obvious lack of doctors able to treat the disease. Almost a hundred years ago John Kenneth Galbraith[2] jokingly said that "the only function of economic forecasting is to raise the reputation of astrology." He is still right, despite all the sophisticated and computerized econometric models. This crisis has finally revealed that economists, just like sociologists, philosophers and meteorologists, cannot forecast the future. All they can do is describe and interpret what they see, and, hopefully, give more or less

---

1 http://www.britannica.com/EBchecked/topic/861479/Luiz-Inacio-Lula-da-Silva
2 http://www.econlib.org/library/Enc/bios/Galbraith.html

reliable short-term predictions.

The ruling, and most likely inadequate economic theory relies on the concept of non-regulated capitalism; it works best if everything is spontaneously governed by the free market. Its magic hand should, supposedly, create continuous growth, efficient resource utilization and long-term prosperity. Believing that human economic behavior is rational and most our decisions is based on logic, the macroeconomists have completely neglected the role of psychology, namely our "animal instincts."

Most people make business and economic decisions not based on knowledge and logic, but relying on emotions and instincts. If it weren't like that, marketing would long ago cease to exist. High quality products would easily beat those that seduce buyers with design and promotion campaigns. Before trading in the stock market, people would first try to learn all there is to know about economics and particular businesses. Believing in rationality and predictable human behavior, the quantitative economists have spent decades in building complex models for managers to follow and obey. Since the authors of the best among them have been honored with a Nobel Prize for economics, no wonder the models managed to seduce bankers and politicians all over the world with their elegance and beauty. However, in times of crisis, the usefulness of these models was close to nothing.

How can we explain that paradox? Most great economists of the past, Smith, Ricardo, Keynes, Marx, Schumpeter and Galbraith, never used models, quantitative analysis and deductive logic. But that age is over. The last half a century no one could even call himself an economist, unless he was a number crunching, model building researcher. Today the only economic theory worth discussing and applying is the one supported by extensive econometric and statistic tools.

The conceptualists who didn't care much about figures, like most founding fathers of the modern economics, from Smith to Galbraith, could never be candidates for the Nobel Prize. Frankly speaking, today they wouldn't even be able to teach at universities nor publish articles in respected economic journals. However, their ideas have made history while even the most elaborate quantitative models quickly disappear into oblivion.

Economics is obviously much more human that most scientists are ready to admit. As such, it is a fragile combination of tradition and innovation; it's formal and informal, rational and emotional, planned and spontaneous, predictable and totally stochastic, just like human behavior. Therefore, economic laws are at the same time objective and subjective, logical and irrational. They set people and things in motion by inspiration and by explanation. As we know from historical experience, any powerful idea is, in the long run, stronger than the common sense.

The key tool of all great economists was not Econometrics and formal logic, but ideas, concepts, arguments and emotions, powerful enough to move individuals, masses, governments and corporations. As pointed out by Karl Marx,[1] it has always been a task of philosophers and researchers to explain the world. But the real challenge is to change it for the better.

In times of emerging paradigms, we don't need tools describing why something looks as it does. We need tools to help us innovate and move forward. Instead of great economists with measurement and modeling skills we need great visionaries and motivators.

1.8. Change or Die

Obviously, the modern economy is half mathematics/statistics and half psychology (maybe even psychiatry). At the same time, modern politics is just a touch of rationality, combined with the abundance of emotion, populism and irrational stuff like (unreasonable or unjustified) fear, and hatred. Therefore, if we want to initiate economic (and political) changes, the most efficient way is to start up an intellectual revolution. It means a change in values and norms, an attempt to develop new and improved global, national, organizational and individual culture.

As far as economics is concerned, we need a new interdisciplinary paradigm relying not just on numbers and models, but on history, psychology, sociology and political theory. Instead of quantitative economics, some authors offer a concept of participatory economics[2] ("Parecon"), a democratic and harmonious search for a balance of interests between government, employers and workers. The first key word is *participation* of all stakeholders in setting goals, as well as in making sure they are attained. The second key word is *harmony*. We need an economy and society able to overcome the conflict-based and anarchic nature of capitalism, and shift its focus from competition, growth and profit towards well-being and happiness for all.

Risking an oversimplification, I offer you a cute example from the colonial past. An African tribe was just taught to play football by a group of British soldiers. The first game they ever played last until dark. The Brits told them they should finish and go home. *We cannot*, answer the Africans; *it is not a tie game yet. No one deserves to leave the football field unhappy.* Can you imagine the world being run by such happiness-for-all value system?

Changes are, obviously, necessary and should start as soon as possible. But are individuals, corporations, countries, political parties and power elites ready to accept changes and replace the existing economic and political model with a new one?

---

1 http://www.historylearningsite.co.uk/karl_marx.htm
2 http://www.versobooks.com/books/85-parecon

In his book titled "Change or Die" Alan Deutschman[1] presents the results of an interesting medical study. Suppose there are six individuals whose health, even life, depend on a drastic change of bad habits (e.g., Alcohol or drug addiction, smoking, bad nutrition, lack of physical activities). Suppose the doctor advises them to "change" (behavior and habits) or they are most likely dead within a year. How many succeed in drastically altering their lifestyle in order to survive? The study proves that only one in six finds strength and determination to change. Two people decide to give it a try but, sooner or later, they give up, and return to the old habits and the suicidal lifestyle. The remaining three never even try to change and thus destine themselves to a deadly outcome.

Isn't that kind of sad? Even under the most drastic pressure, only one in six people can, voluntarily, alter his behavior. The other five choose to resist change despite the fact that it's, literally, a matter of life and death.

Let us look at this problem from a less dramatic angle. Suppose you decide to go on a summer diet because you want to look better in a swimsuit at the beach. You think 10 pounds of weight loss would make the desired difference. I guess we know what would happen. Only one in six succeeds in losing 10 pounds. Two in six start a diet, but after a week or so, go back to the old eating routine and, maybe, lose a pound or two. The remaining three people just talk about going on a diet, but do nothing and hence lose no weight.

Both examples, the dramatic and the funny one, throw a clear light on the human capacity to change. One in six people is for it, two support him, but soon give up, and three are against it from the very start, mostly because they distrust their own ability to change. Ironically, typical human behavior could be epitomized by the following statement: *I am for changes, but please, change someone else, not me!*

Yes, yes and yes, it is so difficult to change habits, behavior, values, political and economic system, or the way we approach and solve problems. So, if we really want to initiate, manage, lead and successfully complete the process of paradigm change we need different people than those who dominate the actual political and business environments throughout the world. As Tom Peters cruelly pointed out[2], "if you want a paradigm shift, it is not enough for the old professors to retire. They must die!"

It is truly difficult to change. Fighting for a new paradigm is like rowing a boat upstream. If you stop for just a moment, you start sliding back, and you get farther from your goal, losing momentum. It is always easier to go with the flow and let the water carry you, instead of fighting your way upstream. That's

---

1 http://www.goodreads.com/book/show/51369.Change_or_Die
2 http://www.brainyquote.com/quotes/authors/t/tom_peters.html

why most people just observe the signs of crisis, try to avoid the outcomes, hope for the best, rely on destiny and let the river of trouble to carry them away. In the end, they get drowned by the currents of recession and crisis, because they did nothing to prevent it. As pointed out by Ancient Roman philosopher Seneca[1]: "No man has become great without hard work, the virtue should be learned." The flaw in human nature is that, in principle, we are easily spoiled. We turn bad automatically; we turn good only with a lot of effort.

Be it as it may, the more we delay the reforms and changes, the higher will be the human and social cost. Some philosophers suggest there is an analogy between the actual state of the world and the demise of monarchism. One after another the kingdoms disappeared and, from the mainstream idea, the monarchy gradually became a marginal concept. Something similar could happen to modern capitalism and the way it runs the economy and society. The best case scenario is a well-planned *refolution*[2], a set of reforms with a revolutionary goal to build "new capitalism," a system which is not a master of economy, politics and individual freedom but a slave, ready to serve them. The worst case scenarios involve varying degrees of massive violence.

The capitalism as a global system is not likely to disappear before a clear alternative emerges. Similar to the concepts of market or democracy, it is deficient and sometimes even ridiculous, but still better than other options.

1.9. What Really Counts: Wealth or Happiness?

By the way, what are our options? Let's look at the economy first. I guess the scope and the size of economic reforms will depend on the dispute between the spirit of Davos, a hierarchical, polarized and conflict-based capitalism, and the spirit of Porto Alegre, a democratic social and egalitarian capitalism.

Since 2006, Brazilian harbor Porto Alegre is the headquarters of The World Social Forum[3], an association of international non-government organizations, dedicated to global economic system recovery. On the other hand, Davos in Switzerland is the place of regular annual political leadership gathering called The World Economic Forum[4]. On that occasion the Global Competitiveness Report is published, presenting a list of countries ranked by competitiveness, defined as the ability of a given country to create economic growth. The 2013 report[5] deals with 147 countries, placed in three groups.

---

1 http://en.wikipedia.org/wiki/Seneca
2 The word was first used in late 80s to describe Russia's peaceful way into modernity after the fall of the Berlin Wall.
3 http://openfsm.net/
4 http://www.weforum.org/
5 http://www3.weforum.org/docs/WEF_Global CompetitivenessReport_2012-13.pdf

---

There are (1) Factor-driven Economies) (2) Efficiency-driven Economies and (3) Innovation-driven Economies.

Hopefully in the future we might need the fourth group: Sustainable growth and personal happiness driven economies. While the three differ from one another based on the key source of economic growth and profit making, I offer the fourth to emphasize the most important goal of any successful economic system: sustainability and pursuit of happiness.

You may be a little suspicious. Why do we need new goals and new methods to measure success? Traditionally, all countries are ranked by GDP (Gross domestic product) per capita or by PPP (Purchasing power parity) per capita. The latter is a technique used to take into account the relative value of currencies. There is a growing concern that GDP and PPP may not be the best tools to measure success of a given economy or society. Basically, they measure just the amount of possible spending (or consumption) per person. It stems from a belief that money is the most valuable resource, and that there is a monetary equivalent to anything that has value.

Imagine, for a moment a peasant living on a small, far off island, who makes his living by selling coconuts at the local market. Every day he brings 20 coconuts to earn 5 US dollars. One day the price of coconuts grows. What does he do? Next day he brings to the market only 18 coconuts in order to earn the needed 5 dollars. This story, which is, by the way true, should make us think. What is more important? Growth, profit and high GDP per capita, or happy and satisfied population?

Driven by such logic, the OECD (Organization for Economic Cooperation and Development) uses a concept of better life index[1]. It was proposed by a group of Nobel Prize winners asked to search solutions "beyond GDP[2]." The Beyond GDP initiative is about developing indicators that are as clear and appealing as GDP, but more inclusive of environmental and social aspects of progress. For example, instead of measuring how much people produce and consume, we may decide to measure the overall quality of life, namely how happy and satisfied they are.

Traditional tools measure success as growth of GDP, which is nothing but purchasing power increase. Many argue, and I fully agree, that the better target would be the increase in happiness and elimination of poverty. Sociological studies show that, when a country reaches 15.000 US$ per capita, individual happiness no longer depends on personal income and earnings. For example, despite constant growth of GDP per capita in most Western countries during the last five decades, the happiness index has not increased. On the contrary! For example, in 1935 only 2% of the USA

---

1 http://www.oecdbetterlifeindex.org/
2 http://www.beyond-gdp.eu/

population under the age of 35 suffered from depression; today it is almost 14% [1]. During the last fifty years "the rich free world" experiences a steady growth in suicide rates, alcohol and drug abuse, mass murders and terrorist activities. Alcohol and drug addiction, as well as violence, are nothing but the blow-off valves, reflecting the growing dissatisfaction and depression. So is consumerism. You are feeling bad and depressed? Go to a shopping mall! There, you will spend money for things you don't need, just to show-off in front of people you don't care about!

Why are we not happy, even though we are richer and have more things? The reason lies in the dominant values. Success and status are overstated and, at the same time, there is a decrease in mutual respect, trust and esteem. For example, in 1960 over 60% of grown-ups in the United Kingdom had "trust in other people." Last year, only 30% of people said they trusted others [2]. The free market practice has imposed a market-based attitude upon the whole society. Everything is looked at from supply and demand, profit, wealth and growth perspective.

In principle, a society based on fierce competition, constant conflict and the Darwinian survival of the fittest is not harmonious and healthy. It pushes the less successful into depression. It forces companies to resort to whatever it takes to make profit and growth, be it cheap child labor, wars to protect economic interests, or ecologically disruptive resource utilization. It makes the whole society insensitive to a growing gap between the rich and the poor, and leads to an overall lack of humanity and solidarity.

How long can we tolerate the fact that one in six citizens in most developed countries suffers from depression or mental disease, while at the same time, one in six kids in the poorest countries dies from malnutrition?

1.10. Who Will Lead the Refolution?

In most countries the growing social separation has melted down the so called middle class. It is not only an important economic, but also a serious political issue. The middle class is a stabilizer of negative trends within a society. Also, it is the key source of public pressure, demanding economic and political reforms. The ancient Greek philosopher Aristotle [3] used to call the middle class *the fundament of any stable state*, and this has become one of the principles of Scandinavian socialism. Countries without a strong middle class tend to suffer from deviations of democracy like widespread corruption, oppressed minorities, various forms of tyranny, even the emergence of dictatorships.

---

1 http://www.mentalhealthamerica.net/go/state-ranking
2 http://www.crest.ox.ac.uk/papers/p106.pdf
3 http://www.brainyquote.com/quotes/authors/a/aristotle.html

The middle class is a proud and organized group of educated people with social status, ready to resist bad leaders, corrupt governments and inefficient bureaucracies. They are not easily manipulated and they strongly advocate democratic rights, fairness and justice. The middle class is like a conscience of the society. It is the basis for recruiting politically organized citizens. In order for people to engage in politics, or in non-government organizations, and be ready to fight for ideas and ideals in the political arena, they must be economically independent. A fear for survival and everyday struggle for existence are the best fuel to power up the engines of dictatorship and despotism.

I guess that is the main reason why, despite the growing resentment for political elites and the unequal distribution of wealth, most common folks are still not ready to protest and publicly question the regime. Demonstrations, strikes and protests are not rare, but they are not populated because, in our selfish society, they are organized to protect interest of particular groups, for example in cases of massive layoffs, and occupational or trade rights violation. One after another, the interest-driven groups roam the streets in protest, the unemployed, the retired, students, veterans or workers in businesses that went bankrupt. Perceived as a fight for particular interests, such protests or strikes have no tendency to attract "masses." And without strong pressure from below, we cannot expect any "refolutionary" movement to take place.

How long will the common people stay passive? The *Occupy Wall Street*[1] can serve as a good case study. Even though the protest is based on a common cause, and the emotional tension about it is very high, the public opinion and the number of protesters never reached the needed critical mass. However, they clearly demonstrated who is, in their opinion, responsible for the crisis, and they obviously sent a strong message that, whenever the American government decides to help the Wall Street, it shows the citizens that it is not far from being its criminal accomplice. Cynical comments about a marriage between the political system and the financial sector no longer come just from the protesters. Even one of the US senators publicly compared the bankers with gangsters[2], reminding the public on a famous Al Capone's quote "You can get a lot farther with a smile and a machine gun than you can with just a smile«.

So, here we are! Common people are afraid and disoriented. The middle class seems to be weaker than ever. The intellectual elites are not willing to fight and have no clear agenda! Who will start the refolution? Can it be the individuals with vision and leadership skills, coming from political parties,

---

1 http://www.foxnews.com/opinion/2011/10/14/understanding-occupy-wall-street/
2 http://www.rollingstone.com/politics/news/gangster-bankers-too-big-to-jail-20130214?page=4

or from global social networking? Are there such people? A loud minority to ignite the silent majority?

The aim of this book is to provide them with needed help and support. Without vision and action, initiated by such leaders, sooner or later we can expect the street unrest, and in such case nobody can predict the type and direction of changes. To avoid that, we need leaders who are really dedicated to genuine public and national interests, and not just chiefs of political or business tribes fighting over power. Their main task must be to start a peaceful and continuous refolution, a reform from within. But it seems there are no such global leaders and no new visions in sight. How come?

We know there are politicians and there are statesmen. The main concern of every politician is to win the next elections; the key goal of a statesman is to find solutions for the burning issues and to lead the country toward its long-term success. The contemporary political arena is filled with politicians, and the statesmen are scarce. How come?

In most modern democracies the political life is organized in such a way to force the party leaders think and behave as politicians, not as statesmen. Their primary concern is to remain in power, if they have won elections, or to gain power if they have lost it. How can they succeed? By obeying the rules called populism, seduction of the masses, expensive public relation strategies, political dealership, quid pro quo tactics, and false promises. What they should not do? They must never hurt any key power structure and interest group, they should never rock the boat, even when it is filled with water and obviously sinks. They often promise change, but they rarely deliver. The less they do, the higher are their chances to remain in power. The devils we know are always better than the angels we don't know.

No wonder most politicians are faceless bureaucrats, working hard to preserve the state of affairs. That may be a good strategy in times of harmony, stability, success and progress. But the present world is characterized by the opposites: it is instable, disharmonious, locked in place and lacking success. The world's political and economic arena is in search of people who are able and ready to walk the talk of change. Barrack Obama promised a change we can believe in. And he failed, mostly because there wasn't much substance behind the nice words, no vision, no courage and no true leadership. In my view, the existing system should not be managed but changed. Maybe, for the first time in human history, we have a chance to make the change globally. Why is that?

We are surrounded by global communication systems, global ecological problems, global economic issues and global political challenges. Managing such an integrated environment calls for a holistic approach, a global vision, and a unified strategy. Exposed to a growing risk of global catastrophe, we need a clear definition of common goals and establishment of efficient mechanisms to reach them. So far, the process of globalization has ignored the need for political and social responsibility, the excuse being that no global goals are unattainable, because there is no Global Government, since no country wants to give up its sovereignty.

What are the answers to that dilemma? One is a growing cosmopolitan attitude, built on the idea that we all travel the spaceship Earth. In principle, cosmopolitanism means gradual withering away of national states and governments. Globalization of democracy and markets is already taking place. It's time for a democratization of markets and globalization. That process should rely on a new moral vision of society and community in which any symbiosis between Capital and Politics would seem unnatural, and completely undesirable. That symbiotic relationship has proven to be a key to all the evils and should be destroyed. At the same time, politics must find a proper distance from the strategic goals of powerful corporations and interest groups; it must cease to service the multinationals, and to promote their economic interests at the expense of individuals and society.

A crisis has always been an opportunity. We would never accept the "change or die" approach unless we realized to be immersed in almost insoluble problems,. The crisis and prolonged recession are a springboard for both, individuals and societies, to jump high, to adopt innovative ideas and to try out original approaches. We need new politics, tailored to the needs and welfare of all citizens. We need new economics, aligned with ethics, aimed at redistributing the wealth in such a way to reduce poverty and provide all people with decent and dignified life conditions. We need a new government, dedicated to sustainable growth, preserved environment, renewable energy, lower pollution, and recycling. We need new leaders, able and ready to fight for a new, better and more harmonious world.

I believe that the speed and intensity of the changes depend on a critical mass of individuals who personify the refolutionary ideas discussed in this chapter. We desperately need new leaders, both in the political arena and in business, to serve as role models for others to imitate and follow. To be in charge makes a leader uniquely responsible and accountable. One of the goals of this book is to give a small contribution to that long-term refolutionary process.

1.11. Questioning the Clear Images

Where does the battle for the new paradigm start? Most likely, it's the educational system. Today, all countries have developed an elaborated infrastructure aimed at teaching, indoctrinating, training and educating individuals, starting from an early age until retirement. Is this system working properly? Do we get necessary knowledge, skills and attitude to become change agents?

Let us start with a simple question: How much of what we learn is ever useful in real life? Seven years ago, while I was the vice-dean for international cooperation, my University performed a research[1] involving a portion of nearly 50.000 alumni of the School of Economics and Business. The reply to the above question was: between 8 and 12%. Simply stated, on the average only 10% of what our students learn during their college education was ever useful in real life. And my school, one of the oldest and most influential in the whole region, is not an exception; similar results have been obtained from studies in different countries. This fact is really disturbing. The schools as we know them, are lacking real output quality. Any system that produces only 10% of useful output should be considered a total failure!

What should be done? Albert Einstein use to say that we cannot solve a problem with the same thinking that created it. Thus, the first step is to redefine the concept of learning.

Allow me to be personal about this. Many years ago, as a graduate student at an American university, while cramming for a tough exam and reading a scientific journal, I came across a poem. It was titled "In Broken Images"[2] and appeared as follows:

> He is quick, thinking in clear images;
> I am slow, thinking in broken images.
> He becomes dull, trusting to his clear images;
> I become sharp, mistrusting my broken images.
> Trusting his images, he assumes their relevance;
> Mistrusting my images, I question their relevance.
> Assuming their relevance, he assumes the fact;
> Questioning their relevance, I question the fact.
> When the fact fails him, he questions his senses;
> When the fact fails me, I approve my senses.
> He continues quick and dull in his clear images;
> I continue slow and sharp in my broken images.
> He in a new confusion of his understanding;
> I in a new understanding of my confusion.

Blinded by the exactness of science and concerned about how much I still had to learn, I found myself angrily contemplating why anybody would misuse the space in a scientific journal to publish a poem. The author should

---

1 School of Economics and Business (2007). Alumni studies. Unpublished internal study
2 A poem by Robert Graves, http://en.wikipedia.org/wiki/User:Dead_goddess

have provided us with facts and findings of his own research instead, thus teaching us something. Why a poem?

The unconscious is sometimes more clever than the conscious. Despite a strong internal resistance, the poem remained in my heart and mind, almost against my will. It took many years, and many experiences, to make me appreciate the complexity of life and the limitations of all the clear images I possessed. An ever growing number of broken images helped me realize how confusing any problem solving situation is, and made me learn that only a few complex life issues can be resolved by recipes and hard knowledge.

As I was writing this book, the poem suddenly crossed my mind. Unlike the first time, I recognized in it an old friend, a lighthouse guiding internal itineraries, a precious jewel in my intellectual treasury box. So, let's start questioning the clear images about learning and organizational culture. They are critical in setting the stage for refolution and defining the role of leadership in it.

Just like Einstein, Thomas Edison used to say that, if you cannot solve a problem, you must change it. When you redefine it, you'll see it differently and, maybe then, you will be able to solve it. However, we are accustomed, educated, mentally programmed and trained to look at problems pretty much the way everybody else does, based on prevailing paradigms.

Yes, we enjoy seeing things clearly. We like our world structured, organized, rational and predictable. The reality, on the other hand, seems to be quite different. More often than not, our clear images fail us and we end up being confused.

What does the starting point for the necessary education refolution look like? The issues we are trying to address here are not new. Mark Twain used to say that he had never let his school interfere with his education. Albert Einstein expressed his opinion on the matter like this: It is a miracle that curiosity survives formal education. An inventor is simply a fellow who doesn't take his education too seriously, is the sentence attributed to Charles Kettering. Margaret Mead's comment on education could be summarized in the idea that people must be taught how to think, not what to think.

Look at the following table[1]. It stresses the difference between the bureaucratic and the innovative approach to education. Without going into details, let's just ask a simple question: What set of ideas more appropriately describes the present educational system? Is it aimed at development or status quo? When dealing with change, is it quick, offensive or slow and defensive? Are the new ideas easily accepted or rejected? From organizational point of view, is it rigid and stable or flexible and dynamic?

---

1 Srića V. (2008), "Social Intelligence and Project Leadership," the Global Management and IT Research Conference, New York, May 2008.

Table 1. Bureaucratic vs. innovative approach

ISSUE	BUREAUCRATIC APPROACH	INNOVATIVE APPROACH
Goal	Status quo	Development
Changes	Slow, defensive	Quick, offensive
Approach	Follow rules	Change rules
Objectives	Follow procedure	Make things happen
Decision Making	Outvoting	Consensus
New Ideas	Rejected	Accepted
Key Resource	Money	Knowledge
Organization	Rigid and stable	Flexible and dynamic
Leadership	Autocratic	Democratic
Authority	Formal hierarchy	Participation and competence
Problem Solving	Empirical	Innovative
Recruiting	Formal criteria	Skills and attitude
Training Focus	Specialization	Multidisciplinary
Ideal Student	Obedient	Independent
Control	Ex-post and imposed	Anticipative self-control

If you go down the whole list, and then conclude that modern educational institutions are characterized by bureaucratic approach, I have another question: What set of ideas should be associated with an educational system which is better tailored to the needs of today and tomorrow? If you agree that it is the innovative approach, I rest my case. If you don't, stop reading this book and start writing your own book titled: *I am a bureaucrat and I like it!* It is destined to become a bestseller.

Not so long ago, education was a boutique, and now it has become a cheap chain store. Every boutique tries to be unique, while cheap stores look alike. Hence, education has lost its innovative uniqueness and gained bureaucratic impersonality. It happened gradually because the goal of most educational and training activities is to teach administrative procedures, rules and well-structured approach that can be repeated and replicated. The very nature of such education is to "produce" administrators (pedantic followers, obedient executors) and not change masters (leaders or innovators).

What is the difference and why is it important? It's the topic for all the chapters to follow. In short, administrators prefer to control, analyze, make plans, communicate and coordinate. On the other hand, leaders[1] are there to set a vision, encourage and motivate, manage change and inspire. Leadership is, above all, a capability to influence behavior of people, including their values. As a result, organizational goals are attained with will, dedication and enthusiasm. Leadership is about commitment, and commitment is about values.

Leaders create visions, and make people follow them, while administrators plan, organize and supervise their teams. Administrators are susceptible to rules and regulations, based on experience. They develop stable procedures and build robust organizational structures. Unlike leaders who want to experiment, innovate, explore and reinvent. Leaders expect initiative and make people fight for a vision while administrators distribute tasks and expect obedience. Imposed control is the key to success in the mind of an administrator. On the other hand a leader knows that self-control is the best control, and self-motivation is the best motivation. Leaders inspire their team to participate in a dream-come-true experience, while administrators deal with trouble shooting.

Administrators are risk avoiders who rarely provoke or fight. On the other hand, leaders are fond of risk and infrequently engage in creative conflicts. Administrators must use power to get what they want, while leaders receive cooperation without even asking for it. It is mostly because our inner values drive our behavior stronger than any imposed rules and regulations.

Leaders are explorers; administrators take the paths already established. An administrator is a perfect response to the challenges of any stable system. On the other hand, a leader is needed to alter the course, to innovate and take chances. Since most present day systems and organizations are fully immersed in change, we need a critical mass of leaders to replace the existing critical mass of administrators, fighters for the status quo. Today, we train people to step on a brake and try to stay on course. Tomorrow we will need people trained to push the accelerator, speed up and move in another direction. That's what should be expected from the refolution-supporting educational system; teach and train for leadership, and not just for administration.

Let's move to another clear image that needs to be questioned. Some ten years ago Peter Drucker wrote that "the corporation as we know it, which is now 120 years old, is not likely to survive the next 25 years. It should

---

1 Srića V. (2008), "A Few Comments on the Role of Social Intelligence and Leadership in Project Management," invited paper and keynote speech, PMI Research Conference, Warsaw, July 2008.

survive legally and financially, but not structurally and economically." The management guru perceived corporations, government bureaucracies and most other institutions (including schools and universities) as old-fashioned organizations based on fear. They have developed strange concepts like cubicles, and standard operating procedures. The rigid hierarchies have bosses and teams appointed by senior management, and the goal attainment is based on command and control. Working within such environment causes alienation and depression.

In a society and economy dominated by knowledge, we need new types of "corporations." Instead of organizations based on fear, we should build organizations based on love. The traditional corporations have been developed in times of hard physical work. Today, most employees are knowledge workers. Their source of motivation is not control and fear, but love for what they do, a feeling of accomplishment and self-fulfillment. Brain-based organizations need a new value system, aligned with passion, enthusiasm, appetite for life, engagement, commitment, great causes, and determination to make a difference. The students and workers of the future must be trained for shared adventures, bizarre failures, and appetite for change. Otherwise, as stressed by Tom Peters[1], why bother?

Recently, I discussed that issue with my PhD students. We came up with an ideal organizational framework, the one that would perfectly describe what they, a bunch of talented and well educated young people, would like to be surrounded with at work.

Firstly, they wanted an environment that would support endless creativity. In the brain-based economy, innovation is the key source of competitive advantage. Next, they wanted an organization to be fully adaptable, internally, as well as externally. The constantly changing environment calls for maximum flexibility. Thirdly, they wanted a non-bureaucratic, inspirational working environment, designed to stimulate imagination and boost their passion for change. They decided they would like to work in an informal organizational setting, based on love in which all the ideas compete on equal footing. They wanted their tasks to be freely selected and not administered, within a hierarchy which is natural, and not imposed by the top management. They would like to work in self-organized teams, and enjoy the authority based on knowledge and results, not on formal position. Last but not least, they mentioned an abundance of resources and possibility to attract them by the quality of an idea or a project. At the end of our discussion they sadly pointed out that such organizational culture does not exist, and, more or less, it looks totally utopian.

---

1 Peters T. (2005). Leadership (Tom Peters Essentials), New York: DK Publishing

But that's not true at all! Over the last couple of decades, such culture spontaneously emerged on the Internet.

For the argument's sake, imagine that a huge corporation with an elaborate hierarchy decided to build The Web, based on a long-term plan, clearly defined budget, and precise goals. No way! The Internet self-developed, step by step, as a self-organized endeavor, feeding on endless creativity, full adaptability, loving and inspirational environment in which ideas compete on equal footing, tasks are selected and not administered, teams are self-organized and authority is not based on position but on the quality of an idea and its execution. Doesn't that look exactly as the "utopian" culture proposed by my students? Why can't that be a model for the organizational culture of the future, the one that is a necessary prerequisite of social, educational, business and political refolution?

Of course, it can. But first, we must stop being obsessed by more-than-a-century old military-like perfect bureaucratic organization called a corporation. Truth be told, traditional corporations are nothing but inhuman hierarchies, resembling concentration camps. Based on rigid plans, often absurd rules, fear of bosses, constant control, obedience and punishment, they are everything but desirable places to work, enjoy and be passionate about. We need new, Internet-like environments designed to support new values, creativity, innovation, and change. In traditional hierarchies, for one thing, the boss is there to catch employees in what they do wrong. We need organizations with bosses who catch the subordinates in what they do right!

Organization of the future should be built on love, friendship, candor and integrity. Imagine a world in which all students, teachers, employers, employees, politicians, bosses and workers are educated and trained to tell the truth, keep a promise, take responsibility, admit mistakes, abide by the rules, win the right way, enjoy life with humor, joy and humility. If you think that's impossible, remember that every crazy idea is considered totally insane until it wins.

Since the beginning of human history there are people who see the world as it is and ask why. We need people who see the world as it could be and ask why not! At present, there are no visions of real change, and there are no concepts and principles on which such a change should stand. Hence, the real problem lies in the fact that politicians and governments (not to mention educational institutions) don't search for new paradigms; instead, they engage in cosmetic changes of the existing one.

Can the old barrels hold the new whisky any longer? Human systems, organizations, institutions and individuals, they all seem to be in search of new ideals and values, in other words a new paradigm. Therefore, education and organization of the future will have to deal more successfully with the "cultural dilemmas" and issues discussed in this chapter.

We have just started to "question the clear images." This methodology is going to be used throughout the book. It is also a metaphor for the innovative leader, a person able to question the existing organization and change it for the better.

1.12. Are there Perfect Leaders?

Everyone likes a good quote. Here are my top-five on leadership[1]: (1) If your actions inspire others to dream more, learn more, do more and become more, you are a leader. (2) A leader is one who knows the way, goes the way, and shows the way. (3) Leadership is the art of getting someone else to do something you want done because he wants to do it. (4) Innovation distinguishes between a leader and a follower. (5) Good leadership consists of showing average people how to do the work of superior people.

Nevertheless, leadership is not defined by witty words, but by its outcomes, results, successes and victories. Based on a commonly accepted oversimplification, most successful systems are headed by good leaders, the winners. Less successful systems are managed by average leaders. Bad systems are usually run by poor leaders, the losers. The greatest historical, economic, political, business, sport, scientific or artistic victories are accomplished by teams who are headed by genuine winners.

It is often said that our future depends on how well we are going to manage knowledge and innovation. But, do countries and companies really "walk the talk" with this stuff? In a brain-based environment, our best asset is people and the way they are organized, inspired and guided. But, are our governments, countries, states or local communities managed by leaders, ready and able to deal with the new agenda? In my experience the answer is mostly negative! Most of the political establishment is old-fashioned and conservative, inadequately equipped for the challenges of the new era. Even the world's best corporations are often dominated by selfish interest, traditional business culture, bureaucracy, poor leadership, and inability to change.

In times of great challenges, the most important leadership skill is the ability to manage change in a harmonious way. The world's stage opens for the masters of economic and political transformation, able to bring harmony to the complex multinational and multicultural environment. We need a critical mass of such leaders, or we won't be able to avoid the global catastrophe!

---

1 By John Quincy Adams, John C. Maxwell, Dwight D. Eisenhower, Steve Jobs and John D. Rockefeller, http://www.brainyquote.com/quotes/topics/topic_leadership.html

"Follow me and I will successfully lead you from Monday into Tuesday," says the boss from a Karel Capek's aphorism. Then he adds: "I am the leader, and you are the follower, unless it's a dark place!" Would you like to follow such a person? What should your favorite boss look like?

There are literally millions of book and articles on leadership. In most of them, the authors and researchers enthusiastically draw models of perfect leadership. Some are inspired by the careers of the most successful practitioners; others build on theoretical ideals; and yet others offer a combination of both. Here are a few definitions by authors whom I have personally met and/or whose accomplishments I especially appreciate.

Jack Welch, who was pronounced "The Manager of the 20th Century," defines a perfect leader with three words: speed, simplicity and self-confidence. According to him, there are two kinds of managers: the quick and the dead.

For Alan Mulally from Ford, positive leadership is an honor to serve and move the organization forward, making sure everybody is included. It starts with a compelling vision and a comprehensive plan.

For Larry Ellison of Oracle, it is primarily important that the leader be self-confident, creative and ready to face challenges. Everyone follows the one who walks first. If you believe in your work, so do your team members.

Steve Jobs from Apple expected his directors to show initiative, courage, readiness to take risks, the ability to delegate, openness to criticism and willingness to search for new ideas.

Ken Blanchard views leadership as a combination of high ethical standards, and the capacity to manage situations at hand. Good leaders are moral, flexible and able to adjust.

Tom Peters, author of numerous management bestsellers, provides an extensive list of traits typical for successful leaders: they help each person develop his full potential; they spend time with the subordinates; they appreciate opinions of others, irrespective of status or hierarchy; they do not escape from problems, or make others do their dirty work; they are persistent, yet tolerant; they are humble and don't seek special privileges; they are simplifiers and motivators; they delegate with trust, and accept responsibility for failure; they stick to principles, especially under pressure; they tend to resolve personal issues "face to face"; they keep promises and are committed to their team; they treat mistakes as learning tools; they are fully dedicated to their organization; they come to work early, and leave late; and they appreciate people with ideas. According to the modest Mr. Peters, the list tells you more about good leadership than most curricula at best American business schools.

As far as Henry Kissinger is concerned, good leadership rests on passion for success, perfectionism and readiness to sacrifice. He describes a perfect boss as a person with soft voice, tender smile and a large stick behind his back.

General Colin Powell emphasizes the most important task of a leader — ability to teach his team self-confidence. Good leaders listen to everybody, but are ready to make decisions quickly. They are ambitious, knowing that only by trying to achieve the impossible, will they achieve great results. According to Powel, leadership is the art of accomplishing more than the science of management says is possible.

Following Mahatma Gandhi, leadership at one time meant muscles; but today it means getting along with people. Ideas and ideals are stronger than weapons and arms.

Akio Morita, the founder of Sony, always advised his managers to understand the employees and their needs. The best leaders are the ones who follow members of their team and gain their trust by keeping all promises.

In some cultures, leaders are just the first among equal, while other cultures prefer (benevolent) dictators. Quite a few successful companies or countries are headed by real tyrants, while others make their progress on the wings of partnership, participation, delegation and democracy.

Of course, I have developed a very elaborate leadership model, and the rest of this book is based on it. Why would I be an exception? Is it any good? You will know only if you try to implement it. You must keep in mind that effective leadership is not defined by concepts and ideas, but by results. As Albert Einstein used to say; a valid theory is always easily implemented. That's why my model represents a combination of theoretical concepts, and actual experiences, gained by their application. It is based on research studies, as well as on personal contacts and real life projects, related to business and politics. It could "humbly" be described as a model of models, a kind of Humpty Dumpty approach.

First, I break the complexity of leadership challenge into pieces. Then I use them as building material to construct a number of simple mental models. Finally, I take all the pieces and put them back together again using storytelling as a glue. The parts and the whole are based on my own leadership experience, or on a variety of practices and cases I have witnessed. Oscar Wilde wrote[1] that "all art is surface and symbol. Whoever digs under the surface does it at his own risk. Whoever interprets a symbol does it at his own risk." I fully agree. So, when you finish reading this book, and decide to apply the model in order to get something practical out of it, you do it at your own risk and take a chance.

---

1 The Picture of Dorian Gray, http://www.goodreads.com/book/show/5297. The_Picture_of_Dorian_Gray

Those of you who like models, concepts and theories, and need a framework in order to grasp the details, should read the rest of this book page by page. Those of you, who want to get practical suggestions, hints and proposals without being bothered with theoretical background, should skip the next section and jump immediately to the Part 3. I wish both groups a pleasant reading experience. Take a chance on me!

PART 2 — THE MODEL

> All mankind is divided into three classes: those that are immovable, those that are moveable, and those that move.
>
> — Arabian proverb

2.1. It Takes Knowledge, Skills and Talent

Do you agree with Harold Geneen, the legendary CEO of ITT: "Leadership cannot really be taught. It can only be learned"? Or, maybe he should have said that leadership can be taught, but it cannot be learned easily?

Many people believe that, if adequately trained, anyone can become a leader. Others see leaders as humans made of special material, shaped through genetics and environment. As proof they offer a list of uneducated CEOs with brilliant careers, none of them having a management school diploma. Moreover, the most successful among them have been college dropouts, from IT industry prophets like Steve Jobs, Bill Gates, Mark Zuckerberg, Michael Dell and Larry Ellison, to the influential and popular Ted Turner, David Murdoch, Oprah Winfrey, Roman Abramovich, John Lennon, and Lady Gaga. Most of these people probably think that while education may not be completely redundant, if you are not born a leader, or a star, no leadership, or starship, program in the world would help you become one.

If they are right, we don't need books on leadership like the one you're reading. Luckily, there are many who believe that leaders also emerge through training and self-development. They advocate continuous learning, leadership seminars, MBA programs, trainings and workshops. They put their faith in trained leaders and the fact that, in the end, knowledge always pays off.

Is there a correlation between knowledge and leadership? Do the experts in a given field make the best leadership material? In the early 1990s, a former McKinsey consultant, Lou Gerstner, was appointed CEO of the staggering IBM. Presenting his strategy to the management board, he surprised them all by admitting that he knew nothing about computers. *That's not an issue*, he added, *you are the greatest experts in the industry, and the company is not in trouble because we don't produce excellent computers and software.* The board members were shocked; their leader publicly admitted he knew nothing about the core business. But what he did know was at the time much more important for the company. They had to deal with problems of lost vision, rigid organization, reduced motivation and lack of respect for customers.

The story addresses the classical question: *Should the leader be an expert?* There is always a need to balance professional competence with human skills, technology with organizational culture, efficient use of resources with motivation for success, good annual income statements with a solid long-term vision. That's why a good leader is not necessarily a top expert in the field. Successful leadership calls for both, professional expertise and human systems management skills.

One answer leads to another question: *Are leaders born or made?* I guess the best answer is: *Yes!* People without a genuine leadership personality, be it inherited through genetics or installed by a supportive environment, are never going to become great leaders. But the other side of the coin is equally important. A path to bad leadership is paved with lack of motivation to study and self-develop, disinterest in theories, and inability to learn from mistakes.

In a book with a very telling title[1], the Gallup Organization researchers Buckingham and Coffman indicate that the individual success of a leader (or a boss) depends on harmony (or a proper balance) among his knowledge, skills and talents.

Knowledge deals with *what it is about*. It is acquired by studying, reading, attending seminars or searching the Internet. Leadership knowledge is found in books, articles, websites and libraries; it is based on facts and can be obtained from expert lectures or from consultants.

Knowledge is easily transferable. Faster or slower, sooner or later, anyone is able to learn anything from others. Throughout our lives, we are trained by teachers, parents, co-workers, bosses, tutors, professors and consultants. Theoretically, all individuals can master all knowledge on leadership, subject to time, intellectual ability and motivation constraints. It is rightly assumed that some leaders know more than others, but it is also true that knowledge (or "theory") is only one ingredient of successful leadership.

---

1 First Break All the Rules, http://www.amazon.com/First-Break-All-The-Rules/dp/0743510119

Skills have to do with *how* things are done; they are practical abilities, responsible for better or worse work performance. There are specific skills like dancing, skiing, driving a car, riding a bicycle, maneuvering a boat, using computers, mastering foreign languages, solving mathematical problems, or bookkeeping. Also, there are mental abilities to analyze balance sheets, to quickly get the overall picture, to listen carefully, to resolve conflicts, to convince or to sell.

Skills are acquired and developed through practice; in a way, they reflect accumulated experience. Leaders with a lot of practice may be less knowledgeable but have more skills. Years of experience and a growing number of ballgames makes us all more skillful.

Skills, like knowledge, can be transferred from one person to another. That's what all the trainers, teachers, mentors, bosses and coaches are for. Even though mastering a skill seems to be more complicated than acquiring knowledge, most people are capable of doing it right.

Talents are personal traits or characteristics by which we differ one from another. There are traits common to all people (a need to be loved, a need for physical safety). Some people are similar to certain groups of people (ambitious individuals, risk takers or perfectionists tend to look and behave alike). However, some of our traits could be quite unique. Here, the term "talent" does not mean a special gift (i.e., talent for music). Rather, it describes a trait that "differentiates" (e.g., to be a risk taker, and to be a person who plays it safe, are two opposing talents).

Unlike knowledge and skills, a talent cannot be acquired from others nor can it be transferred from one person to another (except by genetics). We are either born with a talent or discover it while being brought up, or we don't have it. Before the time of mass education, leadership programs and management schools, all successful leaders were "natural born."

There are many anecdotes about talents and personality. Here is one: Great maestro Wolfgang Amadeus Mozart attended a concert by a twelve-year-old child prodigy. At the end, Mozart praised the kid and his superb performance. The proud child responded: *I want to become a composer like you. When should I start?* Mozart told him to be patient; it would take years of study, a lot of work and many more concerts. Not pleased with the answer, the boy said: *But you were already composing at the age of six. Yes,* answered Mozart, *but I never had to ask anybody when to start.*

Although all categorizations are somewhat arbitrary, we can talk about three types of talents; the first has to do with motivation (why we work), the second explains the behavior (how we do things) and the third describes the relationships (how we relate to people).

What are the motivational talents? They describe our attitude related to what makes us act and move. For example, are we competitive or not? Are we altruists or egoists? Why do some things work for us while others don't? What are we prepared to fight for? How much do we depend on love and support from others? Do we need to be publicly recognized or not? Do we enjoy serving others or are we more self-centered? Do we aim high or let things "flow," not caring what happens to us?

Second come the thinking talents. We differ in terms of the choices we make and the speed and ease with which we make decisions. We may be dedicated to single or multiple goals. We may be superficial or perfectionists. We may be self-disciplined or disobedient. We may prefer predictability or surprise. We do, or don't, think strategically. We seek risk or avoid it. We analyze options before making a decision (asking ourselves, what if?), or we just impulsively jump....

Third, we have relationship talents. We build interpersonal relations by deciding who should be trusted, and who shouldn't, whom we ignore, whom we respect. We may be in conflict with most people or avoid all conflicts. We may see others as competitors or as collaborators. We may like, or resent, foreigners. We may be globalists or nationalists. We may believe in the goodness of all people or be skeptical and cynical about human nature....

Obviously, everyone can master leadership knowledge and skills if they try hard enough. However, leadership talents cannot be acquired in any management school. In case you have inherited them, people will probably call you a *born leader*.

Fortunately or unfortunately, there is no ideal combination of knowledge, skills and talent that guarantee anyone to become a perfect leader. The world's best leaders are very different; each of them is characterized by a unique combination of knowledge, skill and talents. Buffon[1] is well known for saying: "His style is the man himself." Personality is the content and the form, the inside and the outside, the inherited and the acquired. These are inseparable. A good leader adopts a style and develops an approach that suits his personality. You cannot fake it; you must be it. That's why the perfect leader is best described as a perfect combination of imperfect traits that fit together perfectly.

2.2. There Are Administrators and There Are Leaders

Margaret Thatcher was known for saying: "Being a leader is like being a lady. If you need to explain to others that you are, then you are not." A boss who must repeatedly point to his authority in order to make his employees pay attention is like a parent who must constantly remind his children that they should listen to him, because he is the father. Instead of saying: I am

---

1 http://en.wikipedia.org/wiki/Georges-Louis_Leclerc,_Comte_de_Buffon

the boss, or, I am the father, you should act like one. The authority of a true leader does not depend on titles or hierarchy; it is genuine!

There are many historical examples of genuine leaders. What would the Roman Empire be without Caesar, or early 19th century Europe without Napoleon, or post-war France without De Gaulle, or former Yugoslavia without Tito, or India without Mahatma Gandhi, or the EU in recession without Angela Merkel? Walt Disney, J. P. Morgan and Henry Ford have left behind not only a legacy of good leadership, but also the company name. What would General Electric look like without Jack Welch, or CNN without Ted Turner, or Apple without Steve Jobs, or Microsoft without Bill Gates?

What do they all have in common? The most successful politicians and businessmen have charisma, the ability to seduce, convince and win people over, to motivate, inspire and lead. People with charisma are followed; their ideas are gladly implemented. Charismatic personalities are destined for leadership roles. Organizations headed by charismatic leaders accomplish their goals with ease. However, it works both ways; charismatic leaders are capable of leading followers and organizations to doom and destruction, sometimes after a truly successful and glorious start. History is full of examples, and Napoleon is a prime one.

In principle, there are official leaders who hold a position, informal leaders who possess charismatic qualities, and formal leaders who have both the official position and the reputation of natural leaders. An ideal situation for most systems is to have a formal leader at the very top. It makes the organizational authority stable and unquestionable.

We have already talked about the difference between administrators (they manage an existing system) and leaders (they are involved in innovation and change). The actual training, education and development of most managers, potential leaders, is based on the public/business administration paradigm. The term "public administration" refers to the management of government and public (non-profit) institutions while "business administration" means managing for profit. Hoping to become prospective leaders and executives, many young Americans, Europeans and Asians enroll in Master of Business Administration (MBA) programs. The degree usually entitles them to management and executive roles in profit and non-profit organizations. Most actual managers are formally educated and trained in business or public administration, and not in leadership, because such a degree doesn't exist.

Why is that important? There are fundamental differences between administrators and leaders, and there should be a difference in the way they are educated and trained. Today, we educate all managers to be administrators, and we hope that the fittest among them will fight their way up to the top. Why do we do this? Most likely because, deep inside, we believe that leaders are born, not trained.

As already pointed out, the capacity to lead evolves from charismatic power. There are many soldiers in every army and only a few generals; and amongst the generals there is but one Napoleon. Charismatic personalities are, above all, genuine and original, never to be mistaken for someone else.

A charismatic individual is a person with integrity, strong convictions, stable goals and endless energy to overcome obstacles on the path to success. Charisma relies, among other things, on the ability to communicate in a simple, straightforward and attractive manner. A charismatic leader is able to make an impact on the minds and the hearts of his followers. Why the minds? Because he is perceived as the expert, able to do the job. Why the hearts? Because people tend to get emotionally attached to his personality.

Aside from the style, there are differences in the content. Managers administer, control, analyze, make plans, communicate and coordinate. Leaders set a vision, encourage and motivate, innovate and inspire. Leadership is, above all, a capability to influence people's behavior, including their value systems. Leadership is about commitment and passion.

Administrators are in-the-business guys; they focus on current operations and the fiscal year, their main goal is to run the system "as is." Leaders are on-the-business people; they focus on transformational change, and the future shape of the enterprise, "as it should be."

Typically, administrators are risk avoiders who rarely provoke or fight. On the other hand, leaders are susceptible to risk and frequently engage in conflicts. However, administrators must use power to get what they want, while leaders receive full cooperation without having to ask for it.

Having a manager-administrator is a perfect response to the challenges of a stable system. On the other hand, leaders are needed to alter the course, to innovate and improve. Administrators keep the system running while leaders save it from failing at times of transition. Leaders are explorers, and administrators prefer well-trodden paths.

True leaders are known for their desire to lead. Power is passion, power is sweet, and power is like a drug! On the other hand, administrators never truly enjoy managing others, and they don't get a kick out of organizational power and authority. They dislike responsibility and risk, and try to avoid conflicts at any cost. True leaders crave for the leading position and the challenge it brings. They look at the leadership role with strong desire; they want and must lead.

This is a book on leadership, so forgive me if I sound emotional and euphoric about it. It only proves another important point. Administrators are serious and rational people, leaders are known to be playful and sensitive.

Not every manager can or must be a leader. A system run by leaders only would very quickly end up in disaster. Therefore, the ideal top management of any organization consists of a balanced combination of people with managerial and leadership traits. However, it is difficult, if not impossible, to find a person who is able to play both roles. The winning combination is to have a leader at the top surrounded by a team of administrators. He or she brings the vision and the others provide conscientious and dedicated effort in its implementation.

2.3. Leader from Within: Self-Developed Internal Harmony

This chapter is dedicated to conceptualists, the ones who want to grasp the big picture. If you are not that kind and you just want to get practical and useful ideas on harmonious leadership, feel free to skip the next chapters and jump directly to Part 3.

In physics, there are concepts of potential energy (what can be done) and kinetic energy (what is done). Potential energy is a possibility; roughly speaking, it is the amount of energy available for work. On the other hand, kinetic energy is the one doing the work. A big stone at the top of a hill stores a lot of potential energy, but it can do meaningful work (i.e., break city walls) only once it starts rolling down the hill.

As stated before, each person is a combination of knowledge, skills and talents. In a way, the three represent that person's potential energy, the outcome of self-development. The more we have, the more we can do with it. What do we do with it? Our potential energy may be used to accomplish different goals and implement various life plans and projects. Also, our knowledge, skills and personality are the tools we apply in leading others. Like kinetic energy, it enables us to successfully finish the projects initiated and attain the goals set.

The energy metaphor should help you understand how to become a better leader. In short, if you want to grow as a harmonious leader, you must invest time and effort to self-develop (increase your leadership potential). Also, you must engage in developing your team (effectively use your leadership potential).

The goal of your self-development is to be in harmony with yourself in order to become a better person and a better leader. At the same time, your improved capabilities and personality help your team succeed. Being a better leader, you can help your organization "harmonize" and achieve its goals with less effort and more quality. Simply stated, as a leader, you must simultaneously develop internally (by building your potential energy) and externally (by using your kinetic energy). That's the basis of the leadership model established in this book.

The first part of the model shows that leaders grow from within (through self-development). They build up their personality in order to achieve internal harmony. What is internal harmony? It is a balance between what you believe in, what you hope for, what you can do and dare to do, and what you wish to achieve with respect to your life, your organization and its environment. Part 3 deals with that.

The second part of the model shows how you perform externally and lead your team to success; first you help your teammates understand where the system stands, then you help them set a vision, and, finally, you mobilize and motivate them to implement the vision and meet the goals. Part 4 deals with that.

It is not easy to become a better boss and a more harmonious person. The model used in this book starts with the idea that, before trying to influence others, each potential leader must search, find and maintain his inner balance. In order to successfully lead your team, you must learn to lead yourself first. There are four components contributing to the "internal harmony" of each person, as shown in Figure 1.

The spirituality of every person is his deepest essence. It responds to the questions *Who am I* and *How do I see myself as a person.* Spiritual harmony depends upon balancing what you believe in, what you love, hope for and are prepared to fight for. We have already talked about the global epidemic of depression. It is a direct outcome of our neglected spirituality. As Martin Luther King Jr. would say[1], "the means by which we live have outdistanced the ends for which we live. Our scientific power has outrun our spiritual power. We are surrounded by guided missiles and misguided men."

The second, cognitive segment describes our relationship with the environment; it responds to the question how we experience the world that surrounds us, including our existence. Cognitive harmony is achieved when we manage to base our work and everyday life on the principles and values in which we trust. It enables us to understand how we feel about ourselves, how we perceive the world around us, how we interact with it and how we fulfill our needs. Today, more and more people are troubled by so called "cognitive dissonance." It is the distressing mental state that people feel when they find themselves doing things that don't fit with what they know. A search for cognitive harmony simply means that we want our expectations to meet reality, creating a sense of equilibrium.

The third segment is strategic harmony. It reflects our ability to answer the question *what* (vision), *why* (mission), *where* and *when* (goals) and *how* (specific actions) you intend to live your life. Finding the right answers enables you to understand how much you are prepared to persevere in

---

1 http://www.brainyquote.com/quotes/keywords/spiritual.html

order to obtain your personal and business objectives. It serves as a set of guidelines in dealing with the following dilemmas: where are you headed, what do you expect from yourself and how do you intend to achieve your goals? In principle, your strategic harmony delineates the territory in which you seek to be unique.

Figure 1. The Leader from Within — Internal Harmony

Operational harmony is the fourth segment and it reflects the way we perform in a given space and time. For leaders, it is important to be productive and effective, to feel independent (financially, emotionally and physically), to build cooperative relationships with partners, clients, voters and coworkers as well as to develop a feeling of belonging to a system, a community or a country, and a hierarchy. Being in operational harmony really means to be in an efficient balance with what we do. Efficiency is our ability to climb the stairway of success; and our operational harmony must ensure that the stairs lead to the right floor.

Even if it sounds philosophical and sophisticated, the concept of harmony has been well understood and practiced by many cultures in the past. Let's consider just one example, the Native Americans. Traditional "Indian people"[1] have been fully dedicated to living in harmony with other human and non-human beings, as well as with the environment. While individual freedom was highly esteemed, there was recognition that decisions must be made for the common good, based on the question: *How will this impact the seventh generation?* Harmony with the environment rested on the idea that everything has a soul, like a living person, and thus the same courtesies afforded to humans should apply to the environment. The role of the human people was to understand and maintain a long-term, internal and external harmony with the plant people, the animal people, and the water people.

The chapters that follow are, more or less, concentrated on helping you develop your harmonious self. Part Three focuses on self-development (the

---

[1] See "Traditional Indian Leadership and Harmony," http://nativeamericannetroots.net/diary/1525

leader from within); and Part Four deals with team development (the leader from without). In this book, *the team* means the group the leader is in charge of. It can be anything from a work group, family, task force and project team to a department, company, political party, city and state administration or a whole government.

I love a certain story from Africa. Every morning, a gazelle wakes up, aware that she must run faster than a lion in order to escape and survive the day. Every morning, a lion wakes up, aware that he must run faster than a gazelle if he wants to catch his prey and survive the day. Basically, when they both wake up, they should start running. It is a nice metaphor for self-development. Every morning when a leader wakes up, he should start working on the four layers of his inner harmony. The goal of self-development is to build a better person and a better leader. It means a constant struggle to harmonize the interaction between cognitive, spiritual, strategic and operational aspects of one's life.

So far we have touched upon self-development and issues related to inner harmony. Before we move on, let's briefly discuss the leader-from-without; what leaders must do in order to help their team develop and win.

2.4. Leader from Without — Explanator, Visionary, Mobilizer, Motivator

Imagine a situation that actually happened some time ago. An airplane crashes in the Andes peaks, hundreds of miles away from any human settlements. Twenty-five survivors find themselves in the middle of an icy desert, poorly stocked with clothing and food. What are the odds that they are not going to freeze and die of starvation? What determines the likelihood of their survival?

The situation is complex, but the answer to that question is simple — their survival depends on whether there is a leader among them, able to organize the group and help them find a solution to the problems they are faced with.

The challenges are numerous and complicated. Quite a few crash victims are overcome by panic; some engage in fighting and quarrels; others are at peace with destiny, and crawl into the remains of the wreckage to vegetate. Once they fully realize the difficulty of the situation, a struggle over limited resources, like water, food and clothing, may break out. If there is no leadership, in times of severe distress, destruction is inevitable. Sooner or later, someone must step in and start to lead them. What should that person do?

First of all, the prospective leader should explain to all the surviving passengers what has exactly happened to them. By drawing a true and a persuasive picture of the actual situation, he will gain their trust. In this particular case, they have to be convinced that no rescue mission will find them; the only hope for survival is to get organized and start searching for help.

Next, a leader must propose a solution and explain how the problem should be dealt with. His task is to provide the group with a common vision and convince them to act accordingly. In order to succeed, they must define the specific tasks required and find the ways to accomplish them. For example, the leader will ask the group to look for those who are strongest, most likely to endure a long journey down the mountains, and then equip them with the best shoes, warmest clothes and supplies of food.

The third task of a leader is to mobilize all members of the group and instruct them what to do. In order to solve such a difficult issue, all heads must be put together. Those who stay, and those who search for help, must feel that they are working side by side, and contribute to the common goal. The leader should also be able to make them believe that they can handle the situation at hand. He must encourage them to fight instead of giving up. Any individual action or conflict should be avoided; all members of the group must be persuaded to fully cooperate, if they are to reach the common goal.

The final and the most difficult task of the leader is to motivate all members of the group to hold on and give their best. He must set an example, lead the way, and remain calm. Full of enthusiasm and confidence, he should feed the group with positive energy, determination and endurance. In times of hardship, the task of the leader is to inspire members of his team to give more than they think they can.

Maybe you find the example too drastic to serve as a model for everyday leadership challenges. French philosopher Jean-Paul Sartre[1] used to say that "truths are best understood when they become acrobats." It is easier to see what really matters in the most drastic situations. Becoming an acrobat, the truth is cleared of unnecessary details which blur the overall picture. Our story does just that; it pushes the practice of leadership to the limits. In principle, all business and political teams face the same challenges as the group of people hopelessly stuck in the Andes after the atrocious accident. If they want to become a winning team, they need to understand where they are, then they need a vision how to get out of trouble, and, finally, they need to be mobilized and inspired. This applies equally to a team eager to win the next basketball match, and to all of us who dream of preventing global catastrophe!

Harmonious leadership means trust. What exactly makes us trust the person in charge? First of all, he must be able to sell us the picture of our

---

1 http://www.brainyquote.com/quotes/authors/j/jeanpaul_sartre.html

situation in such a way that we believe him. I call this role *the Explanator*. We expect our leader to know exactly *where we are*. We follow him only if we are convinced that he is aware of what's going on, and sees it better than the rest of us. The leader must be good at formulating and selling the picture of a problem, or a situation, we are faced with.

Secondly, a good leader must be able to come up with a plan, and persuade us to be on top of things. We expect him to tell us where to go from here and provide solutions to problems we might meet along the way. This role is referred to as *the Visionary*. We gladly follow people who seem to know exactly *where we should be going*. Also, they must be successful in selling us a vision, and in making us believe that it can be accomplished.

The third role of a leader is to launch all the members of the group, or at least the vast majority, in a desired direction. We may call this role *the Mobilizer*. In order to set us in motion, the leader must make clear *why we should stick together*. According to an old Croatian saying, there are as many opinions as there are people. Members of any group usually come up with a number of ideas, proposals and standpoints concerning what should be done, or how a problem could be solved. Without leadership, a group is divided in terms of direction, point of view, behavior and actions to be taken. Hence, a significant portion of the available energy is wasted in an internal power struggle. However, everybody is better off if all members of the group end up being mobilized towards the common goal. More than others, this role distinguishes a good leader from a bad one.

Figure 2. Leader from Without — Harmonious Team Leading

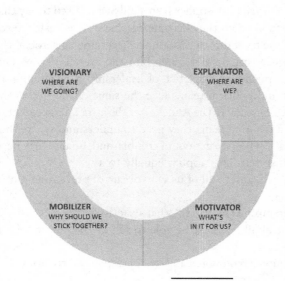

The Explanator must sell us the idea of where we are, the Visionary shows us where to go, and the Mobilizer keeps us moving together in the chosen direction. Doing that, he must steer our ship in such a way to survive storms, fight resistance and doubt, and bypass the obstacles we come across.

This brings us to the fourth role of a good leader, his ability to stimulate us when we are ready to give up, to lift our spirits when we are down, and to renew our faith when we have lost it. It's the role of *the Motivator*. Good leaders are able to convince us why something should be done, and explain *what's in it for us*. They provide us with inspiration to give our best, they motivate us to work harder, to endure longer and try the impossible. Of course, it takes the right emotion. Poetically speaking, if a leader wants us to build a ship, he must not drum us up to collect wood, or assign us tasks and work, but rather teach us to long for the endless immensity of the sea.

The four roles are symbolically presented in Figure 2. Good teamwork heavily depends on the leader's ability to successfully play the four roles. All the great leaders, from Jesus and Buddha to Gandhi and Mother Teresa, succeeded because they have been good Explanators, Visionaries, Mobilizers and Motivators.

The true goal of every teacher is to bless his students with knowledge, skills and morality. Self-development produces a harmonized person and a solid leader. Team development produces a powerful group, able to win even when the boss has left. Since the times of Aristotle, a good teacher must be able to "produce" students who are more competent than him. This is equally true for good leaders. They set an example and let the followers complete the task by saying: *We did it on our own!*

2.5. What Makes a Harmonious Leader?

In the Saint-Exupéry's masterpiece, the wise fox explains to Little Prince that "it is only with the heart that one can see rightly; what is essential is invisible to the eye." However, the search for harmony is not just a matter of the heart. If it were, we would be nothing but slaves of our feelings. It is only natural that we want to live in harmony with ourselves, with other people, with our goals, thoughts, feelings, hopes and everything that surrounds us.

In principle the life of every individual consists of many conflicting segments. It can be described through a series of opposing requirements that need to be balanced and harmonized. First, we have to balance the private and the business sides of our life. Many people are unable to do it right and easily become victims of disharmony. The outcome is either lack of success at work, or a failure with respect to family and friends, or both. We also need to find a proper balance between the individual and the social side of our lives. If we don't, we either identify with ourselves at the expense of ourselves, or we lose contact with others and remain alone and lonely. There are other sets of needs and realities that have to be balanced if we want to harmonize our life, i.e., the local and the global, the actual and the expected, the planned and the accomplished, the emotional and the rational, the existing and the ideal...

One of the key ingredients of internal harmony is our ability to love and care. Actually, inner harmony could be poetically described as a balance of the four H's: Hope, Heart, Head and Hand. First, whatever we do is triggered by Hope, which gives us a vision and direction. A passion of Heart follows, providing emotional support and strength to endure. It is reinforced by the stability of our Head, responsible for rational analysis, self-confidence and a propensity to succeed, which, in turn, enables our Hands to work effectively and help us attain goals and make our visions come true. Harmonious people keep all the four H's in harmony. What they Hope for is aligned with what they think in the Head, feel in the Heart and are able to accomplish with their Hands. If this book was intended for the poets only, I would stop here and offer a 5H model as presented in Figure 3.

Figure 3. The 5H Model

However, since poets have been mysteriously silent on the subject of leadership, let me return to our serious prosaic model. It describes harmonious leadership as a two-step process. The first step is what the leader does internally, and the second deals with what he does for his team.

The following figure captures the essence of my Harmonious Leadership Model.

What the leader does internally is a lifelong process of self-development. Its goal is to build and improve the leader's harmonious personality. The goal of self-development is to attain and maintain an effective balance of leader's spirituality, cognition, strategy and operating efficiency. I build on the assumption that only leaders with internal harmony can lead and develop harmonious teams. The main outcome of the self-development process is the leader's self-confidence, enhanced willpower and readiness to lead others. The leader's inner balance is a powerful tool in leading other people; its outward appearance is often called charisma, integrity or natural talent for leadership.

Figure 4. Harmonious Leadership Model

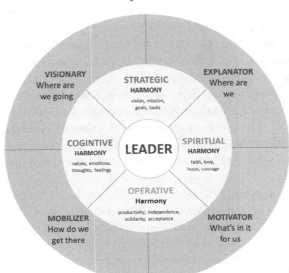

The second step of the harmonious leadership process describes how the leader enables his team to win.

Basically, he must be able to successfully play the four roles of Explanator, Visionary, Mobilizer and Motivator. The task of the Explanator is to clearly define the actual situation (where we are). The task of the Visionary is to explain the future and provide solutions to all problems (where we are going). The task of the Mobilizer is to put the team in motion and ensure unity and efficiency (how to get there). The task of the Motivator is to inspire, provide optimism and energy, as well as to build commitment (what's in it for us).

The rest of the book is dedicated to explaining every single leadership-related piece of knowledge, skill, or talent associated with this model. It explains in full detail how to work on oneself and one's team, what a leader should know and be capable of, as well as what makes him and his team succeed, or helps him and his group achieve their goals in a harmonious way.

The model is simple and straightforward. The leadership journey starts with the four elements of personal harmony and ends with the four leadership roles. I hope you find it intuitive and natural.

Talking about natural, while writing this book, I came across the concept of Natural Law[1] or the law of nature (Latin: *Lex naturalis*). It's a system of law that is purportedly determined by nature, and thus universal. Natural Law is considered to be the ultimate source of order and harmony displayed

---

1 http://en.wikipedia.org/wiki/Natural_law

throughout creation, and it determines what is good or bad, right or wrong, acceptable or detestable. The idea that there is a supreme law standing behind everything as the ultimate truth sounds appealing. No wonder the scientific, legislative, economic and political community, from the times of Plato and Aristotle until today, seems to be puzzled and intrigued by it. One of its strange outcomes is the Natural Law Party (NLP), active in more than 60 countries, including the USA[1] and Canada. The party claims that political problems could be solved through alignment with the Unified Field of all the laws of nature, through the practice of Transcendental Meditation (TM). At one time, Mahesh Maharishi Yogi, the father of TM, was a very influential person. However, after his death in 2008, the global TM movement gradually dissolved.

I am not an admirer of the Yogi, the TM or the NLP. However, I must admit that, to a certain extent, my model and some of these ideas are in tune. As already pointed out, the actual business and political world are headed down a one-way street due to the distorted value system (not aligned with the Natural Law). To foster change, we need a critical mass of harmonious leaders with balanced personalities and skills. Eventually, they would bring long-term harmony (the Natural Law) to the disharmonious world and its institutions. We have gone too far in twisting the harmonious ways of Nature. Only by realigning our personal and social values with the laws of nature can we avoid a global catastrophe.

I believe that a good text can be interpreted at your convenience. The following chapters are, above all, aimed at helping you ask better questions on leadership, the traditional type or the harmonious type. Only by asking the right questions will you get closer to the right answers. At times, the book provides you with solutions, but, all in all, it sets you on a journey to search for your inner harmony, to find the ways and means that work best for you. In any case I hope to help you become a better person and a more effective leader, one who brings harmony to your own personal life, to your team, to your organization and to the world.

---

1 http://en.wikipedia.org/wiki/Natural_Law_Party_(United_States)

PART 3 — SELF-DEVELOPMENT

> The difficult is done at once; the impossible takes a little longer.
>
> — Charles Alexandre de Calonne

3.1. Leaders are Dolphins

Chuang was a troubled ruler in the Lu region of China. He went to a temple to seek advice from a famous teacher, Mu-Sun. Together, they walked to the banks of a river and the teacher ignited a huge fire. They sat in silence until dawn, beside the river, and watched the flames slowly disappear. As they were gazing into the sunrise, the Teacher said: *The immense flame is now but a handful of ashes left behind. The fire was strong and destroyed everything in its way. Finally, it became a victim of its own power. At the same time, the quiet river continued to flow, becoming deeper, wider and stronger on its journey to the sea, carrying food and drink for everyone.*

There are rulers who resemble fire, and others who are like rivers. The former exercise their power and authority, while the latter humbly serve their followers. Some leaders are oppressive and aggressive, capable of destroying themselves and their teams while trying to achieve their goals. Others are prepared to serve the people they lead, ready to search for long-term solutions based on mutual harmony.

The story basically talks about two opposing leadership styles; there are traditional bosses, and there are true leaders. In order to make as clear distinction as possible, I offer you a set of metaphors.

Traditional bosses resemble *old-fashioned parents*. Instead of trusting their children, they act like supervisors. Convinced that nobody would do anything right without close monitoring, they build their authority on rigid control. Strict orders, total obedience and use of force are very much to their modus operandi. They are also accurately described as officers, judges, animal tamers, or bookkeepers. Like *police officers*, they seek unconditional obedience just because they represent the law and order. Like *army officers*, their authority may never be questioned. Their role is to give orders and ask for subordination, no matter what. Like *judges*, they pronounce a verdict that must be respected; the authority of justice is not to be questioned.

Traditional managers are like *slavers*, or *wild animal tamers*; in dealing with people, they gladly use a moral whip and easily hurt the feelings of their subjects. Resembling *bookkeepers*, they are focused on figures and dislike faulty human nature. They always prefer a nice balance sheet over employee satisfaction; and they would never trade short-term goals and the bottom line for long-term harmony and good interpersonal relationships.

Traditional leaders believe in formal authority and obedience. They dislike opinionated workers; they don't respect people and tend to achieve results through strict control, punishment for negligence and the use of formal power and authority whenever necessary.

Harmony-based leadership calls for different metaphors. A modern boss should, above all, be a good *coach*. He must put the interpersonal harmony on the top of his list, even at the expense of short-term results. The boss is trusted because everybody feels his love and appreciation. The leader-coach cares for us, and does his best to turn us, metaphorically speaking, into world class athletes. Motivation is on the top of his agenda; he praises, encourages, supports and develops. He may even hurt or punish us, if such behavior would make us change for the better. In any case, he would treat his team like a parent who adores his children and wishes all the best for them.

A good leader is like a symphony conductor who knows how to inspire his business "orchestra." Classical managers say: I expect you to play that (do it) as stated in the score (business plan) and that is all. I expect good work because you are professionals. On the other hand, a leader-conductor must be able to inspire his orchestra and enable all individuals to give as much as possible, and more. He might, for instance, say: This evening we perform Vivaldi's "Four Seasons." While we play 'Spring,' imagine the sounds of the beginning; everything is in bloom, everything is possible and the world is filled with hope and great expectations. Spring is the time of youth; little babies are born and some will grow into Nobel Prize winners. Blossoms will turn into beautiful flowers, and the mountain streams have just started their long journey to the sea, carrying the fresh fragrant water towards the ocean.

A leader-conductor is not only going to get the job done. He intends to inspire us to play his vision. And, if he does, we do our very best and try very hard to please him. To a traditional boss, we give only as much as required, while a true leader usually gets from us more than we believe we are capable of giving.

A harmony-based leader is a *catalyst*, able to speed up the process of change (e.g., to enter new markets, to implement new organization, to introduce new information technology). He is like a *midwife*, helping us "give birth" to change as painlessly as possible. Like a strategic-harmony-seeking *visionary*, he is able to see farther and better than the rest of us, hence we gladly follow. As a person, he dwells on friendship and positive emotions, and we are happy to be in his company.

Many traditional leaders resemble *sharks*. They are perilous, aggressive and unscrupulous individuals, ready to tear down all the obstacles in the way. They are powerful and dangerous, their goals justify the means. All methods are allowed, even if it means breaking moral and social norms, hurting innocent people or ruining lives and careers.

Not all traditional leaders are like sharks. There is a passive, old-fashioned boss who resembles a *catfish*. Instead of reacting to changes in the environment, he buries his head in the river bed and waits. Instead of hunting the prey, he prefers to stake out and wait for smaller fish to swim into his mouth. The catfish-boss will occasionally stir up the water, hoping to be better than other fish in coping with the muddy environment. This skill is especially well developed with political catfish.

To this list we could add a *swine-fox*, a common species among political and business leaders. It's not found in nature, and could be described as a dirty low life smart ass. The swine-fox boss is corrupt and sly. He attains his goals through fraud. In boxing terms, he is ready to hit below the belt. His tools are political maneuvering and bribery, media hiking, blackmailing, searching for legal loopholes, exploiting system deficiencies and profiting from human weaknesses.

It is difficult to push the analogy to the other side, but let's give it a try. Harmony-based leaders resemble *dolphins*. A dolphin is an intelligent and spiritualized creature. He exhibits a high level of decency and integrity, and is always ready to play. A leader–dolphin enjoys winning but does not humiliate nor torment his opponents. He is a team player, ready to help and inspire. He is sociable and elegant. He does not adhere to dishonorable deeds or dirty tricks. He is known to avoid unclean and foggy situations; he lives for today, and thinks about tomorrow; he is ready to work, play and win through joint effort. Metaphorically speaking, and this chapter is nothing but a chain of metaphors, we may describe harmonious leadership as a process of transforming sharks into dolphins.

3.2. Leaders Are Proactive

In most religions, God is love. Allow me to paraphrase this thought: A harmonious leader is love. Because I love my job, my company, my country, the world, the system, co-workers, plans, my career and success, I care, I try harder, and I am prepared to fight and sacrifice. Those who love are ready to suffer, struggle, make efforts and face difficulties. Those who love try to be better, more successful; they invest in self-development and growth in order to make their dreams come true. They know what they want and try relentlessly to achieve it, irrespective of the price.

Facing a final battle after long years of war, a Chinese ruler asked a wise man what the outcome would be. General Su was eager to win and ready to die for it, but his army was small in number and unequipped. His enemy, General Li, led an army larger in number, better equipped, well fed and destined for victory. The wise man took the ruler to the lake, picked a flower and tossed it in. They watched the flower for a while, as its whiteness lay calmly on the surface of the water, and then continued to walk. The Wiseman picked another flower and threw it in the stream, which quickly carried it into the distance.

The stream is small, but it flows and carries away the flowers, which the lake is not capable of doing, stated the Wiseman. *General Li is similar to the lake; large, with many weapons, yet slow and immobile. Sure of his victory, he will stay behind and do nothing. On the other hand, General Su will be in constant motion, leading his men from the frontlines of the battlefield. His desire for victory will inspire his whole army. That's why he is going to win.*

Arms and weapons are important, but leader's personality is the key to victory. Every day, our political and business arena indeed resembles a battlefield, with executives and politicians behaving like generals. The success of each battle fought by various political or business armies depends on ambition, capability, knowledge, decisiveness and determination of the leaders.

General Su is active and venturesome. General Li is passive and motionless. Relying on his strengths, he does nothing. The two of them have differing views regarding the future and their behavior differs accordingly. General Su is proactive and General Li is reactive.

Reactivity is the attitude exhibited by most people in business and everyday life. When something happens, I react. Until then, I wait. Biologically stated, there are incentives (or causes), after which a reaction follows. If there is no action, there is no reaction. To most reactive people, private and professional life unfold however they unfold. Hoping for good luck and circumstance, they let destiny do the job. When it turns its back on them, they complain about their fate and bad luck. Their main goal is to go with the flow, or at best to keep up with the Joneses. For example, if everyone invests capital in stocks, so will they. When everyone sells their stocks, so will they. When everyone moves to a specific market, so will they. When everyone retreats, so will they! Reactive reasoning is like a sure bet. Those who don't take risks probably won't make big mistakes, but they rarely achieve anything truly valuable. Why are most individuals like that? It is easier, more common and more "natural." Reactive behavior requires only reflex action; and proactive behavior requires will and vision.

Proactivity is rare but rewarding. As Steven Covey[1] points out, "the most effective people are not problem-minded; they are opportunity-minded. They feed opportunities and starve problems." Good luck, opportunity and chances must be seized because they might not come again. Something new must always be attempted! Be the first to try! Do something original and success is sure to come! Make the first move and everyone will follow you!

Proactive people know what they want, and consequently, they invest time, money and energy in materializing their dreams and visions. Their life and business motto is to turn fantasy into reality. They are prepared to take chances, knowing that's the only way to gain. They usually swim upstream and do not follow the direction of the herd. If everyone turns left, proactive people consider turning right. No wonder, proactivity is a typical trait of great leaders. Proactive individuals dare to err or go astray, and proactive organizational environments try to encourage initiative by rewarding creative mistakes.

There is an often-told story about a manager from IBM, who, wishing the best for the company, undertook a huge risk and made a decision which caused the firm to lose ten million dollars in a single day. Horrified by the outcome, he thought it would be better to leave than to be thrown out. So he brought his letter of resignation to the CEO the following morning. *You want me to let you go? Are you out of your mind?* said the CEO. *We just invested ten million dollars in your education!* A mistake that made you learn a valuable lesson is a huge intellectual capital for the whole organization.

Philip Knight, the CEO of Nike Corporation, used to motivate himself and his employees by saying: "The only way to avoid mistakes is by never trying! Therefore, we must reward creative mistakes and punish mediocre success!"

Proactivity is a typical trait of the most successful leaders, but also of some who have ruined their professional careers due to excessive risk taking. Proactive people are innovative and ready to venture. They constitute a minority, but they play an important role in changing the world. At the same time, the reactive majority will always adapt, produce average results, and,

---

1 http://weekplan.net/be-proactive-best-quotes-from-stephen-covey/

of course, have no problems with survival, if all remains stable. Proactivity often means no pain, no gain! Reactivity always means no gain, no pain! Proactivity generates potential casualties for a good cause; reactivity is survival; but *why bother*?

Many years ago, as a Fulbright student, I proudly stood amidst three hundred colleagues, facing the Dean of Graduate School of Business at Columbia University in New York, enrolled in the MBA program. I wondered what he would tell us in his opening speech. First, he pointed out that we are enrolled in one of the most prestigious and expensive programs in the world and congratulated us for beating the tough competition. Then he explained the role of his faculty. Their job was not to prepare us for positions such as directors of banks and companies, financial, marketing or information officers, but rather, teach us to become winners.

At the time, I considered these to be empty words and did not grasp the importance of such ambition. Now I hope I do. There are many bank and company directors, even more financial, marketing or information officers, but there are only a few leaders who possess self-confidence, belief in themselves and a winning spirit, enabling them to succeed in every endeavor they attempt.

As a visiting professor at the Renmin University in Beijing, I learned approximately two hundred Kanji symbols. Among these, there was a word composed of two ideograms. When unified, they mean *crisis*, when separated, the first means *danger* while the second stands for *opportunity*. Isn't that a wonderful definition? Every crisis is dangerous, but it is also an opportunity. Without a crisis, there would be no opportunity to change and improve. Leaders are barely needed in times of stability, but their role is crucial in times of a pending organizational or global catastrophe.

Let's not be too serious; it's time for another joke. Two shoe salesmen arrive in Africa in order to test the market. After they have walked around and collected some data, each reports to his headquarters. The first complains in a sad voice that his visit was in vain. There is no market for shoes, everyone is barefoot. The second salesman excitedly reports: Wonderful news! Everyone is barefoot; the market is huge and boundless!

If we perceive a situation as trouble, our behavior becomes reactive. Instead of doing, we wait, or hold back. The situation is seen as a problem; and we try to defend ourselves from it, counting on good fortune. If we see the same situation as an opportunity, we become proactive and take advantage of the circumstances. An experienced leader could benefit from such difference in perceptions. All he has to do is to propose a simple rule: on our team, there are no problems, just challenges.

A good thing about a crisis is that it offers a chance to do something different. If we perceive it as a problem, a nuisance, or a danger, we pick defensive attitude; in the worst case scenario, we are paralyzed, devastated or mentally destroyed by fear. If we view the crisis as an opportunity, we start acting as entrepreneurs, and try to take advantage of the circumstances. Metaphorically speaking, we grab the destiny's hair in our hands, like Kairos, the ancient Greek god of the opportune moment. As Bertrand Piccard[1], the famous adventurer and balloonist points out, "adventure is the crisis you accept; and crisis is the adventure you reject."

As leaders, we must nourish our proactivity. It is a result of equilibrium between what we hope for, what we see as our mission, what we feel about ourselves, and what we are ready to do, in order to succeed. Proactivity is an outcome of internal harmony, providing us with self-confidence. The winners are aware of their capabilities, they are ready to set high goals, they know what they want, and are prepared to self-develop, learn and grow, in order to win.

The famous Roman emperor and philosopher Marcus Aurelius[2] pointed out three cornerstones of proactive behavior: courage, patience and wisdom. It takes courage to change the things we can change, it takes patience to accept the things we cannot change, and it takes wisdom to distinguish one from the other.

3.3. Leaders are Ethical

They say everything is allowed in love and war. Many believe that the same applies to politicians and business executives. They are powerful and mighty, their decisions can change our life and destiny. The way our political and business world is structured puts a lot of responsibility in their hands. Do they deserve it? Can they cope with it? Are they, as should be expected, made of the best human material?

I come from a post-communist country. A good number of transitional leaders might be best described by the already mentioned swine-fox metaphor. They succeed by being dirty and clever. They look you in the eye while stabbing you in the back. Their leadership style, and overall behavior, is slimy and corruptive. Being relatively isolated from the market capitalism and western democracy, we thought that the grass was greener on the other side of the fence, and we tended to idealize business and political leaders of the "free world." But, once the Iron Curtain was fully open, we saw too many swine-foxes roaming freely on both sides. Today, just by watching the evening news, we learn on a daily basis about political and business leaders who break or circumvent the law, ignore ethics and twist around all moral

---

1 http://en.wikipedia.org/wiki/Bertrand_Piccard
2 http://www.butler-bowdon.com/meditat

norms. For them, it's quite normal to lie, cheat, "beg, borrow or steal." The real problem begins when the public gets used to it and starts accepting it is normal.

It is difficult to achieve inner harmony without adhering to strong standards of morality and ethics. Not only because it is the right thing to do, or because it feels good, or because ethical behavior improves the society as a whole, but because true leaders are aware that, in the long run, morality produces results, makes a profit and creates value. Besides, every leader is a role model. Therefore, it is important to set a good example.

Some time ago, I learned an interesting fact from a lawyer friend. The population of Japan amounts to 130 million, yet they have about the same number of lawyers as my homeland Croatia, with less than 5 million residents. How come?

Whenever two Japanese businessmen (or politicians) shake hands and make a deal, both undertake a moral obligation guaranteed by their honor. If one party is unable to fulfill the promise, even without a signed contract, his career is terminated. Such people are marked as dishonorable and no one would do business with them. In an environment with such high ethical and moral standards, naturally, courts and lawyers are not very busy.

How about Croatian politicians and business people? A swine-fox will sign a contract, and before it's even implemented, will start coming up with excuses: they cannot deliver the goods on time, cannot guarantee the quality and prices, cannot pay overtime or are unable to meet the financial obligations. You'd better have some understanding! ... Or sue me!

My American students occasionally ask what type of environment their Central European colleagues work in, and what major issues they deal with as managers. I attempt to accurately portray the nightmares they face: Will the customer pay for the material delivered, and what will be the delay (in most cases the major debtor is the government)? Will the supplier deliver the goods purchased and prepaid; will the judicial system take more than five years to bring wrong doers to trial... Then my students concede that the West is not really doing much better.

The fundamental moral dilemma faced by most leaders on a daily basis can be narrowed down to an aphoristic question: *Is there a good way to do a bad thing?* The answer is very simple: No, there isn't, and don't bother looking for one! Harmonious leaders must do good things, and avoid doing what is bad!

The answer leads to a new question: How do I know if something is good or bad? Experience and literature on leadership[1] provide us with sub-questions. So, in case you have doubts, ask yourself: Is it illegal? Does

---

1 One such book is The Power of Ethical Management: http://books.google.hr/books/about/The_Power_of_Ethical_Management.html?id=ohuwFJBt4hwC&redir_esc=y

it violate any laws or corporate governance? Is it righteous? Will it hurt someone's feelings in the short or long run? Does it enable us all to win? How would I feel if I do this? Will I be proud? Would I feel good if I read about my decision on the front page, or hear about it on the evening news? Would I feel proud if my family learned of this?

The moral dilemmas faced by business leaders and politicians are often more complicated and deep-set than perceived by the media and the general public. From personal experience I assure you it is never easy to make seven-and-more-digit decisions that have considerable impact on people's destinies, personal wealth, business, and political, scientific and professional careers. Whenever I was unsure what to do, I would go through the above list of questions.

The first part is quite simple: You must never do anything illegal, regardless of how appropriate you think the specific laws concerned (or any political standards) are. Legislation is often bad and insufficient, but as long as the rules are there, we must obey.

The second set of questions is more complicated. Nothing is as natural as the pursuit of justice and fairness. We spontaneously want to achieve satisfaction for all. Nevertheless, someone will have to be hurt as a result of the decisions we make. It is impossible to please everyone, all the time. If everyone is rewarded in accordance with merit, some will be hurt. If everyone is treated equally, irrespective of what they deserve, only the best and most capable feel abused. Even though we are all driven by a desire to be accepted by everyone, only mediocre leaders try to please everybody. By trying not to get anyone mad, and by treating everyone equally, regardless of their contributions, we hurt the most creative and productive people in the organization

This question boils down to the dilemma: If I truly must, whom should I hurt by my decisions? The answer is as simple as the question. The person who deserves it most!

The best leaders aspire to be accepted by their best workers. If they must hurt someone, let that be the worst workers. No one can be liked by everyone, so it is important to be appreciated by those who, according to our criteria, deserve it most. Unfortunately, it is only human to do just the opposite; we hurt those closest to us (e.g., friends and family members), and treat best those who deserve it least (e.g., strangers and casual acquaintances).

The third set of questions is very helpful because it takes into account our feelings after a certain decision is made. Lacking a better orientation, personal feelings can serve as good guidance. For example, you must choose among several options, and you are not sure which is best. For each option, you should ask yourself the questions above: How will I feel? What if this ends up in the news? Will I be proud or embarassed?

Whenever lacking better criteria, you may question your feelings; that's the least deceitful of all approaches. Why is that? Our feelings are clear reflections of our internal harmony. We cannot trick them because somehow they already "know" what is good for us, and what is not, what is moral and what is unacceptable, what we really want, what we aspire to and what sort of decisions we can live with. No wonder high moral standards are the bedrock of personal and organizational harmony.

3.4. Leaders Hold out a Second Longer

At the end of my teaching experience in Beijing, I decided to make one of my childhood dreams come true. I visited the site made famous by Bruce Lee. At first glance, Shaolin does not differ from other Buddhist temples, situated on the romantic slopes of a Chinese mountain range. However, the monks adhere to utterly unusual methods in perfecting the secrets of martial arts. The great master Li Xiaolong explained that secret in his broken English: *Many believe we teach how defeat your enemy. It just the opposite. The martial art teach you fight enemy inside.* The moment he said that, I had shivers and I knew that was it. I have to defeat the enemy inside first. He is not out there, he is in my head.

As a kid I came across a strange definition of a hero: a person who can hold out a second longer than others. Never knowing when the other guy would give up, he should find enough strength to endure. The energy for withstanding one second longer is entirely mental. In terms of this book, that energy comes from tapping into our internal harmony, our power of self-perception and self-determination. A more traditional term for that would be *autosuggestion*[1]. It's a very strong leadership tool, mostly because, in order to succeed in what they do, leaders need strong willpower based on a self-fulfilled prophecy: "I believe in myself and that is why I shall succeed."

It is quite clear that every person is what he believes himself to be, and that every individual, to a certain extent, becomes what he decides to be. Therefore, if you want to be a leader, you must learn to think big and to look at your abilities and actions from the positive side.

You know about the placebo effect. Research proves that any drug, even an aspirin, works up to 70% better if the patient believes in its effectiveness. In many cases a placebo, or a fake medicine with no healing properties, can cause a patient to be made well just because he persuaded his mind and body that by taking it he had overcome the illness. The same thing applies to leadership.

---

1 The term was introduced by Émile Coué, a French psychologist in his book Self Mastery through Conscious Autosuggestion (1922)

Placebo leaders are successful because they believe in themselves and their abilities. Human mental energy is extremely powerful. It has been recorded that, in ancient Greece, women from the warlike city of Sparta gave birth to strong children, while women in the intellectual city of Athens bore intelligent children, because this is what each mother desired and expected to happen.

That's why leaders should be characterized by a high level of self-motivation. Self-development strengthens our will and builds self-confidence, affecting our spiritual life and improving mental ability overall. Experience tells us that we are more creative, stronger and more successful if we convince ourselves of it. We all have potential; we just have to learn how to unleash it!

Many great minds in human history, from Leonardo and Michelangelo to Tesla and Edison, felt they had a "mission." They were propelled by a feeling that they were predestined for something unique and grand. Such autosuggestion helped them release all their creativity and talent. The same holds true for contemporary leaders. There are many examples of this you-can-do-anything-you-set your-mind-to attitude, from a multitude of innovative products to impossible missions successfully accomplished, despite a strong resistance from the environment. You don't know what you're capable of doing until you try!

However, it is never easy to make decisions which are difficult to implement. First you must convince yourself of the reality you aspire to, and then you have to turn conviction into action, to make the new reality come true. This is why all diets begin on Monday, and all big decisions are made through rituals. Following Li Xiaolong's advice, we must defeat the enemy inside us. According to French leader Charles De Gaulle, to quit smoking is the easiest thing in the world; he managed to do it at least a hundred times. Even when he made a firm decision to quit, he failed to do it. How did he finally succeed? One day, he told his Chief of Staff, every member of his Government, his personal secretary, his wife, his children, all the foreign politicians with whom he talked, all his relatives, neighbors, and journalists he bumped into that, as of tomorrow, he would no longer smoke. When "tomorrow" came, he had to make a tough choice; to resist the temptation each and every time, or to be humiliated in front of so many people. And that's how he managed to defeat the enemy inside and overcome his weakness.

Self-control and self-motivation are two main pillars of self-development. The capability of a leader to master his weaknesses and discover hidden fountains of energy is often a key to success. In his book on emotional intelligence, Daniel Goleman[1] describes an experiment from the early 60s.

---

1 http://www.danielgoleman.info/

A group of four-year-old children was put in a room and each was given a chocolate bar. The teacher explained that they could eat it. However, anyone who was able to wait ten minutes without touching the candy would receive yet another chocolate bar, and get two instead of one.

Guess what happened! Most of the children finished all of the chocolate immediately. Others ate it piece by piece, some fiddled and poked it around, some even tried to fall asleep in order to resist temptation. But only a few succeeded. Twenty-five years later, a detailed analysis was made of the school and life success of each subject. The results indicated that the children who were patient and exhibited a high level of self-control achieved much better results in their lives. They had the ability to *delay pleasure*. That idea is very important for leaders, who must be ready to sacrifice and have endless patience whenever necessary. They should believe that working hard, and investing a lot of time, money, energy and effort must pay off eventually. Short-term pleasures are never as sweet as long-term satisfaction. Overnight success is almost always based on many years of hardship and sacrifice.

A long-term orientation and persistence are essential ingredients of inner harmony; so is pride. Good leaders are proud of their knowledge, capability, skills, experiences, points of view and results. That pride is responsible for great self-expectations which enable leaders to achieve internal peace and fulfillment whenever they do things right. It also means that they need not be admired by others in order to feel important. The strongest feeling of pride comes from within, from self-assessment; from the awareness that we have achieved something valuable. However, a mature leader should never be arrogant, self-absorbed, and boastful about his results and accomplishments.

A person genuinely satisfied with himself doesn't need external confirmation and approval. Self-control, self-motivation, a long-term view, pride, and ability to delay pleasure; all these are reflections of internal harmony achieved. There is only one person whom a true leader should constantly try to please and impress; himself.

3.5. Leaders Persist

Once upon a time, the urban legend says, Sir Winston Churchill was invited to give a lecture at Cambridge University. The Dean introduced him as follows: *Listen carefully to each word from the greatest speaker of our times. His message will alter your lives.* Rising to the podium, Churchill gave them a serious gaze, said only one sentence, slowly stepped down, and then left the hall in silence. Some of the students were disappointed by the shortness of his speech and began to whistle. It was not until later that they comprehended the depth of his message. All he said was: *Never, never, never give up!*

Persistence and *perseverance* can be considered the most valuable leadership virtues. We should stick to our beliefs and hold onto our convictions, even when there is no immediate value earned. We must believe that every problem can be solved if we remain persistent, consider it from all angles, pay it sufficient attention, and never give up.

As a part of inner harmony, persistence stands next to trust in our abilities, self-confidence and a winning spirit. Mark McCormack, who used to coach some of the top world athletes, strongly believes there are three features that make sport superstars different from ordinary people: (1) dissatisfaction with the results, aspiration to improve, (2) capability to reach top form for major events and (3) the ability not to fear any opponent.

Let's make an analogy. Leaders achieve results which are admirable to others; however, this never pleases them indefinitely. After one goal is achieved, another is set. And when conditions change, the goal may be adjusted as necessary. As soon as one difficult project is completed, a passion for another, yet more difficult, emerges. The best leaders are constantly dissatisfied with what is accomplished because they truly believe more can be done. The best is yet to come! The process of improving oneself is endless; it keeps a leader in motion forever, in a constant search for rejuvenated supplies of energy and harmony.

The ancient Chinese teachers of martial arts have developed a strange concept of challenge. Two masters face each other as if preparing to fight. After a minute or so, the fighters decide who is the winner, without having exchanged a single kick. The winner is the one who managed to impose his authority on the other, it's the one with more self-confidence, whose attitude and posture succeed in sending the message: *You'd better surrender! If we fight, you are going to lose and suffer!*

As a samana (hermit-saint) on his spiritual journey of self-discovery, Siddhartha[1] from Herman Hesse's book had to learn three things: to contemplate, to be patient and to starve. This reminds us of yet another key to success. It takes a lot of patience. A good leader is supposed to be patient, especially when the prospects do not appear very bright. He should rest his inner harmony on the belief that, with time, everything falls into place. Success and results need not be desired impatiently, irrespective of the circumstances.

In one of my favorite Westerns[2], the old Indian chief decides that it is time for him to die. So he climbs the mountain, chants his song of death and makes his bed, ready to meet the Great Manitou. Next morning he wakes up, still alive. Patiently, he packs all his things and starts a long walk back to his village, chanting: *Magic sometimes works, sometimes it doesn't work.*

---

1 http://en.wikipedia.org/wiki/Siddhartha_(novel)
2 http://www.imdb.com/title/tt0065988/quotes

One has to come to terms with things once they have happened. The past, over which we have no influence, shouldn't entangle us in its web, preventing us from moving on. Patience and persistence play important roles in achieving spiritual, cognitive, strategic and operative harmony. Internal balance and stability give leaders strength to endure when everybody else has given up.

3.6. Leaders Think More and Work Less

Patience is important, but so is impatience. "We want it all, and we want it now," is a saying most likely invented by a leader. Even the greatest ideas and visions are worthless if they can't be implemented rapidly and efficiently. Most leaders are fast decision makers, able to cut through argument, debate and doubt, to offer a quick solution.

However, there are many problems that must not be solved in haste. If something is truly important, it should never become urgent. Good leaders should take time when making key decisions regarding life and work. Strategic issues are not bound to short deadlines. A good leader knows that his deeds should not be completed in terms of quantity but in terms of quality, and it is better to think more and work less. All visions, strategies, plans and actions must be harmonized. This can only be done through a continuous process of rethinking and rebalancing all facets of the leader's private, political or business life.

I often ask my students and colleagues where they see themselves five years from now. Where will they be, what will they be doing; how they perceive the future. Many have trouble in answering the question; some have never given it a serious thought. As in the song *Que Sera, Sera* by Doris Day, *whatever will be — will be*. I do not know what will happen and cannot influence it. It's destiny, after all.

However, if you don't think about the future, you may not even have one, says an aphorism. Any individual or collective vision, mission, long-term goals and plans should be defined without time pressure or tension. Does it surprise us that in real life, it is just the opposite?

As a member of the Zagreb City Council, I often participated in discussions leading to annual plans, budgets and strategies concerning the future of the Croatian capital. According to a typical bureaucratic habit, it was done within rigid time constraints and under pressure of impossible deadlines. No wonder, most decisions were of poor quality. The time "saved" by rushing into inadequate visions, strategies, plans or budgets resulted in a lot of time wasted to correct the mistakes.

There are many ways in which leaders manage time in order to increase efficiency. A good leader must have clear goals and know what is important.

Also, he must be prepared to cope with unforeseen circumstances, to eliminate unnecessary procedures and minimize paperwork. Successful managers personally deal with the work of great importance, and delegate everything else to co-workers. In order to do it right, they must have well-defined priorities.

During a gala dinner, I happened to be seated at the table with a president of a multinational corporation, and a leading business consultant. The conversation eventually touched upon the topic of consultancy — what is it worth, and are consultants really useful? The president laughed ironically, his experience having shown little value extracted from consultants. Besides, he complained, they were unable to solve his greatest problem. Due to his heavy workload, he was spending more than ten hours a day in the office. He was willing to pay an extravagant fee to any consultant who could provide a solution, but he had already lost hope.

Now everyone looked at the consultant. He took a deep breath and responded: *I have some free advice for you. Tomorrow morning, when you get to the office, cancel all telephone calls, meetings and appointments. Take a blank sheet of paper and write down the three most important problems that you, as CEO, must solve. Take as much time as you need. When you are satisfied with your list, dedicate all your knowledge and energy to the first problem. Work on it until you come up with the solution, and then remove it from the list. Make a new list with only three problems and repeat the steps. Always deal only with the issues of primary importance. I think this might help.*

A few months later, the consultant received an envelope from the CEO with a big check. The envelope also contained a message: *Thank you! Your advice was most helpful.*

Good time management depends on good priority setting. Leaders shouldn't waste time doing non-essential tasks! That is why all routine organizational processes ask for standard procedures (i.e., ISO quality standards). Once we standardize the routine tasks, it is easy to teach new operators to perform the tasks, to plan and control them, reward the employees for the work done and motivate them to achieve better results. It also means that more time is left at the top for vision, strategy, innovation and initiation of new projects.

What does your daily routine look like? Whatever appears on your desktop, whether you are a politician, a manager or an employee, falls into two categories: the relevant, and the irrelevant; things which are important, affecting your work results significantly, or unimportant stuff, creating barely any effect. The Pareto principle teaches us that 20% of the work we do accounts for 80% of the impact, while the remaining 80% is only 20% relevant. Good leaders must distinguish which matters are of greatest importance, in the mountain of tasks that seem to require attention. They should focus on fewer problems of greatest significance.

Systematics sometimes helps. Here is another two-category situation. Leaders deal with things which are under their control and things which are beyond their control. The things under our control can be altered and influenced by our decisions, while the things outside of our control either occur or do not, irrespective of our will.

We have already explained a leadership rule: *Deal only with relevant things!* Good leaders have discovered a related rule: *Most energy should be directed towards the relevant things under control.* It is our battlefield, the place to fight and win. Only the controllable part of the system is influenced by our decisions. As far as the relevant things that are outside of our control are concerned, it is wise to accept them as they are and to adjust to them.

Sun Tzu offers some advice that is two and half thousand years old: "When you are in trouble, change, and you will survive. It is unwise to persistent in confronting the inevitable. Winners are those who know when it is time to fight, and when it is not."

Irrelevant issues deserve minimal attention; one must ignore them, if possible. The relevant things outside of our control call for accommodation and adjustment. However, you should never give up on the relevant things. Therefore, there is yet another rule: *Try to gain control over as many relevant things (which are at present outside of your control) as you can!* Wise leaders adjust and conform if they have to, and try to increase their influence over important matters which affect the bottom line. For example, they can lobby, in government or the media, before a new law is passed; they may control the inputs (e.g., raw materials) by taking over some suppliers; they might create a strategic alliance with key partners, or they might sponsor a business school program impacting the quality of human resources.

It's a typical mistake to spend time on noncritical issues instead of dealing with what is essential. The things outside of our control are used as excuses for not doing what we are supposed to (e.g., We are victims of circumstances, we are affected by poor laws and exceedingly high taxes, no one can succeed in the face of such competition...). It is useless to get angry at important items that we have no control over, because we cannot change them. Instead of finding excuses, it is always better to seek for ways to make a difference.

Without priorities and clear, long-term goals, our short-term behavior cannot be efficient. A good preparation is half the task completed. As Sir Winston Churchill[1] once said, "Take care in the beginning, and the end will take care of itself."

I have seen many managers moving in a vicious circle. When asked

---

1 http://jpetrie.myweb.uga.edu/bulldog.html

about their strategies, visions, plans, projects and priorities, they say they are overcrowded with routine tasks and don't have time for things like that. We must be fully aware that the lack of strategic harmony affects our day-to-day efficiency. Operative disharmony is a result of deficient strategy. If I don't know where I want to be in five years, it is difficult to make any good operative decision today. People without strategy are constantly struggling, even though they may work very hard. They waste a lot of energy and resources, they are always behind schedule and, somehow, they always seem to be doing the wrong thing.

3.7. Leaders Know What They Want

How does success emerge? What makes a politician win elections, why is a company great; what makes an idea work? Why is a career brilliant; why does a team win?

As a teenager, I played in a band, as I mentioned. Like most such groups, the four of us used to read pop magazines and shared a dream to make it big. One day, we found an article revealing the secret of becoming a pop star, claiming that success depends on only two things: image, and a hit.

Image means to be recognized. As soon as you are spotted by someone, they should say: that's Bob Dylan, Madonna, Sting, Michael Jackson, or Norah Jones. A *hit* means that you have done something truly excellent, something that is recognized as a success. Something that will gain media attention, reach the top of the charts, take over the hearts and wallets of fans.

In the business environment a good image means brand-name recognition, an established market position, a famous organization, integrity, good customer relations, positive feedback from the public and the media. In business, a great image is one of the key competitive advantages. In politics, image is the chief asset of a political party, a movement or a leader. If the image is blurry, or gets obscured, by an incident of any sort, elections can be lost and careers go down the drain. The image of a political or business leader is primarily tied to the results of the organization they run. The leader's image is also heavily affected by his or her personal appearance, communication skills, the things he or she stands for, and public reputation.

Our *image* is the most distinct reflection of our internal and external harmony. It reflects our values, our integrity, our readiness to self-develop, as well as our ability to develop our team and the whole organization.

In business environments, we can talk about "hits" such as: growth of market share, launch of a successful product, revolutionary innovation, new business models, professional respect, attention-grabbing marketing campaign, and decades of reliable profit growth. In politics, the possible "hits" are election results, GDP growth, global recognition of a country, new highways built, increase in employment, and the overall well-being of citizens.

It has already been pointed out that success finds those who fight, who are proactive and ready to take chances. If you wish to succeed, regardless of your profession, that simple advice still holds: *All you need is a good image and a hit.* My teenage rock band didn't have either one. So I ended up as a university professor, a politician and a consultant!

Several years ago, my school enrolled fifty students in a new MBA program for ICT managers. As the head of that program, I decided to invite the best student, after completion, to stay with us and help us teach the others. As the first in his class, that person ought to have rather unique skills and knowledge. So, by the end of the introductory session I explained this idea to the group and asked them openly: *Who do you think will be the best in your group?* One student replied: *The smartest one among us!* Some nodded in agreement, but the majority disagreed. Having some life and business experience, they understood that a brilliant mind is not the key to every door. They had seen quite a few bright individuals who did not succeed. Also, they remembered a few not so smart ones who did.

If it's not brains, what is the key to success? After some debate, we concluded that business and life success (there was some disagreement about what that really means, and how it could be measured) depended on two things: clarity of goals and persistence in achieving them. A person with a small number of clear goals always wins over an individual who lacks focus. To hit one target right is better than to go for many targets and miss.

We are clear about the goals if we manage to view our business or life situation from a long-term perspective. However, clear goals are not enough if we have a propensity to quit easily. In order to attain ambitious goals persistence is necessary, not to mention hard work and readiness to sacrifice. As Mr. Churchill suggested, good leaders never give up. Their self-developed inner harmony must provide their actions with perseverance and continuity.

Yes, goals are important. That fact can never be overemphasized. Therefore, goal setting deserves as much time and energy as needed. If we define the right goals, the only mistake we might make is not to achieve them. But if we pick the wrong goals, we go the wrong direction, and solve the wrong problem. Obviously, goals need to be checked and probably adjusted as we move forward. People with clear goals know what they want; they are balanced individuals who are aware of their internal harmony sources.

What is the goal of your company, your department, you as an employee, you as a person, you as a parent or marital partner, you as a leader, you as a friend or a human being? Can you state the majority of these goals quickly, without getting confused, because you already know the answers and need not think about them?

In Lewis Carroll's famous children's book that is really for adults, a Wonderland rabbit looks at Alice as she approaches, first through a telescope, then through a microscope, and finally through an opera glass. Then he reaches an irrevocable conclusion: *You are traveling the wrong way.* In the same book, Alice asks the Cheshire Cat which way she ought to go. *That depends on where you want to get to,* wisely answered the cat. *If you don't care where you're going, it doesn't matter which way you go,"* said the Cat. Only if you are sure about the destination is it easy to choose the right path.

Experienced leaders probably have a funny addition to the cat's wisdom: Even if you don't know exactly where to go and you are supposed to lead, act as though you do. Eventually, the fog clears and the true path becomes obvious.

The Chinese wise man Lao Tse would probably comment: *A path which is a path is not the path.* This is why true leaders often dislike following in other people's footprints. As the poet Robert Frost[1] tells us: "Two roads diverged in a wood, and I took the one less traveled by. And that has made all the difference."

3.8. Leaders Take Time

Time is our greatest resource. It is the terrain on which all business and life battles are fought, gained or lost. Every task evolves through time and makes use of time. Even so, the availability of such a unique, irreplaceable and powerful resource is often taken for granted. Successful leaders respect time and treat it with special concern and care. A lack of time is a major constraint in every project and activity.

Time is the seed of the universe, says the Mahabharata, an ancient Indian poem. Time is also in its properties; it always comes, but never returns. Unlike other resources that can replace each other (e.g., capital, and labor), time is completely non-exchangeable and indispensable. It cannot be harnessed and saved for later. Irrespective of the demand, the supply cannot be increased. You can't save it to spend it on another day. When it is gone, it has vanished forever. Not even the best scientists can invent new minutes. Time is a very equitable resource because it cannot be rented or bought. Each human being has exactly the same number of hours and minutes every day. The wealthy and clever have no more than the poor and stupid. Time is inelastic. Even so, time is amazingly forgiving. No matter how much time you've wasted in the past, you (probably) still have today.

Perhaps even more than people and money, time is a key resource, necessary for any type of activity. Needless to say, harmonious and efficient

1 Robert Frost, http://www.poetryfoundation.org/poem/173536

time management is a must. The minutes, hours, days, weeks and years ahead of us bring opportunities that should not be lost.

Yesterday is history, tomorrow is a mystery, today is a gift, we learn from oriental wisdom. Time brings change that must be managed, and every new day initiates the remainder of our business and private life. If you want to be efficient, make sure to balance the three segments of your time: for work, family, and yourself as a person.

For most ambitious leaders, work means life, and the rest just happens "along the way." A settled family life, providing satisfaction and happiness, is as important for career success as a battery for starting a car engine. Energy is not just there to be spent; it needs to be rejuvenated. A harmonious leader will, therefore, devote time and affection for his family or friends. It is still one of the major pillars on which our internal harmony stands. As suggested by Herb Kelleher[1] of Southwest Airlines, it is wise to employ "people who have balance in their lives, who are fun to hang out with, who like to laugh (at themselves, too) and who have some non-job priorities which they approach with the same passion that they do the work." Bitter workaholics and grim professionals should find jobs with the competitor. Why? Because such an attitude is disharmonious; its effects on the overall work culture and values is negative in the long run.

Every individual must have time for himself, his hobbies, his self-development outside of work and family. Otherwise, if they happen to lose their work or family, they are left with nothing.

While I was studying management in New York, I heard of a successful businessman from the West Coast who was offered a new job in the midst of his career. Very pleased with his current position, he was suddenly faced with an offer that was hard to refuse: the current job, which he truly liked, and the challenge of a great new career. What should he do?

He remembered a school friend who had, in the meantime, become a famous career consultant, and he called him to seek advice. *I'll help you free of charge,* said the friend. *I only ask that you come to New York by train.*

I can charter an airplane, a rocket ship, and get there right away, said the businessman. I don't have time for half-a-week journey by train. *Please, do as I tell you, or solve the problem on your own,* responded his friend. I'll be sorry for the rest of my life if I don't make the best decision, contemplated the businessman, and finally he decided to board a train for the Big Apple.

He spent the first hour reading a newspaper, irked by the very thought of the long train ride, wondering how much his job was already suffering because of this. Then, he stared out the window for a while, counting telegraph poles alongside the tracks. Next, he drank a cup of coffee and

---

1 http://en.wikipedia.org/wiki/Herb_Kelleher

finished reading the newspaper. He took a short walk, glancing through a window at the shadows of the mountain range, reddened by the evening sun. Soon, as it was too early to sleep and there was nothing left to do, he started to reflect upon the reasons for his journey. He suddenly realized that he had not pondered his ambitions, wishes, career, or personal goals for over a decade. Struck by a unique feeling of pleasure, he started a long conversation with himself about the purpose and meaning of his career.

Somewhere in South Dakota, half way to NYC, he finally recognized what it was he wished for in his life. Eventually, the train reached Grand Central. Smiling at his friend who was waiting for him in the station, he called out: "I've got it! I don't need your advice." *I asked you to ride a train*, said the career consultant, *so that you would think about your dilemma with no distractions. I knew you would come up with the best solution. You just had to take time to find it!*

An old Irish prayer[1] teaches us: "Take time to work; it is the price of success. Take time to think; it is the source of power. Take time to play; it is the secret of perpetual youth. Take time to read; it is the foundation of wisdom. Take time to be friendly; it is the road to happiness. Take time to love and be loved; it is the privilege of the gods. Take time to share; life is too short to be selfish. Take time to laugh; laughter is the music of the soul."

Self-development is a search for harmony and it takes time. In order to take a look at their career and life from a distance, every once in a while harmonious leaders must pull themselves out of the everyday routine. It is important to know that the days and hours spent on thinking, strategy, vision, planning, contemplating — paying attention to personal or group goals — are not wasted time but rather the best investment in the future. How you spend your time is how you spend your life. Wouldn't you like it to be harmonious and balanced?

3.9. Leaders Don't Fall for Mantras

There is a well-known story shared among people who dislike consultants. A sports car stops alongside a large flock of sheep, and the driver says to the shepherd: *If I tell you the exact number of sheep, will you give me one?* The shepherd reluctantly agrees. The driver connects to the Internet via his mobile phone and quickly retrieves the information from a satellite. *You have 342 sheep*, he says to the surprised shepherd. As the stranger puts his prize into the trunk of his car, the shepherd hazards to ask: *If I guess your profession, would you give me back my sheep?* The driver agrees. *You are a management consultant*, says the shepherd. *How did you guess?* asks the surprised driver. *Piece of cake! First, you told me something I already know. Secondly, you charged a high price for it. Thirdly, you*

1   http://www.democraticunderground.com/discuss/duboard.php?az=view_all&address=298x1040

don't really understand my business, because you took my dog.

If you happen to read any respectable business magazine, in every issue you will be overwhelmed with an old or a new management fad like Activity-Based Costing, Balanced Scorecard, Benchmarking, Core Competence, Customer Retention, Customer Segmentation, Cycle-Time Reduction, Merger Integration Teams, One-to-One Marketing, Pay-for-Performance, Shareholder Value Analysis, Strategic Alliances, Supply-Chain Integration, Viral Marketing, Virtual Teams... If you open any journal on leadership, you will be flooded with ideas and concepts like Change Leadership, Transformational, Transactional, Invitational or Contingency Leadership, Ad Hoc Leaders, Situational Leadership, Trait and Behavioral Theories, Leadership Style Analysis... Certainly, no trade exists without tools. It's true, the management and leadership professions are changing dynamically and continuously, followed by a number of consulting "tools" emerging on a daily basis.

No doubt, leaders are expected to master new knowledge and always be at the cutting edge. But how to live in harmony with an ever growing inflow of leadership/management fads and mantras?

In the pre-Google era, I used to ask my Californian students to analyze articles and books whose titles contained a managerial fad, whichever term was "in" at the time. We wanted to find out which tools were most popular during a given decade and how long its popularity lasted. Aside from analyzing the circulation of university library titles (all items borrowed), they also studied the number of "hits" (items with the same key word) in professional databases, made by business people, students, professors and other users of the UCLA information system which is, by the way, one of the best in the world.

The analysis indicated that most managerial tools are nothing but short-term fads, similar to pop music and hit movies. When a tool is in, the users borrow and read all kinds of books and articles on Re-engineering, the Balanced Scorecard or Viral Marketing. It mostly depends on their popularity in professional magazines, management development programs or consulting practice. When a tool is no longer popular, the interest withers away. In the meantime, a set of new "tools" is sure to appear. One year, most companies were implementing ISO standards, followed by a set of re-engineering projects. The next year, every respectable company was working on its vision and mission statements, aligned with strategic plans, while the following year everyone was running business intelligence projects or buying new CRM (Customer Relationship Management) software.

The managerial profession is captured by a mania for fashionable tools and consulting fads that come and go with waves of expensive marketing campaigns. They last for some time and, after being replaced by another fashion, they fade away forever. Only a few tools manage to survive. Used on a long-term basis, they return the money and energy invested.

In the meantime, next to good consultants there are many "fog sellers." As soon as they detect a new trend shaping up, rubbing their hands in anticipation of demand, they intensively invest in marketing and turn themselves into instant prophets and gurus. As such, they start offering expensive workshops, seminars and lectures, laughing at naïve managers while counting their earnings.

Most of these are nothing but *managerial or leadership mantras*. In Buddhism, this term describes the sentences containing God's wisdom and message. The mantra is an idea which, if repeated often enough, becomes a part of us. Upon its acceptance, we change our attitude and start looking differently at ourselves, the world, our life or the environment.

In principle, the successful sale of managerial/leadership mantras depends on two things: (1) the quality of the marketing campaign used to sell the story to the business profession, (2) the inferiority complex which many managers successfully mask with an aggressive and self-confident exterior.

Of course, wise leaders should be open to help and new brainware. How do we resist fallacious mantras and false prophets and, at the same time, tap into true sources of wisdom, knowledge and authority?

Mantras are only one side of the management/leadership tool coin. On the other side, we see the consulting services market. The question remains: which advice to follow?

Here's a dirty little secret from consulting: any solution or suggestion by an external expert is trusted twice as much as the same idea when it comes from an internal expert. This rule of thumb is a key source of income for many consultants. Being a well-paid consultant, I guess I have a right to tease the profession. Every joke contains some truth, anyway.

Don't be over-impressed by experts! They may have more information than you, but not more wisdom and understanding. Their major assets are their reputation and the fact that they (presumably) have broad experience throughout the profession. By contrast, experts focused on their specialty can find it hard to clearly see and solve many real life problems.

Transitional countries like my Croatia have long been a pasture for "foreign experts" and their consulting services. After all, transition from one economic and political system to another is a complex, timely and costly affair. Numerous regional cases ended up as failures and misinvestments (less gained than spent). There are many reasons for that.

First, the transitional market was not perceived as a priority by the leading consulting houses. They either avoided it or provided second-rate consultants. Western experts usually find it difficult to adjust to the local business and political environment. If they want to succeed, they have to devote a lot of time and energy to learning in order to get accustomed to the region and its specifics.

One has to choose one's sources of knowledge carefully. Good leaders should make a practice of learning from the best. Furthermore, academic knowledge often doesn't translate well into reality. Above all, blind acceptance of any mantra must be avoided. "Trendy" does not mean "effective." It's not the tools that do the job. It's people who make the tools bad or great!

3.10. Leaders Cope with Stress

You wake up screaming, and realize that you have not slept at all. You used to be on time, now you're late... You used to be focused, now you lose concentration... You were an optimist, now you see everything painted black... You were open to people, actions, and ideas, and now you hold back... You used to be cooperative, now you're hostile ... You were creative, now everything seems like a routine... You used to look forward to each new day, now everybody is getting on your nerves... What's going on? You're suffering from severe stress! And you are not alone. According to the WHO (World Health Organization), stress has become a global epidemic.

I had a chance to visit the best Japanese corporations, Hitachi, Honda and Sony. One of the meetings ended at 8 pm. On the way out, we passed by a dozen ambulances. I asked my host if there had been some accident at work. He looked at me as if I had fallen from Mars and said: *Karoshi!* Later, I learned that this gentle word that sounded like the name of a gourmet dish, has a terrible meaning: death from exhaustion at work.

I went to teach in China. Upon my arrival, I was greeted by eight colleagues from the University (I learned that 8 is their lucky number). They took me to dinner and we enjoyed Beijing duck, eating and drinking Maotai until dawn. A week later we met again, but this time there were seven of them. With sad faces, they explained the absence of the eighth professor: *Gualosi!* Death from overwork.

As a visiting professor in the United States, I was invited to meet the dean with whom I had communicated via email and phone for half a year, discussing the details of my work and residence. We had chatted about various topics ranging from curriculum and literature to my off-campus accommodation. I could hardly wait to meet him in person. But, upon my arrival, the vice-dean informed me with a bemused smile that the Dean had ended up in a psychiatric institution: *Burn out!* This time I knew what he meant: complete emotional exhaustion at work, loss of desire to live, due to long-term stress.

Obviously, leaders consume a hefty daily portion of stress. It comes from making responsible decisions, managing costly and complicated projects, solving interpersonal issues, communicating with many different people, controlling behavior and balancing conflicts of interest. Without inner harmony to lean on, such constant external imbalances may strongly affect physical and mental health. What is the enemy and how can we fight it?

Stress is defined as a state of long-term tension resulting from responsibility in facing complex situations. As we all know, stress causes physiological and psychosomatic reactions which may result in fear, frustration and physical exhaustion. If such a state persists, it has an impact on overall health. That's the bad news. But there is also good news. Exposure to challenges produces an excess of adrenaline in blood, which can temporarily improve intellectual and physical capabilities, making people under stress more focused and efficient.

Many people are at their best when under pressure. Top business and political leaders thrive on excessive workloads that would be impossible for average people to manage. A person whose daily schedule is loaded with ten or more obligations has to organize his work and learn to be efficient, just like children who, in addition to regular school hours, take music lessons, study foreign languages and engage in sports training. A Croatian proverb states: *What must be done, will be done.* Nevertheless, there are limits. Therefore, keep in mind that your operative harmony (and the resulting efficiency) are a consequence of good personal strategy, coming from spiritual and cognitive balance.

Management literature is rich with suggestions on how to fight stress. Stress is internal; it does not necessarily have external sources. Stress is in the way we see and respond to ourselves, our work and our environment. A situation could cause panic, or leave us completely calm, depending on how we choose to look at it. Understanding this fact should help us control tension and restlessness. We must learn to take things as they come, whenever we are unable to alter them. The level of stress depends on our internal harmony: if what we expect (our goals, ambitions, wishes and needs) is balanced with what we are able to accomplish under the circumstances, there is a little or no stress. Our inner harmony should be our stabilizer. Then you won't lose your temper over a problem or an issue. If you can solve it, then go ahead, without losing your peace of mind. If the problem cannot be solved, let me remind you that it is all a matter of perspective. The same situation looks horrifying to some and pushes them to despair, while others stay cool and calm. It always helps to say: *Don't panic! I have solved similar problems before; I can solve this one as well...* We must keep in mind that the source of stress is our perception of an event, not the event itself. If a problem seems impossible or too difficult to cope with, we should try to see it with different eyes. Things are as we see them; it pays to see them as being to our benefit; then we may think of different and more successful approaches when responding to them.

Self-development helps us win the battle against stress. Every man is responsible for his own reactions and emotions, for his mental and physical health. It has been proven that people who are optimistic cope with stress more easily. They are more productive and live longer, happier lives.

Harmonious leaders control their instincts, temperament and feelings. Control does not mean repression, but rather direction. We cannot change our emotions, but we can decide what to do with them. We alleviate stress by dealing with ourselves! What is the most important secret? Find time to relax, to consider the outcomes of your actions, to prepare defensive strategies for situations in which you may lose! Doing it, you find stability and improve your internal harmony.

It is not that difficult to practice self-control. For example, follow the old Indian advice: Before you raise your voice at someone, count to ten. Before you raise your hand against someone, count to one hundred. It will give you time to reconsider. The truth is that, whenever you act impulsively, you are likely to regret it later.

Impulsive behavior lacks balance and perspective. More stress means less harmony, and vice versa. In order to avoid stress, you should stop doing disharmonious things and stick to the values that produce balanced outcomes. In essence, the fight against stress is a battle with oneself. You may "win" not by altering your nature but, rather, by understanding your true self, your reactions, goals, fears, weaknesses and strengths. To master stress means to tap into hidden sources of strength. Sometimes it means changing one's perspective. According to Marcel Proust[1], "the magic of discovery is not in continuous search for new landscapes, but rather in the capacity to look at old landscapes with new eyes."

3.11. Leaders Are Ready for Femaleadership

The last chapter on self-development for leaders is dedicated to Femaleadership. What is that? Before I answer that question, let me ask you another. Did you know that women's impact on consumer spending decisions[2] amounts to 83%? The female influence is highest when buying furniture (94%), choosing a vacation destination (92%), or buying a new home (91%), and lowest when buying new car (60%) or purchasing consumer electronics (51%). However, we still live in a male-dominated

1 http://www.brainyquote.com/quotes/authors/m/marcel_proust.html
2 http://www.she-conomy.com/facts-on-women

world, and being a woman leader is a difficult task — mostly because it consists in dealing with men.

Female emancipation is a recent phenomenon. In April 1944 a proposal to ensure women's suffrage and equality was presented to the French parliament. The presenter gave a lengthy speech, trying to emphasize the idea that women and men are actually the same. There is only one small difference. He never finished the thought, because everyone in parliament started to shout: "Long live that difference!" (*Vive la différence!*)

Some historians claim that, in human history, patriarchy alternated with matriarchy, but the present is characterized by a disproportionately small share of women in the structures of economic and political power. Representatives of the "fair sex" do play an increasingly important leadership role, but the process is slow and got a late start. The first woman graduated from Harvard Business School only in 1965. Fifty years later, female students at that school are 40%. In the former socialist bloc, women were legally equal to men as far as possession of property, the right to work, and salary were concerned. They rarely occupied leadership positions, but they were highly represented in expert positions. Over half the doctors, dentists and pharmacists in Eastern Europe are women.

There are many reasons for the scarcity of women in management positions. They have not been trained as leaders and managers. Also, they are victims of cultural norms, legal restrictions, the power balance and their own indifference or lack of ambition. In most cultures there is a strong division between male and female roles. A woman is too often in a position to be either a housewife (the politically-correct term is home-maker) or a career woman. In Arab countries, Latin America and the less developed regions of the world, managers can only be men. Women are expected to be dependent, and to serve. Even in the developed societies where women enjoy formal equality, the cultural stereotypes are not completely eradicated. One of the reasons for the modest representation of women in power structures is their own lack of interest in leadership or managerial career. Interesting enough, male resistance to female executives is stronger in Europe than in North America. Polls in Italy and the UK show that almost half of men reject the idea of having a female manager. In the U.S. and Western Europe only 3% of directors in large corporations are women, and they occupy 12% of middle and lower management positions, although they make up 45% of the employed.

Even though the power structures in both politics and corporations are dominated by men, psychological studies point out a number of "small differences" which indicate that female leaders have some competitive advantages. Experts agree that, in principle, female bosses are more focused on organizational relationships and not on action, like most men. Female managers prefer to share power and information, and they encourage participation. Other female leadership qualities include a tendency to develop organizational structures resembling family networking. Women are more understanding of people's emotions and problems, they are able to avoid conflicts and encourage cooperation; they are known for intuitive and emotional problem solving approaches, and especially for readiness to admit mistakes. All these female leadership traits contribute to more harmonious relationships with less conflict and more personal satisfaction. In addition, women are emotionally stronger and more resistant to frustration at work; they exhibit greater self-control, patience and stability in attitudes. Being more intuitive, women are less prone to fall for superficial effects and it makes them harder to cheat. In principle, men are more naive, and easily become objects of manipulation. This is explained by evolution, because the "stronger sex" used to resolve the issues with the environment by force, while the "weaker sex" had to develop more subtle methods to defend themselves without muscle power. Although we all know that "women are from Venus and men from Mars"[1], the associated stereotypes are often wrong and sometimes dangerous. Not all women are the same and not all men are alike. Many women exhibit male behavior, while many men present typical feminine qualities.

However, taking all that into account, it is not surprising that female bosses are more and more appreciated, both in business and in political life, which makes women the key pool for selecting future leaders. This book is written in he-form. Since English is not my native language, maybe I can't do better. But, whenever I use "he," I actually mean both sexes, with a slight preference for the ladies, mostly because of their actual under-representation. We are definitely entering the era of *femaleadership*. In this context, I am fond of the prophetic proposal by director Kevin Smith in his movie "Dogma"[2] that the manager of all managers, or God, is actually a woman.

---

1 A Book by John Gray: http://www.goodreads.com/book/show/1274.Men_Are_from_Mars_Women_Are_from_Venus
2 http://en.wikipedia.org/wiki/Dogma_(film)

> By three methods we may learn wisdom: First, by reflection,
> which is noblest; second, by imitation, which is easiest; and third
> by experience, which is the bitterest.

> — Confucius

4.1. The Explanator

> The person who tells the best stories is destined to lead.

> — A Native American saying

4.1.1. Leaders See through the Eyes of Others

Dissatisfied with his progress, a student of Buddhism decided to leave the temple, situated at the top of the Ping Mountain. One evening, he knocked on his teacher's door to say goodbye. *Leave, if you want to, but let me accompany you tomorrow on your way down the mountain*, responded the teacher.

When they set out in the morning, the teacher asked the student to look around and tell him what he saw. *I see the valley, encircled by mountains; in the center there is a lake and an old city*, said the student. When they were half way down, the teacher repeated the question. *I see the walls of the city, the brown rooftops, the port and many boats sailing on the lake*, answered the student. When they arrived to the city walls, the teacher repeated the question. *I see dogs and children playing, a group of traders taking livestock to the market, a few sailors loading wooden boxes onto boats and a bunch of noisy children throwing rocks into the lake*, answered the student.

The path to knowledge is like a journey down the mountain, said the teacher.

Wisdom can be attained by understanding that what we see from the top is not identical to what we see from the mid-point, or from the bottom. Knowing this helps us reject prejudices, opens our mind to learning, and teaches us to respect what we don't see from where we stand.

In a romantic novel, the author uses the following example: On the table there is a glass containing some liquid. For one person it is "half full," yet for the other, it is "half empty." Different people often see the same thing from differing perspectives. In "Rashomon," the cult Japanese black and white film based on a short story of Rynosuke Akutagawa and directed by Akira Kurosawa, an infamous robber attacks a travelling couple, kills the husband and rapes the woman. During the investigation, the event is described by the murderer, the woman, the magically evoked spirit of the victim, and by two random witnesses. Each one's testimony is totally different and a spectator, or a reader, must be totally puzzled.

Both oriental examples remind the harmonious leader that most situations can be seen differently by various participants and onlookers. People have differing ideas regarding the same issue, depending on their perception, as well as their goals or interests. What is even worse, they often change their mind about the same situation or a problem. No wonder, an aphorism states that a man who has never changed his mind should not be trusted.

The main task of the Explanator is to sell his image of the present situation to his teammates. In doing that, he must be able to manage the *organizational Rashomon*. Leaders must be aware of differing perceptions, because human behavior is like this, often strange and unpredictable.

Perceptions are derivatives of a prevailing organizational culture. We bring to the work-place our values, norms, attitudes, ideas, misconceptions, prejudices and ways of perceiving problems. Luckily, we can learn to change. Therefore, one of the key tasks of the explanation is to balance diversity. On one hand, he is supposed to generate a favorable organizational climate, in which differences in opinions are valued and stimulated. On the other hand, he must enable his teammates to find a common denominator and try to reach consensus.

In order to overcome the Organizational Rashomon, Andy Grove, the legendary CEO of Intel, allegedly had a genuine boxing ring installed in his office. Whenever there was a conflict within the company regarding a particular suggestion, project or technology (in any high-tech environment, that's a rule rather than an exception), the representatives of the competing groups were invited into the "ring" and Mr. Grove would tell them: *Please, discuss the issue! Feel free to argue, even quarrel, if necessary. I will just listen. Pretend that*

I am not here, if you can!

And so, they would debate the pros and cons of the different options in front of their CEO. For him, it was the best way to weigh their arguments and learn about the situation at hand. Each of the conflicting parties was best aware of the strengths of their arguments, and each knew the best counterarguments for the other proposals. Once they had had their say, the leader was able to come up with the best, most balanced (we would say "harmonized") decision.

Before inventing this idea, Mr. Grove used to resolve such situations just like the vast majority of executives: he would call representatives from each side and listen to them, one after the other. The first would usually be very convincing; educated individuals are quite capable of making their point. Then, for the sake of justice, he would listen to the other side. The opponent would also sound very convincing, resulting in complete confusion for Mr. Grove.

The Explanator should always try to see the world through the eyes of others, be it co-workers, clients, partners or competitors. While I was consulting a major regional food company, I persuaded the CEO to climb into a delivery truck at the crack of dawn, and deliver his products to customers (local supermarkets) along with his drivers. This allowed him to learn from his clients, or his employees, things he would never have known otherwise. It is hard to be a successful and well informed leader from the comfort and security of your posh office. There, surrounded by murals, impressive furniture, smiling secretaries and chiefs of staff, enchanted by the scent of fresh flower arrangements, you are isolated from real-life problems, unable to view their full complexity.

People tend to believe their current world outlook. By closing their minds to what is unseen from their positions, they miss the opportunity to learn from others, to consider their points of view and understand their positions. As our Zen teacher would say: *What is not seen from here can be seen from another part of the organizational mountain.*

Good leadership and governance rest on our ability to change the viewpoint in order to see more clearly. Organizational Rashomon happens because each of us perceives the world, and the people in it, from our own perspective. Our perception of the problem is not always complete or correct. Others may also have valuable insights. Differing positions in the organizational structure, and responsibilities, may have a strong impact on perception of goals, demands, values, and opinions of the people involved. This makes it difficult for them to understand each other, but it makes each of them a potential contributor to understanding the full picture. The wisdom of the Explanator is to see all relevant pieces of the organizational puzzle through the eyes of others. It is one of the cornerstones of harmonious leadership.

4.1.2. Leaders Sell

In New York's Central Park, near Chess & Checkers House, a beggar was sitting next to his hat with a handwritten note: *I am blind*. During lunch break, a marketing expert passed by, bent down and added something to the note. When he returned in the evening, he asked: *What kind of a day did you have? Never better*, answered the beggar, laughing — *what did you write for me? Nothing special*, said the marketer, *I just wrote: "It is spring and I am blind!"*

When I ask participants in my workshop what is their most important activity, many of them say: I have to sell! Everything I do passes or fails in the marketplace, and everything is reflected in the sales report. Total sales and the profit achieved show how successful I have been.

Some always disagree. They don't sell anything to anyone. As a matter of fact, they despise selling. Instead, they do important stuff like developing human resources, purchasing materials and equipment, managing information technology, controlling quality, developing new products, dealing with prototypes and design, researching the market, accounting, keeping track of finances. Some of them even seem a little offended: *Thank God we are not salesmen! Why such a fuss about sales?!*

Where does the negative attitude towards selling come from? Why is it that some people perceive trading as akin to smuggling or conning? It is quite obvious that, if there are no sales, all the other business activities don't matter!

Traditionally, a sale can be defined as a relationship between a seller and a buyer; one does something to the other. What does he actually do? Salespeople are perceived as individuals who will do anything to succeed. The seller will attempt to charm the buyer, work him over, convince him, sometimes even misinform him, just to make a sale and earn some money. The seller doesn't necessarily solve the buyer's problems, nor does he always intend to. Both sides, in principle, don't trust one another and don't exchange available information.

As far as the other group from this chapter's introduction is concerned, namely the people who despise selling, they live in denial. Everything we do, irrespective of the job or position, boils down to sales and selling. Of course, the notion is used in a much wider sense than selling products and services. No matter what your job description, be it production, back office, management, business information systems, finance, research and development, or human resources, you sell are in the business of selling something to someone. For example, you sell your reports to your superiors and your decisions to your subordinates. You sell plans, budgets, project proposals, as well as standards, organizational rules and procedures. Therefore, you'd better learn how to sell in order to do your job right.

Business is all about sales, but so is politics. Political leaders must be the best salespeople of all. They sell the party program, they trade ideas and ideologies, and, in order to succeed, they must successfully sell their personality to voters, and offer good explanations for any mistakes.

Some sell ideas; other sell skills, and still others sell knowledge. Some sell information; others sell projects; yet others quality standard manuals. Leaders most often sell visions, goals, decisions, plans and reports. Parts of the system which are not directly exposed to the external market participate in an "internal" market, even though it is rarely perceived as such, where they offer their products and services to the rest of the system.

The organizational simplicity and efficiency of Toyota is a good example of such philosophy. The executives teach all Toyota workers that they are all buyers and sellers, all the time. Regardless of your job, your customer is any worker who needs something from you, and you are a customer of any worker who does something for you.

Our uneasiness to admit that, in essence, we are all "in sales" evolves from a negative perception of selling in most contemporary societies. Traditionally, selling was something an honorable man would try to avoid. Friedrich Engels pushed these ideas to the extreme by describing the trade as a "legal fraud."

Contemporary marketing gurus invest extraordinary efforts in developing theories and practices to do away with such a stereotype. Today we define selling as helping the buyer (client, user, or customer) to succeed.[1] The concept is aimed at pushing the classical "buyer–seller" concept towards a relationship between a consultant and a client.

What is the difference? Any cynical manager would gladly remind us that most consultants he knows are the worst kind of sellers. Maybe so, but we shall, for the argument's sake, use the non-cynical meaning of the word. Consultants, by definition, don't do anything to their clients just to earn their fee. Their goal must be to help the clients succeed and, in doing so, both sides should be satisfied. In order to do it, the consultant must become a partner, assistant and friend of the client, protecting his interests, sharing information and developing a relationship based on trust and full cooperation.

The Explanator must be perceived by his team as just such an advisor.

---

1 E.g. Mahan Khalsa, http://www.goodreads.com/author/show/102985. Mahan_Khalsa

He should make sure that all members of his team see him as the person in charge who helps them succeed in whatever they do. Only then can a leader properly sell his vision, mission and goals, giving his followers a strong reason to work for him. Poor leaders don't know how, or don't try hard enough. Or, sometimes, they try too hard to be convincing. While communicating, they are perceived as touts pitching some idea, not as consultants.

Once we openly admit that we are, and all the time must be, "salesmen," the need to develop our selling skills becomes crystal clear. Otherwise, we destine ourselves to be unsuccessful regardless of what we do.

Most often a leader sells ideas. He is supposed to convince someone of something. We've enumerated the range of ideas he has to sell, from a common view of reality to goals, deadlines and detailed tasks to be completed. Furthermore, he sells to his team the importance of work discipline, the need for quality control, the reason why rules and regulations should be obeyed, and, finally, he sells a positive attitude, motivating his teammates to give their best and to win.

Obviously, throughout this book I am "selling" ideas to you. Imagine that tomorrow morning, I knocked on your door and said: *Hello. Please let me in and I will show you something important. Here is a book you can buy from me. It will change your life and make you a better leader.* Most likely you would shut the door in my face and, in a patronizing tone, tell the people you live with: *Another salesman! I just got rid of him!*

Why would you do such a rude thing? Because I knocked on the door as a salesman, I looked, acted and spoke like a salesman. You have learned by experience that "salespeople should not be trusted." They sell you something you don't really need just to earn commission. In such a mental environment, the seller's chance of reaching you is like the survival rate of a snowball in hell.

My goal is to convince you that I wrote this book because I want to help you become a harmonious leader. Only if you are convinced will you allow me to "sell" you a number of mental models and suggestions. Only if you really feel that the book helps you improve your personal leadership style and philosophy might you decide to finish reading it, and even recommend it to others. At no time should you become overly conscious of my "selling."

People instinctively resent "sellers." Anyone who looks, speaks and acts like a salesmen will be discredited from the start.

Thus a persuasive leader must not give away a single piece of evidence identifying him as a salesman. His intentions must be genuine, and the methods of communicating his personality and his goals must be sincere and effective. Political or business leaders who want to deceive us, by pretending to be advisors or counsellors, are detected and disclosed, sooner or later.

As we know, It is well known that you can fool all the people some of the time, you can fool some of the people all the time, but you can't fool all the people all the time. A leader must sincerely want to be an advisor; he must truly believe that he is not a salesman. He must honestly wish to help his teammates succeed in solving their problems. It's the best way to make them invest all their energy and knowledge in solving his problems as well.

One of the major reasons why politicians are distrusted is the widespread belief that, after coming to power, they usually follow their personal interests, not ours. In other words, they seem to behave like salesmen. A desire to work and act for the common interest, and to lead in such a way to please the followers, has always been a characteristic of harmonious leaders, the true advisors to their team. You may be a genuine leader-consultant and still lose, but if you are a leader-salesperson, you will lose big time.

4.1.3. Leaders Speak and Listen

An Indian maharaja set his son off to a temple to learn how to be a good ruler. The teacher sent the prince into the forest and then asked him what he had heard there. The prince listed the chirping of birds, the bustling of the wind, the rustling of leaves and the grumbling of a bear. Dissatisfied with the answer, the teacher sent the prince back, advising him to listen more carefully. Upon returning, the prince described the sounds of bees buzzing, streams flowing, grass swaying; but that still did not satisfy the teacher.

The prince went into the forest once again, and stayed there much longer. When he finally returned, he told the teacher about the sounds of buds turning into flowers, the whisper of the sun that warms bird wings, the sound of grass drinking the morning dew. The teacher told him that he had finally mastered the skills of a ruler, because now he could hear the inaudible. The new skill would enable him to listen to the hearts of his followers, not only to their words. He would be able to hear their true emotions, thoughts and wishes, not just those which they openly show and express.

One of the most important principles of good leadership is provided by human anatomy. We have two ears and only one mouth; therefore, it is twice as important to listen as it is to speak. However, most people do just the opposite. To them, good communication means the ability to talk and persuade, or the competence to give presentations and convince others. Most people, above all, enjoy listening to themselves; they lack patience and interest in what others have to say.

Of course, it is extremely important to develop the skills used to persuade, influence and convince. But not all leaders recognize the equal importance of listening to others, in order to be able to satisfy them as well as to learn from them. The golden rule of communication says: *First try to understand the person you are speaking with. Then, it is much easier to explain your position and send your message through.*

Research points out that business and political leaders spend about 70% of their time communicating. No wonder they are expected to speak efficiently, to formulate ideas in such a way as to easily tell, explain, justify, motivate and convince.

Selling ideas is the key task of the Explanator, and he must be successful in convincing others. In ancient Greek tragedy, a chorus was used to better explain the play to the audience. Before the show starts, the chorus tells you what the story is all about. Then the drama takes place, twisting and turning in all its complexity. At the end, the chorus appears once again to retell the whole story in a nutshell; to highlight the key messages and the lessons learned. This is the principle oral communication should follow, as summarized by Dale Carnegie: tell them what you are going to say, say it, and finally tell them what you said. This helps the audience to grasp key ideas, proposals, conclusions and suggestions.

It is always good to provide people with new data in combination with facts already known. Regardless of the occasion (e.g., explaining how to handle customer complaints, a presentation to potential buyers, presidential address to the House of Congress, or farewell speech for a retiring employee), a good speaker introduces no more than 30% new information to the listener. Any more than that, and the speech is tedious and difficult to follow. If it provides less than one third new information, the speech is boring.

The Explanator speaks in an illustrative and emotional manner, using examples, anecdotes, jokes, stories and experiences. The words are pronounced with feeling, to provide greater impact and make the message stronger. A leader who says he is happy must radiate positive emotion; if he's speaking of serious matters, he must look genuinely concerned; when presenting ambitious plans, he must seem victorious and self-confident.

Good communication is also often funny and witty. A sense of humor can be extremely helpful in overcoming barriers, solving problems and resolving demanding situations. Some leaders have built their image on the ability to joke even in serious situations. Nevertheless, it is important not to overdo it; it's one thing to break the tension and another thing to divert attention from the serious message.

A leader is expected to communicate energy and optimism. These emotions are contagious and stimulating for the listeners. Energetic leaders fill our batteries, increase our motivation and provide encouragement.

Good communication leads to discussion, questions and comments. Such feedback makes sure that the message is well understood. I used to teach a course on *Multicultural Management* on several continents. I was puzzled by the fact that, in many cultures, people are not likely to ask questions. Some people in leadership positions feel defensive when questions are raised. However, there is a proverbial truth that "he who asks does not stray," and leaders should welcome an opportunity to be sure everyone understands.

In selling ideas, simplicity plays a very important role. The Explanator should use clear and unambiguous language and simple vocabulary, abundant with examples from personal experience. In response to criticism or questions, he should not act disinterested, insulted or touchy. Such an attitude may cause a loss of trust and respect for the speaker.

Communication research has shown that we are slow speakers but quick listeners. The speed at which we process the words we hear is much higher than the speed of normal speech. An average person speaks at 120 words per minute and is capable of comprehending between 400 and 600 words per minute. Thus, only one fourth of the listener's capacity is occupied by the speaker's words. The remaining three fourths can be spent to analyze what was said, to prepare questions or comments, or to fantasize and daydream.

Indian chiefs and wise men always speak last. They are expected to conclude, wrap up and give the communication its final meaning. Silence is at times more effective than words. Perceptions take time to sink in; most things are better understood and seen with a little distance in time.

Let's take a look at another serious communication issue. In a song, a boy is complaining about his girlfriend. She keeps shouting *No, No, No,* but her eyes cry: *Yes, Yes, Yes!* What is to be trusted, the words, or the gestures and expressions? The nonverbal portion of human communication is responsible for more meaning than the verbal part. It is more important "how" we say something than "what" we say. Research has indicated that only seven percent of face-to-face communication depends on words. A leader who wishes to convince his team that there is no crisis, must send this message using gestures and not just words. His calm voice and steady hand must be accompanied by optimistic look, and powerful statement of arguments. Such body language will send a message of stability, determination and strength. Any nervous movement, tense body, eyes that cannot calm down, or a shaky voice, would instantly communicate to the audience that his words are not to be trusted.

Of course, communication styles depend upon local culture, traditions, habits and attitudes. The same issue is likely to be described differently in Zagreb, Berlin, New York or Beijing. The same words might be understood differently in Los Angeles, Baghdad, Rome or Tokyo. Young people speak differently from old people, the educated communicate differently from the uneducated, religious believers speak differently from atheists, women read between the lines differently than men.

The success of any human interaction, be it marriage, friendship, a business partnership, or teamwork, depends heavily on trust and harmony. Both are outcomes of pleasant and efficient communication.

In this chapter we have mostly talked about technical and conceptual truths related to harmonious communication. Other chapters will deal with issues like simplicity, candor, value of information and specifics of organizational communication. Needless to say, the Explanator must constantly improve his communication skills. He must pay attention to his verbal and nonverbal communication, how he dresses, his looks, his voice, his eyes, his posture, his gestures, his overall behavior and everything that reflects his personality. Everything we do is some kind of communication; what we are is what we communicate. Effective communication is just a little of what we know and a lot of how we feel about what we know. As the well-known expert on public speaking James Humes[1] likes to point out, "the art of communication is the language of leadership." The Explanator must use every opportunity to practice. Because every time he speaks, he is auditioning for leadership.

4.1.4. Leaders Value Information

After my workshops or seminars, some participants hesitantly approach me and ask if they can get copies of my presentations and files. I always surprise them by saying it's already on the web, or I provide them with an electronic copy on the spot. They have adopted a cultural norm that information is to be kept for oneself, instead of being shared with others.

Information is power and wealth! You share it only if you must; otherwise, close it in your drawer or file, codify it in your database! Keep it secret! Why would anybody give away something of value, especially if it took a lifetime to prepare and compile?

Imagine Ali-Baba in front of the secret door of the treasure cave, desperately trying to recall the magic words which open it. He should say "*Open, Sesame!*," but the words simply do not come to mind. He could try taking a dictionary and reading all the words systematically, first one by one, then two by two, followed by three by three, until he eventually uncovers the magic combination. If he knew the right words, he would get his hands on the extraordinary treasure and become immensely rich. Being unable to recall the password, he is doomed to endlessly try and fail.

Some people find themselves in Ali-Baba's shoes whenever they have to instruct their workers, persuade partners or please customers. If they manage to select the right data, pick the right words, make the right guess

1 http://www.harpercollins.com/authors/4705/James_C_Humes/index.aspx

how to communicate a message, their idea is accepted, a proposal adopted and a problem solved. But what if they do not find the right words or the necessary information?

Let's play around with still another Oriental hero. Imagine Aladdin in the middle of a huge warehouse. All the shelves are packed with lamps. One of them is magical, but how is he to find it? If he starts searching randomly, rubbing the lamps one after another until he discovers the magic one, it might take forever. Having the right information would save him a lot of effort and time.

Without the magic lamp, Aladdin is just a poor shepherd, similar to the rest of his folk. But, if he happens to find the magic one, he gets an almighty Genie at his service. The right lamp gives him the power to manage events around him, including his own fate. And it all depends on simple information.

A leader finds himself in the position of Aladdin and Ali-Baba many times a day. At first glance he may seem to be lucky, compared to the fairy-tale heroes. Living in the age of smart machines, he is equipped with all kinds of gadgets, tools and toys, from the Internet, smart phones, cloud computing, and expert systems, to knowledge bases, data warehouse and competitive intelligence. However, it is still hard to find the right information.

Obviously, in knowledge we are talking about a specific organizational resource. It is not consumed when used, nor is it diminished through distribution. It can be applied to many different situations by various parties, all over the globe. Information processing requires little matter or energy. Information or knowledge is not lost when shared with others. Communication (information sharing) makes people richer, not poorer. My knowledge is not spent if I use it to teach others. It is always there, and I can use it whenever I want. And the global information infrastructure makes it available at practically no cost. As Michael Dell humorously pointed out, the only thing cheaper than the Internet is telepathy.

Information most often meets needs that cannot be satisfied by matter or energy. At the same time, it is possible to substitute material, or energetic requirements with information. It saves time, energy and money to transport information instead of people or goods, whenever possible.

The Explanator values information because he knows the importance of being well informed. It means constantly researching, studying, inquiring, analyzing; in other words, learning, from everybody and everything, be it media, co-workers, customers, training institutions, consultants, colleagues, friends, competitors or opponents. The ever-growing need for information has given rise to the management consulting specialty known as Business or Competitive Intelligence. Instead of undercover or illegal activities associated with industrial espionage, or stealing information from competitors, today's leaders acquire valuable information concerning technology, markets and competition using sophisticated tools like Data Warehousing, Data Mining, or Intelligent Agents. The same is true for politics or government intelligence.

When the flow of information in an organization is based on a set of rules and procedures, managers can control all operations using ERP (Enterprise Resource Planning) software. However, business and political leaders as well must understand that their Information and Communication Technology (ICT) support consists not only of hardware and software. There are other equally important components. By analogy, we can call them: Lifeware (ICT specialists and users), Orgware (organizational procedures, standards and rules), Dataware (stored data, information and knowledge), and Netware (communication infrastructure). The quality of the overall system is a product (not a sum) of the quality of all the six components. Like a chain, the overall system is as good as its weakest component. Many managers believe that a good information system means top-quality hardware and software. The truth is that if we want a superior system, we must also invest in superior human resources, excellent organization, communication, and data storage.

The quality and availability of information are dependent on organizational culture, mutual trust, openness and cooperation. Successful leaders rarely keep information and knowledge to themselves; they share it with subordinates and other people within the system. Although it may, perhaps, threaten the "information monopoly" of leaders (they know things that other people in the hierarchy are not supposed to know), in most cases it can significantly increase the overall efficiency. And, of course, open information exchange contributes significantly to harmonious work and interpersonal relationships.

To live productively requires we be well informed. The success of the Explanator is fully dependent upon quality of information as well as on the technology and methodology used in processing and distributing information within his organization. However, he must be fully aware that technology is just a tool, not a magic wand. Today, we are able to develop a faster mind, but it's not necessarily deeper, broader and smarter.

4.1.5. Leaders Simplify

Sherlock Holmes and Dr. Watson went camping. After they washed down a good meal with wine, they went to sleep in a tent beside the camp fire. A few hours later, the famous detective opened his eyes and looked around in surprise. Then he woke his friend who was sleeping like a log. *Watson, look up into the sky and tell me what you see!* Still sleepy, Watson rubbed his eyes and said: *I see a million stars in the brightly lit summer night.*

What do you conclude from that, asked Holmes. Watson thought for a moment before responding: *From an astronomical point of view, I conclude that there are thousands of galaxies and millions of planets above us. From an astrological point of view, I have been able to see Saturn in Cancer. From a logical point of view, I conclude it is half past midnight. From a theological point of view, the universe above illustrates how God and nature are almighty, and we, people, are small and insignificant. From a meteorological point of view, all indicates that tomorrow will be a warm and sunny day. What do you conclude from all that?*

For a moment, Holmes remained quiet, and then he said: *This is elementary, my dear Watson: someone has stolen our tent.*

During a strategic weekend, the future of Rolex was discussed. Some Board members asked the CEO, who had just returned from a professional trip, what's new in the watch business. *I have no idea,* he responded. *We are not in the watch business. We are in the luxury business! Nobody buys our products because they are perfectly accurate.*

A director of Black & Decker used to describe their company mission as follows: *We make perfect holes for our customers.* The mission of Walt Disney Corporation is to create the perfect adventure; the mission of Revlon, similar to that of a political party, is to sell hope.

Many years ago, a journalist asked Bill Gates what made him the wealthiest man in the world. *The belief that money is not important, and hard work is all that counts,* he stated. *How did this actually help?* insisted the curious journalist. *I managed to implant that belief in the heads of all my employees,* responded Mr. Gates.

Arthur Schopenhauer,[1] an eminent German philosopher, used to say that "all thoughts obey the law of gravity"; they flow from a head to a piece of paper quite naturally. When we write, we know exactly what we mean, and want to say. However, when we read what someone else has written, a strong force holds the thoughts to the paper, making it hard for them to climb into our minds. Therefore, the key task of a good writer is to help the reader in overcoming gravity.

It is not much different when we speak. One must give his thoughts (words) enough clarity, illustrative power, conviction and emotional strength to make them fly from his mouth to the ears of the listeners, like a cannon ball, following a ballistic curve on its path to the target. If we don't give our words enough speed and power, they fall short, trapped by *communicational gravity.*

Clear speech is the most powerful weapon of the Explanator. But it is not an easy tool to handle. For example, you should never expect to be fully understood by others, regardless of what you say and how you say it.

1 http://www.brainyquote.com/quotes/authors/a/arthur_schopenhauer.html

Your messages should be carefully and considerately formulated, so that they correspond with the experience, knowledge, age and perception of the people who listen. It is easier to speak to a hundred doctors, a hundred enraged workers, or a hundred IT engineers than to a hundred ordinary, completely diverse individuals.

Harmonious leaders must be great simplifiers. They should be able to summarize, in a few words, not only great ideas but also the small truths concerning everyday problems. From a pile of facts, they should be able to pull out the most important and offer solutions which everybody understands. Simplicity also contributes to organizational harmony. All good organizations are based on a small number of relatively simple rules which are strictly obeyed. Bad organizations usually stand on a large number of complicated rules and norms that no one knows and everybody thinks are impossible to implement.

Let me give you another example of the power of simplicity. As a guest to the parliament of a large European state, I happened to listen to the speeches of two distinguished politicians. The first spent half an hour describing three of his party's proposals in boring detail and monotonous, bureaucratic language. The second took the floor only for half a minute and, with a strong voice and persuasive gestures, stated that all three suggestions presented by his predecessor deserved only one comment: A huge NO!

At the onset of the Second World War, Sir Winston Churchill offered the British a clear message: "I have nothing to offer but blood, toil, tears and sweat... [O]ur aim is victory. Come then, let us go forward together with our united strength."

John F. Kennedy informed his fellow Americans of the ambitious space program, costing billions of dollars, using two simple sentences: "Before the end of the decade, one American will set his foot on the moon. With him, the entire nation shall walk on the moon." When it finally occurred, the astronaut Neil Armstrong described this event in even simpler terms: "That's one small step for a man, one giant leap for mankind."

The visions of great business leaders can often be summarized in an easily understood sentence. *Every family will have a car*, said Henry Ford when there were barely a few hundred cars in America. *Every family will have a computer*, said Bill Gates at a time when personal computers were just emerging. *We are not going to make better, but different, computers*, said Steve Jobs upon his return to Apple.

The best criticisms can also be summarized in a simple joke. For example, the one about the depth of the current crisis: *Ten years ago, the world was perfect, there was Steve Jobs, there was Bob Hope and there was Johnny Cash. Today, we have no jobs, no hope and no cash.*

A good leader knows the importance of the KISS principle (Keep It Short and Simple). Everything under your control should follow that rule. For the members of your team and for all the employees alike, simple goals are just as important as clear instructions and plain words used to explain, motivate and inspire.

Yes, simplicity is always the best tool of the Explanation. Suppose your boss tells you that you have to complete the assignments within the deadline, otherwise customers will be complaining about the terms and delivery dates, and this could jeopardize your market position, resulting in your inability to pay all the workers at the end of the accounting period. How about this: *If you don't meet the plan, you won't get paid!*

4.1.6. Leaders Dislike Communicational Bicyclism

Organizational communication is like a bloodstream; it provides a leader with a tool to protect the health and efficiency of the system he is in charge of. If this important liquid does not flow as it should, or if it piles up or leaks, causing a lack of oxygen and nutrition, or if the immunological system becomes incapable of resisting external infections, the organism becomes sick. And sickness is nothing else but a state of disharmony.

Good communication provides balance, increases motivation, creates a common feeling that people belong to an efficient, dedicated and goal-oriented whole in which it is nice to live and work. Psychologically, communicating means belonging. Conceptually, as already stressed, communication means harmony. Technically, communication means organization. In a well-organized system the leader is trusted, and the members of his team trust each other.

In a hierarchy, there are three communication styles: courteous, aggressive and assertive. Most corporate or political cultures grow and develop within a hierarchy. It means that there is a tendency to promote *communicational bicyclism*. Communicating style within a hierarchy resembles a bicycle ride. While pedaling, the rider puts pressure on those who are under him. By leaning on the handlebars, he bows down for those who are above him.

Hierarchies are never customer-oriented; they are boss-oriented. As Jack Welch humorously pointed out, standing within any hierarchy, you turn your head to the boss and your rear to the customer. It means that the bicyclists carefully communicate with all those who occupy higher positions. The superior is never told the whole truth; any upward-going message is formulated according to the principle "tell the superior what he wants to hear," and "be courteous." A true leader, of course, doesn't want to be informed in such a way, because it means that he never knows what is really happening in the organization.

While being extremely polite towards the boss, the bicyclist is an aggressive communicator with respect to those who are below his hierarchical pedals. Typically, he treats them with no respect, and raises his voice. Also, he may engage in petty complaining and criticism, sometimes even insulting subordinates. Such behavior reflects the I-am-the-boss and I-can-do-what-I-want attitude. If the leaders support such bicyclism, the communication bloodstream is polluted and the entire system is sure to experience a heart attack, sooner or later.

Obviously, the courteous and the aggressive style are not OK. How should we communicate, then? Assertively! No wonder that word hardly exists in most languages! It means many things. For example, say what you mean while being polite! Treat everybody fairly, be honest and open towards all. Do to others only what you would let others do to you! Don't be offended by constructive criticism! Don't take such information personally, but rather focus on the problem!

All of this sounds reasonable, doesn't it? But leaders are like other people, bloody under the skin, vulnerable and vain. The heritage of communicational bicyclism is many centuries old. It could be traced back to the traditional family. Its tracks are still very deep in many institutional systems, especially those based on heavy administration, such as government, army, school and other powerful bureaucracies.

I was most exposed to communicational bicyclism when I worked for the government. My subordinates would simply race in, smothering me with flattery. Every second word was "Mr. Minister" or "Mr. President," and it was accompanied by a real bow and a fake smile. At first, I complained about such sucking up, and then I went so far as to forbid it completely. Nobody openly said anything, but very soon I discovered that my reaction was to no one's liking. They were accustomed to this "courteous" communication style; it was expected and supported by all my predecessors. It is hard to get rid of the bicyclist mentality because most people are enslaved by habits. And a habit can easily become man's (or an institution's) second nature. Remember the five monkeys?

During the Middle Ages, Turkey was one of the most powerful nations in Europe and Asia. Their sultan was "the ruler of the world" and the emissary of Allah on Earth. One of the most influential members of the Sultan's court had a title of Evet-effendy. His only role was to excessively flatter and court the Sultan, praising everything the Ruler said or did, making such behavior unbearable. The real task of the Evet-effendy was to make the Sultan sick and tired of sucking up. Similarly, in ancient Rome, the emperor was constantly reminded that he was only mortal, like the rest of the people. Many present-day managers and politicians could learn a lot from both practices.

Assertive communication is supposed to teach business and political leaders that they are like everybody else. A traditional Italian proverb states that, if a fish stinks, the stench must have started from the head. Only after the assertive principles are adopted at the top of an organizational hierarchy can they be accepted by the rest. The methods at the leader's disposal range from seminars and workshops to the introduction of formal communication standards. Bosses must never forget that they are role models. To lead means to set an example!

Assertiveness is a friend of honesty and an enemy of hypocrisy. If a Japanese company suffers a reduction in demand, and has enough work for 100 while there are 120 employees, they announce that the excess employees are now "window watchers." Even though there is no real work for them, they are expected to be in full attendance. Are they going to spend the whole day window-watching? Normally, they would be doing unimportant tasks, from cleaning facilities and equipment to putting the company library and files in order. However, if there are no such jobs, they would literally sit down and watch through the window. The work that can be done by 100 is not going to be "watered down" and divided among 120 people. Also, there will be no false statements such as "We are working at full capacity; there are enough contracts to keep us all busy."

Truthful communication builds trust, pride and objectivity. I know that my leader does not try to make a fool of me. He tells me how things are and I trust him. If I am a "window watcher" today, tomorrow it will be somebody else. Today, someone is working for me; tomorrow I will be working for them. Whether the news is good or bad, the truth is always out in the open. I don't have to worry that something might be going on behind my back.

In most cultures, 120 people pretend that there is work for all, and the tasks are "watered down." Since the employees are not stupid, they know what is going on, but they have learned to pretend. Due to insufficient workload, there is plenty of time for gossip and arguing. Interpersonal relationships deteriorate and people start playing political games. It is clear to everyone that there is not enough work to go around, but organizational lies are perceived as something normal, something in the "common interest." Yes, the superiors pretend, they misinform us and tell us nonsense, but that's the way it should be. Such behavior gives us the moral right to do the same, to pretend, misinform and hide the truth from our bosses.

Obviously, only assertive communication builds trust and allows for growth of organizational harmony. Assertive leaders are known for still another thing; they don't conceal their intentions. We usually distrust people who, willingly or unwillingly, hide what they really expect from a communication partner. For example, someone asks: *What are you doing this evening at 8 p.m.?* Not knowing his intentions, you might come up with an excuse, fearing that he would play some trick on you. If this person wants your true reaction, he has to openly declare his intentions: *What are you doing this evening? I have two tickets for the soccer game.*

Good leaders (especially politicians) are known for their "perfect" memory. If they happen to bump into a business partner, party sympathizer or ordinary citizen whom they have already met before, they recognize the person in a flash, showing that they care about people and consider them important. In order to do that, a leader needs not have a perfect memory. There is a saying: what does not fit in the mind will fit on the paper. Whenever you discover an important fact regarding any of your employees, customers, suppliers and partners, write it down — on a piece of paper, or in a database; or instruct somebody else to do it. When you meet this person again, you are ready to astonish him by showing that you haven't forgotten. Databases with detailed personal information regarding important business or political personalities are sold at extraordinary prices — mostly because they enable leaders to improve harmonious relationships with people they deal and work with.

The Explanator must protect his organizational culture from communication pollution, coming from the described communicational bicyclism and hypocrisy. Even though at times it can be very costly, honesty is the best foundation for cooperation, good and balanced interpersonal relationships, and success in business and political communication.

A company in which everybody knows who are the workers and who are the window watchers provides a more harmonious and pleasant environment than a company in which, while pretending to work, everyone is looking out the window.

4.1.7. Leaders Learn and Unlearn

According to an old Chinese proverb, if you plan a year ahead, plant rice; if you plan ten years ahead, plant trees; if you plan a century ahead, educate people.

At the beginning of every school year I ask my students: *How much do you think I know about the topics we are going to deal with in this course?* They always dislike the question. A normal professor is supposed to ask how much the students know, and not vice versa. When I insist, they reluctantly answer: *A lot, professor, you have written tons of books on the subject.*

I try to be more specific: *Imagine a scale from 0% (nothing) to 100% (everything). Now, what is your estimate of my knowledge?* Somewhat more intrigued, the students come up with a number between 50 and 70%. I give them a look as though they have said something ridiculous. Quickly, they change their mind: *It's 90%; you know almost everything there is to know on the subject.* No, I tell them, *wrong direction! I guess my knowledge on the topic amounts to 3%.*

Now all the students uncomfortably stare at the floor. The professor has just admitted that he has no clue. I try to explain my position. *Let's Google the course title. There are a few dozen million hits. If only one thousandth is relevant, what is 3% of that; how much time would I need to read it all? And to follow the daily changes? How many books and articles in various languages are published on the topic each week, and how much time would I need to read just 3% of that? How many lectures are being held on the topic right now, anywhere in the world, how many seminars and workshops? How much is being said on radio or TV broadcasts, and how much time would be needed to capture just the pitiful 3% of these events?*

Soon the students start to nod their heads. Truly, the amount of knowledge on any topic is colossal, and keeps increasing. Then, it's time for me to make the point: *I am proud of the 3% that I know, but I must constantly be aware that there is still 97% that I do not know.*

Now I can ask them the other question: *How much do you know about the topic?* Of course, the students propose any number less than three. It is only logical; I am their professor, and they are here to learn from me. Anyway, this short discussion helps us understand that we do not know, but are prepared to learn. I even ask them to say this sentence out loud: *We don't know, but we are ready to learn!*

Most likely, for the first and the last time in their lives they pronounce "I don't know" with pride. In a business or political environment, this sentence is considered shameful, discreditable or inappropriate and must be avoided. Pretending that we know, we try to look superior for no good reason. Such an attitude prevents us from being curious researchers open to new knowledge and inspired to constantly and continuously self-develop.

The search for knowledge is the search for harmony. An average American manager spends up to 10% of his working days attending seminars, conferences, retreats, professional training or company workshops, including management development programs. Western European business leaders spend about 7% of their time learning, while the Japanese invest close to 20% of their work time in various types of academic and non-academic self-development. In case you are curious about transition economies, according to a research by Zagreb University, top Croatian managers, on average, dedicate one day per year to learning and competence development, and middle managers up to four percent of their working days. Of course, the most successful Croatian companies invest more in management development; the low average has to do with the old-fashioned majority. Once they get appointed or elected, most managers and politicians start believing they know enough and stop working on self-development. They are no exception; the same trend can be observed worldwide.

In order to become a better and more successful leader, the Explanator must be exceptionally dedicated to learning. He must constantly self-develop and consider it the most important lifelong project. The purpose of learning is not, as one aphorism states, to understand and explain the world in which we live and work. The true challenge is to change it.

There is a story about Nanin, Japanese teacher of Zen.[1] One day a university professor from the West, who was eager to learn about this school of Buddhism, paid him a visit. According to the old tradition, Nanin personally served tea to his guest. But, even after his cup was full, he continued to pour. Unable to watch the tea flowing all over the table and dripping on the floor, the professor decided to interrupt him by saying: *The cup is full, you can't pour any more.*

Just like this tea cup, Nanin answered, *you too are full of ideas, concepts, views and prejudices. I cannot teach you Zen if you are not ready to empty your cup.*

It's equally important to learn and to unlearn. Some of the things we know may no longer be right, correct and applicable to situations at hand. The values we believe in may not be the right ones anymore. Our experience and cases on which we base our action may no longer hold true. Our attitudes may be the very source of trouble and failure. In times of rapid change, the problem is how to get new, innovative thoughts into our mind, but also how to get the old ones out!

A true leader must regularly empty his "cup" of concepts, views, ideas and approaches that no longer function; only then he becomes ready to refill it with new content. We must keep in mind that it is equally important to learn new tricks, and to forget the old, outdated ones. According to a Croatian proverb, *It's no good putting young wine in old barrels, because it will get spoiled.*

Nan-in and his guest carry a valuable message for any environment in transition, for example, for my homeland Croatia, struggling to become a successful capitalist country after five decades of self-management socialism. It is not easy to abandon the unproductive, irresponsible, stable, secure, but uncomfortable half-way behind-the-iron-curtain heritage. The cups of the new era do not rid themselves easily of the old content. The issue gets even bigger if there is no change in leadership. In most cases the same people who used to lead the old, are still in charge of the new. They have, perhaps, changed ideologies and adjusted their wording to the new circumstances. However, their minds, habits and actions often remain as before.

In recent decades, many drastic changes have taken place due to rapid

---

1 http://www.zenguide.com/zenmedia/index.cfm?id=6

technological development. The best example is the removal of traditional boundaries between home and office; the local and the global; a product and a service; a buyer and a seller; work and play; a student and a worker; competition and cooperation; business and private life. We used to go to the office, and now, equipped with telework software, we carry the office with us. Smart products like the iPhone or intelligent refrigerator provide us with all kinds of information services. The Internet enables us to buy and sell simultaneously, and participate in global auctions. More and more, our work resembles a creative playground. Studying has become an essential part of any working experience and vice versa. It is getting more and more complicated for the multinationals, and the governments, to say where the cooperation stops, and turns into a competition.

Harmony-based leaders must be constantly aware that the world of falling boundaries is the world of fast and continuous learning and unlearning. It changes, and we must change along with it. In times of a paradigm shift, our most valuable knowledge is the stuff that remains after we have forgotten what we have learned in school.

4.1.8. Leaders See the Whole

An airline was faced with a small crisis. One of their planes had technical difficulties at Airport X. A quick analysis indicated a minor malfunction which the maintenance worker could fix within a couple of hours. However, he would have to travel to Airport X from Airport Y in order to fix it. What should be done? The head of maintenance concluded the following: If I send a serviceman immediately, he may fix the plane by 3 p.m., but he doesn't have a flight back the same day. This means that he stays overnight in a hotel, costing $150 from my budget. If I send him early tomorrow morning, he can fix the problem and be back on the noon flight, and I save 150 bucks.

Saving that money must have made the head of the maintenance department feel useful to the company. However, his decision actually cost the airline $90,000, because they didn't have the plane fixed the same day and had to rent another one in order not to cancel the afternoon flights. The cost-sensitive maintenance manager may even have received a bonus at the end of the year for keeping "his" costs within budget, while the damage was attributed to *force majeure*.

The problem stemmed from his lack of a big-picture view. The goal of the whole, for some reason, becomes less important than the goals of the parts. Obviously, this sort of thing happens on a daily basis in most organizations. Responsibility for the well-being of the whole is not given priority over responsibility for its parts, or sub-systems.

We all know that good leaders must develop a holistic view; they need to see the total entity and the interdependence of the diverse parts. However, it is not as simple as it seems. You know the story. Four blind men are asked what an elephant looks like. The first crawls under the stomach of the huge animal and describes the elephant as a big balloon. The second takes hold of the animal's tail and says: *It's not true, an elephant resembles a snake.* The third man screams in protest, holding a long tusk in his hands: *An elephant is like a twisted spear.* Leaning back on the elephant's leg, the fourth strongly disagrees: *You are wrong, an elephant is like a trunk of a tree.*

We always perceive a whole based on the parts we see or belong to. Those who work in the manufacturing department see the management building as crowded with unproductive, lazy folk who rearrange papers, hold useless meetings, drink coffee and enjoy the anarchy. On the other hand, people in the management building perceive their role to be of utmost importance; they plan, design, research, develop, organize and manage crises created by the manufacturing department. It is crowded with workers who fall behind schedule, make mistakes and create problems of all sorts.

Within every system, the different parts sooner or later see themselves as "us" against "them." Such an attitude is a sure source of trouble. It can lead to interpersonal battles over budget resources or a tug of war over projects, priorities and positions.

The Explanator must always try to see the whole picture. His task is to fight for everyone's interests, not just for some. His goal is to harmonize the system and not the subsystems. He needs the systems approach, based on the idea that every whole is more than the sum of its parts. The interaction of the parts should be aimed at achieving the goals of the whole. The systems approach means that, whatever happens in an organization should be seen from the point of view of the whole, taking into account its vision, mission, goals, projects and programs. Only then can the system be organized, the tasks delegated to subsystems, and finally completed. A true leader is never interested in small wins which might lead to a big defeat. It is often necessary to lose a battle in order to win the war.

The key idea behind the systems approach is the concept of synergy, symbolically described as 2+2=5. I prefer to call synergy "organizational harmony," and it is just another way to say that each system can be more than the sum of its parts. The ability to achieve synergy in teams, companies or political parties provides them with a strategic advantage over the competition.

An optimum for the whole usually equals to the sum of the sub-optimums of its parts. Therefore, we must do what is best for the system and not what is best for its segments. Typically, we all agree that the success of any system as a whole is more important than the success of its parts. In real life, however, that often calls for individual or group "sacrifices," which we resist. Nevertheless, if we wish to win as a team, we must be coordinated. Joint victory is often made up of individual defeats. By the same token, a joint failure might sometimes be a result of personal maximums, which, due to interpersonal conflict, may cause the system more harm than good. The aircraft that needed repairs is a good example.

Effective leaders always keep an eye on the whole, knowing that it occasionally means sacrificing particular interests and hurting some groups within the organization. Such decisions are not easy to make, but should be made for the greater good.

4.1.9. Leaders Think Kaizen

Do you know the joke about a young manager promoted to a demanding CEO position? His experienced predecessor handed him over three envelopes and said: *Whenever you come across a problem, open an envelope, and follow the instructions. They are guaranteed to get you out of trouble.*

Initially, the new CEO was doing fine, but a year later a crisis emerged and his workers went on strike. Not knowing what else to do, he reached for the drawer and opened the first envelope. Inside, he found the following advice: *Blame your predecessor for all the problems.* So he took a stand in front of his employees and explained that the problems they were facing could all be attributed to the mistakes made by the former management team. He asked for some patience and cooperation.

The idea worked, but not for long. Half a year later, the crisis escalated and the strike was followed by a drastic decrease in market share. The CEO opened the second envelope, which read: *Blame the government and its policies.* So he faced the owners and workers with arguments proving that the new taxes, some stupid laws and a few ridiculous government decisions accounted for their poor business results. He pleaded for additional patience, cooperation and self-sacrifice.

The workers and the owners calmed down temporarily, but a few months later, all the problems surfaced again, along with a threat of bankruptcy. The CEO opened the third envelope with a shaky hand, hoping for a solution. There, he found the following advice: *The time has come to prepare three envelopes for your successor.*

That pretty much sums up the typical attitude of many business and political leaders.

The Japanese word *Kaizen* can be best translated to English with the rather long sentence: *It's good, but it could be better.* The term originates from TQM (Total Quality Management) literature and describes a technique of continuous improvement. For me, it is the key concept of successful change management and a paramount of harmonious leadership.

Kaizen is based on positive thinking; it aims at the deliberate elimination of criticism. In essence, it combines two good ideas into one. First, it reflects the leader's belief that nothing is so great that it doesn't require a change. Kaizen leader is open for improvement. Secondly, it helps prevent unnecessary conflicts which are so common in most change management projects.

Our culture is dominated by the view: *It has to be changed because it's bad.* Such a view is responsible for a vicious circle of blame and antagonism towards the predecessors. We explain the need for change by attacking the forefathers and blaming them for the mistakes from the past. It always ends up in fruitless battles, negative energy and perception of change as a problem, rather than as a solution.

By saying "it's good," a harmonious leader has indirectly praised all who are responsible for it. Therefore, he is not burdened with the past, nor does he let it hold him a hostage. By adding "everything can be better," a leader has cleared a path for action, calling for an initiative to change the existing system in a natural, hopefully conflict-free way.

The mindset of most newly appointed leaders reads often like this: *Some idiots have ruined the system (company, country, project, organization), and now, it's my duty to put everything in order.* This is a bad start. It causes unnecessary conflicts with predecessors who feel attacked and insulted. Their most natural reaction is resentment for the new leader, his supporters, his proposals, ideas and actions.

A newly appointed leader may have strong reasons to hold former management responsible for having done a poor job. Nevertheless, should he openly express this view, he would instantly be faced with strong resistance from the "former power structures." A wise leader avoids unnecessary battles. Don't do anything disharmonious, if you can avoid it. Whatever you do to others comes back to you. Take a look at the following story.

A father and his son climbed the mountain. Suddenly, the son stumbled and fell. Angry and humiliated, he screamed *Ouch!* To his surprise, the mountain replied with *Ouch! Who are you,* the kid asked curiously. *Who are you,* answered the mountain. *You are creepy,* cried the kid again. *You are creepy,* responded the mountain. *A coward,* cried the little one. *A coward,* the mountain was sure to reply. *What is it, Dad,* the kid asked his father. *Watch this, son,* said his father and shouted: *You're the best! You're the best,* replied the mountain, and then the father explained: People call it echo, but it's actually life itself. It returns everything you say or do. Life is simply a reflection of your actions. If you want more love in the world, create more love in your heart and your voice. If you want more success in your team, improve their knowledge and skills. This is true for all you do; life will return everything you've invested in it. Whatever happens to you is not a series of coincidences, but rather a reflection of your actions.

Of course the moral of the story is simple; if you give Kaizen, you will get Kaizen. According to Sun Tzu, the supreme art of war is to subdue the enemy without fighting. Harmonious leadership calls for Kaizen logic. The Explanator should always try to introduce change in a non-conflict manner; his task is to search for harmony and consensus instead of blaming predecessors.

4.1.10. Leaders Are True Globalists

Our globe is the biggest whole we have. No wonder holistic leaders must also be globalistic. When did globalization begin? Some people say it can be traced back to the European age of discovery and voyages to the New World. Others see it as an outcome of the recent technological revolution (communication and transport in particular), coupled with the new world economic order.

Let's take a look at a few examples. In December 1987, American Chrysler promoted the Eagle Premier, a new car on the market. The chassis was created in France, the exterior was designed in Italy, the transmission was produced in Germany and it was assembled in Canada; the promotional campaign was run by a US marketing agency.

During the same year, the city's tax bureau stated that one third of the property in downtown Los Angeles belonged to the Japanese. The next spring, a container of Honda automobiles, the first in a series produced in the State of Ohio for the Japanese market, was unloaded from a Chinese trade ship at Narashino Port. Thereafter, a container of Hondas produced in Japan was loaded onto the same ship, to be sold on the American market.

Even a small country like Croatia is heavily impacted by globalization. We are world players in ship building (100% exports), and tourism (85% foreign guests). In chain stores (which are booming), people can purchase products from seventy-eight countries including Italy, Slovenia, Greece, Israel, Spain, Germany, USA, India, China, Taiwan, Chile and Ivory Coast.

Advances in transport and information technology make the world smaller; all its inhabitants are becoming closer and more alike. The growth of multinational corporations creates a huge global market, allowing for the international exchange of knowledge, technology, services, products, skills and managerial talents.

In an old joke describing the charm of European integration, Heaven is a place with a French chef, an Italian lover, an English policeman, and a

German mechanic; it is organized by the Swiss. But there is also a Hell. It has an English chef, a German policeman, a Swiss lover, a French mechanic and everything is organized by the Italians. Is globalization a heaven or a hell?

In search for local harmony, the Explanator must learn to think globally and act globally. Even so, many people are not pleased with all effects of globalization. It brings in new values without question, it endangers the cultures of small nations, it undermines nonstandardized products, and it turns into into mass production what used to be handicraft.

Antiglobalists equally dislike English as a language of global communication, the Internet and mobile networks as a Big-Brother infrastructure, and the world's policeman — America, ever ready to "protect" global interests, whether the rest of the world likes it or not. The trouble with globalization is that, each time there is a global gain, there is a lot of local pain.

Today, the most successful major leaders are harmonized globalists. Their mindset is based on a proper balance of global and local interests; they support the affirmation of small economies and isolated cultures, but opt for open and fair cooperation. In today's business and political arena, cooperation goes hand in hand with competition. You can use a name for that child of globalization: *"Comperation"* or *"Coopetition"*, depending on your taste.

Strangely enough, there are at least two great world problems that could force us to act globally for real. One is pollution control. Focusing on harmony with nature should make us appreciate true globalism, because we can never stop polluted air, or water, at the border, asking for customs forms. The same is true for (political) terrorism. If we are not united, it becomes an issue which no nation, army, intelligence agency or police can isolate, fight and prevent. Living in the world of ozone holes, greenhouse effects, suicidal bombers and data pollution, one could wonder whether globalization still has a chance.

Without understanding global trends it becomes increasingly difficult to cope with change on any level, political, economic, business, social or ecological. If the world is really facing catastrophe, as we have repeatedly tried to point out, harmony-based leadership is desperately needed. Only a critical mass of new leaders, as role models for harmonization of global business and political processes, can help us survive. We need a global paradigm shift. However, we see nothing but slow adjustments.

We are in hot water, and it's getting hotter all the time. Meanwhile, in discussions of the world's problems, we are told that everything is fine, and getting better all the time. At least, we aren't cooked yet. True! Contemporary business and political life are exposed to a gradual value change with respect to leadership style, people's expectations, decision making processes and management practices. The importance of hierarchy is diminishing, and so is the influence of autocratic leadership. There is a growing tendency towards workers' participation and collectivity of all sorts. But are we pleased with such small changes? Do we not deserve to be a little impatient?

There are a number of reasons why leaders should be fully aware of the globalization issues. Today, over 43% of the world's GDP comes from international business activities, organized by multinational corporations. No industry is immune to the influence of international markets. The past decades have been characterized by the tremendous impact of multinationals. For example, Exxon, the petrol giant, creates 75% of its income outside of its home market; 55% of sales of IBM come from foreign markets. For soft drinks giant Coca Cola, it is 50%, and for the king of hamburgers, McDonald's, it is 30%. Global companies are more and more interested in skills, knowledge and talents of managers trained to become global leaders. The same is true for politics.

Leaders who are unable to speak foreign languages and communicate in multicultural environments gradually become subject to isolation. The world is becoming a smaller place. We work in sophisticated international environments in which local success is achieved through global thinking. Prosperity in any line of work could be measurable only through global benchmarking, supported by a global exchange of experiences. To know and understand other cultures, business customs and value systems, helps all countries to avoid isolation and underdevelopment. Pursuing integration allows for better international business and political cooperation. A comparison in global terms provides each leader with the possibility of evaluating the strengths and weaknesses of his system; it enables him to avoid the threats and benefit from the opportunities on the world market.

Personally, I see at least two big global time bombs, and the countdown started a long time ago. The first has to do with world demographics. If the current population trends don't change, in less than fifty years, 97% of people below 27 years of age will be living in Asia, Africa and Latin America. Only 3% of the young will belong to Europe, North America and Australia. Can you imagine the effect of these numbers on education, health, child care, workforce, sports, retirement plans and consumption patterns, not to mention the military issues?

The second time bomb is closely connected; its outcomes are already obvious. The work force of China amounts to almost 800 million relatively well-organized, educated and hard working individuals. The work force of India is not much smaller. The labor cost of China and India is 8 to 30 times lower per capita than in the so-called developed countries. As a result, no production involving significant labor is economically justified anywhere but in these two countries. How will that affect the rest of the world? A major increase in petroleum prices, due to the high growth of oil and gas consumption in China, is just a small hint.

But let's look at the world from the optimistic side! Being equipped for globalization, the Explanator must also get acquainted with the local business and political cultures in which he operates. Every country is specific; successful management strategies in one part of the globe could be a total failure in another. Success in any business and political environment depends heavily on a good understanding of the local culture and values. Harmonious leaders should cherish and maintain a proper balance between the local and the global. More often than not, it's a vital source of sustainable success.

Leadership and management are deeply culture-based activities. It is virtually impossible to transplant any management or leadership knowledge, practices, methods and principles from one culture to another without having to tailor them to local conditions. Cultural environments differ in everything from measurement of success to definitions of quality and notions of efficiency. A good leader should master globalization trends in parallel with the specifics of a given cultural environment, taking into account global criteria as well as local peculiarities. This is probably what Henry Kissinger[1] had in mind when he said that one task of a leader is to get his people from where they are to where they have not been.

4.2. The Visionary

> It is always wise to look ahead, but difficult to look further than you can see.
>
> —Winston Churchill

4.2.1. Leaders Organize and Disorganize

Once upon a time there lived a peasant in China. He had a son who worked on the farm with the help of a horse. One day the horse ran away, and the local farmers said, "Bad luck." The peasant frowned and replied, "Perhaps." Next morning, the horse came back, followed by a whole herd. When the local farmers saw them, they said, "Great luck." Again, the peasant replied, "Perhaps."

After a couple of days the peasant's son broke his leg while riding one of the new horses. The local farmers again commented, "Bad luck," and

---

1 http://www.brainyquote.com/quotes/quotes/h/henryakis130663.html#b6KlswCRJQlLG13d.99

the peasant repeated, "Perhaps." The next week, a war broke out and the emperor's army did not conscript the peasant's son because of his broken leg. The local farmers said, "Great luck," but the peasant just whispered, "Perhaps."

This traditional story actually talks about Yin and Yang, the union and harmony of opposites.[1] According to Taoism, the nature of Yin and Yang lies in the interchange and interplay of the two components; as they bounce around, and cycle back and forth, a state of imbalance leads to harmony, and then the state of harmony soon gives way to imbalance.

The concept of Yin and Yang nicely describes the first two leadership roles. The Explanator is interested in now, addressing questions about the system *as it is*. On the other hand, the task of the Visionary is to deal with the future, describing where to go from here and how to get there. His primary interest is the system *as it should be*.

The Explanator deals with what the present system looks like, the Visionary wants to build a new system. According to our model, the two roles are closely connected; they must be subsequently played by the same person. It takes an Explanator to tell us where we are, and a Visionary to tell us where we are supposed to go. In practical terms, it means that the job of a leader is to be the chief organizer, but also the chief disorganizer. *The organizer* makes sure that every facet of the existing system functions as it should; *the disorganizer* wants to destroy the existing system in order to introduce a totally new system.

A need to, on one hand, optimize the existing system while it still functions, and, on the other hand, destroy it, in order to build a better system, seems to be one of the greatest challenges for any leader. Our harmony-based leadership model explains this paradox through two concurrent roles of a leader. It takes the Explanator to understand the present. It takes the Visionary to envision and introduce changes. And it takes harmonious approach to turn the present into the future with as little transition cost as possible.

Most leaders truly believe that every system should develop and grow and that only constant changes can ensure survival and long-term success. Nevertheless, while they still exist, old systems must be efficient. We cannot destroy the old before we have developed the new to replace it. Therefore, management of every system consists of two, at first glance conflicting tasks: mastering the present and creating the future.

Mastering the present means to manage all existing organizational processes in such a way to ensure their quality and efficiency. The existing processes are not designed to last forever, but until changes take place we

---

1 http://chineseculture.about.com/cs/religion/a/aayinyang.htm

try to make them as profitable and successful as possible. In order to deal with this problem, two types of approaches are developed in each system, or better said, two strategies. The first strategy is aimed at ensuring the optimal performance of the existing system, while the second means the demolition of the existing system in order to introduce a new, better system. Speaking in terms of harmony, we need to come up with a balance between the past/present and the future.

Research indicates that most systems either have no strategy or they have one strategy, one plan, and one control system which deals with both issues: running the existing business and preparing for the future. Can both tasks survive under the same roof?

We have already stressed the fact that, in order to master the present, a leader must be an organizer. In order to master the future, he must be a disorganizer. It is often impossible to find both roles well-played by a single person. That's why many systems have one leader to take care of the existing system and another to develop a new system and do away with the old one.

Speaking in terms of this book, the task of both is to search for harmony; only the organizer's view is short-term, and the disorganizer is supposed to look behind the corner.

Steve Jobs, one of the founders of Apple Computers, was a Visionary, a true master of the future, and an ideal project leader for development of a new generation of computers. When a project was ready to kick off, he was noted for motivating co-workers, ensuring their round-the-clock commitment and feeding them with endless enthusiasm.

However, once they created a brilliant new product, the company needed a shift in focus. There was a new market niche and the opportunity had to be seized. In order to satisfy the growing demand, they had to establish procedures for large-scale production, ensure reliable supply of components, and organize regular delivery to customers. In a word, they were supposed to construct an efficient system for mastering the present. Jobs' motivation to engage in such activities was zero. He was a master of the exciting future, not of the boring present.

As soon as the project of creating a computer named Apple was completed, he lost interest. Turning the innovation into a successful business campaign was not his calling. He dedicated all his energy towards developing a new computer called Lisa, and then still another called Macintosh. As a typical disorganizer, Jobs enjoyed destroying the old in order to build the new. However, the company rightfully wanted to reap the fruits of developmental efforts and take advantage of the market potential for Apple. The Board invited John Sculley, the former manager of PepsiCo, to do the job. One of his first strategic moves was to fire Jobs because his mania of disorganizing and innovating was considered destructive in the company's future.

Here comes a sports analogy. While a soccer team is aggressively trying to score a goal, a coach may give the leadership role to an offensive player, the best shooter. However, during the second half, when the team needs to hold onto the advantage they have achieved, the task of leading is taken over by the goalkeeper or the best defensive player.

In every successful company, a period of innovation and change is naturally followed by a period of stabilization and organic growth, and vice versa. It is necessary to understand this process and support it with an adequate, dual strategy[1]. This calls for two types of leadership roles. Lacking a better term, we can call them the organizer and the disorganizer, or, using the terms of my model, the Explanator and the Visionary. Either way, they are responsible for harmonizing the whole team with their (temporary) mission.

A good leader must be able to recognize which of these two roles deserves priority in a given stage of development. If he cannot play it well, he must find adequate assistance or a replacement. The Apple case makes it obvious that many leaders cannot be good organizers and successful disorganizers at the same time. That's why a new developmental cycle often calls for change in leadership.

However, a leader who takes over the role of disorganizer, in other words, becomes the change agent, always runs the risk of entering into conflict with people who prefer the status quo. Ultimately, as John Kenneth Galbraith pointed out,[2] in any organization, "it is far safer to be wrong with the majority than to be right alone."

4.2.2. Leaders Prefer Binoculars to the Rear-view Mirror

Do you know the story of three stone masons? They were asked why they were performing such demanding work. The first humbly responded that he had to cut stone in order to feed his large family. The second self-confidently stated that he was doing it because he did it well; he was the best stone-cutter in town. The third proudly exclaimed that he was cutting stone in order to build a cathedral, the most beautiful building in the city.

The story is sometimes used as a test for potential leaders. By choosing which mason they empathize with, the candidates disclose their attitude toward work and career. The first stone-cutter looks at his job as a necessity. His trade is a tool for survival, providing an existence for his family. He probably does not enjoy his job but works because that is the way things are.

The second mason is proud of his trade. For him, it is a means of self-

1 http://www.amazon.com/Managing-Dual-Strategies-Derek-Abell/dp/0029001455
2 http://www.brainyquote.com/quotes/quotes/j/johnkennet121862.html

approval. While carving, he does not pay much attention to the meaning of his work. Instead, he enjoys using and perfecting his skills. He is a specialist, an expert who tries to meet and exceed the standards of his profession.

For the third mason the stone cutting skill is not just a trade. It is crucial for making a vision come to life. The goal of his carving is absolutely clear. He does his very best because he wants to achieve his life's mission — to build a great cathedral.

A steady job is a source of survival and bare existence. It is a strong motive for most employees, especially at lower levels of the organizational hierarchy. This is why most test respondents in a random sample choose the first stone-cutter and favor his noble, emotionally tinged goal to feed his family.

The second stone mason is a good professional. He is chosen by people who are focused on technical skills and knowledge. They place the principles of their trade at the top; they are ready to serve and do what they do best, without questioning the purpose of their work.

The third stone-cutter is chosen by people who have the leader's mentality. They need to see the big picture; they have a vision to realize (hopefully their own); they want to do something meaningful and keep control over the way it is done.

The Visionary has a clear goal. He knows what he wants and is ready to fight for it. One of his most important characteristics is enthusiasm about the future. He believes in himself and sees the days to come with optimism.

A few years ago, a regional company invited me to moderate their strategic weekend. They explained that, during the last year's retreat, they had argued about the future of their business so viciously that some of them did not speak to each other for weeks to follow. Even though it was clear that they want me as a buffer zone, in fear of new conflicts, I was tempted enough to accept.

So, one Friday afternoon, we sat down in a sunny conference hall in a luxurious Adriatic hotel and I kindly asked them to begin a discussion the way they had carried it through the last time. I would only observe and listen. They began with an analysis of the previous year, speaking one by one, circling the table, clockwise.

The first praised the results of his department, but did not miss the opportunity to say that their success would have been greater had John's team not messed up certain things. This inspired the second to complain about another department, saying that they had jeopardized the results of his group. By the time it was John's turn to speak, of course, he poured more gasoline on the flames. Within an hour, the room was completely absorbed with negative emotion. The tension and animosity were as thick as ice. Any minute now, pencils and notebooks would start flying across the table.

At that point, I asked them to stop. I reminded them that they were a great company with a solid growth in market share. Respected by customers, they had just made a record annual profit, so they must be doing a lot of things right. I suggested a new discussion rule. Describing the past year, everyone should say what they were most proud of. In other words, they were supposed to brag about their greatest accomplishments. And a second rule: no one should be criticized.

Quite a few were unready to accept my advice because they wanted to continue arguing. But the CEO suggested that they give it a try. It took only ten minutes to feel the difference. Once they started talking about their victories and the things they had accomplished, the room gradually filled with positive emotion. Tension and resentment slowly melted away, the aggression ended, the room spilled over with laughter and relaxation. I turned their attention to that by saying: *It is hard to speak about the future if you are burdened with the past. Forget about the things that cannot be undone. Once you get rid of the rear view mirror, you are able to take the binoculars in your hands and successfully plan the future.*

Negative emotions are destructive and disharmonious. Instead of bringing people together, they are responsible for conflicts and bad feelings. As such, they are key causes of energy loss in companies, groups, families and teams. Antagonistic feelings are contagious; they call for revenge, they affect everybody's self-confidence and spoil interpersonal relationships. Such a polluted working environment makes people lose drive and motivation. Being surrounded by bad vibes is literally a drag, holding us back, a drain that siphons off any energy we manage to bring to the endeavor.

A harmonious leader must try to avoid such feelings, especially in times of change, expected or planned. He should be able to teach his team not to waste time and energy on needless recollection of all the bygone conflicts, mistakes or failures. A disharmonious past must not endanger a harmonious future.

Sun Tzu provides us with the following advice: "Be careful at the beginning and you will not have problems at the end!" The future is potentially brilliant and victorious for all of us, while the past might make us quarrel endlessly. In a good marriage, the couple enjoys talking about the common future, while in a bad marriage the couple constantly argues about the unfinished past. In planning the future, we must be able to throw away the rear view mirror keep our hands free for the binoculars. Like a cheerleader, the Visionary is supposed to encourage his teammates and make them see the future in an optimistic way. If he doesn't look forward to the days to come, what can he expect from the members of his team?

4.2.3. Leaders Create the Future

A humorous definition describes the leader as a dealer in hope. Most our actions are dominated by what we hope for, strive and expect.

A Greek king, prepared to invade a large neighboring country, asked the prophet Pitia what would be the outcome of the battle. *Start the war*, she said, *and you will destroy a powerful kingdom*. Encouraged by such a prophecy, the king attacked his neighbors but was soundly defeated. Expelled from his throne, he returned to the prophet, complaining that she had been completely wrong. *I was right*, she responded. *I foresaw the destruction of a mighty kingdom. Is your kingdom not destroyed?*

Modern leaders also seek prophecies; only today we call them scenarios, analyses, studies, research proposals, simulations and similar products, delivered by a number of modern prophets, called business or political consultants. They try to help leaders define long-term strategies, taking into account trends, competition and crucial risk factors in the environment.

Good leaders should be able to look around the corner. The ability to foresee what might happen is necessary for making plans that avoid potential problems, calamities and losses. The famous Second World War hero, General George Patton, used to say: *A good plan I have today is better than a perfect plan I will have tomorrow.*

Planning the future is the first step towards creating it. Having clear goals and choosing the right strategies to achieve them are roads to success. The Visionary must be in constant search of the competitive edge, and it is situated in the future.

But competitive advantage is a temporary monopoly. For example, we are able to do something nobody else can. We know something others don't. We have discovered, or produced, a thing unknown to others. We are clear about something that still confuses others. Of course, any monopoly is short term because our rivals are not stupid; they soon find out, gain knowledge and develop competence. In the meantime, we search for new opportunities, new temporary monopolies, and new innovation. If we don't, the battle with competitors might be lost.

One of Murphy's Laws states: *The amount of energy needed to correct the outcomes of a wrong decision increases geometrically over time.* Making a mistake during execution is always less costly than making a strategic blunder. But to be right every time is by no means easy. However, a great Visionary is supposed to come up with victorious strategies all the time because they are the only guarantee of a harmonious future.

What are the sources of competitive advantage? A temporary monopoly means to be the best at what you do. The battlefield where you choose to fight and win may be narrow or wide. The first case is called specialization.

In business terms, it is based on a strategic decision to concentrate all efforts on a segment where there is limited demand in order to be the best in that niche. This applies equally to politics, because fighting for customers is pretty similar to fighting for votes.

Diversification is just the opposite case; it means competing in as many market segments as possible, offering a wide variety of products and services. The goal is to win by fighting here, there and everywhere, counting on synergy as the competitive advantage.

Many companies choose a strategy to win by offering products and services with the best price/performance ratio (value for money). Competitive advantage can also be achieved by low prices, so low as to kick the competition out of the market.

In politics this is called populism. Elitism is the opposite choice. Here the source of competitive advantage is found in a narrow niche. A company may try to succeed by selling rather unique, expensive and luxurious goods or services. The customers decide to buy them because of their quality, image, technological complexity, or high prices that can convey prestige. Elitist strategies rely on clients who trust the company or who are impressed by its image (i.e., BMW cars, Ray Ban sunglasses, Dom Pérignon champagne, Rolex watches). The success of such a strategy depends on customer loyalty to the brand name.

In politics, elitism is a sure road to nowhere.

In sum, to create the future through a business strategy, a Visionary can use a list of eight options: (1) search for new markets; (2) develop new products or services; (3) improve customer service; (4) bring new technology; (5) build production capacity; (6) apply new sales methods; (7) use advanced distribution techniques; (8) control natural resources.

Competitive advantage is an outcome of one or more components from the list. For example, a particular company may implement a strategy to enter a new market in Central and Eastern Europe using advanced distribution techniques and improved customer service. Another company may seek advantage through technological development, orientation on e-commerce and investment in new production plant. The key issue here is to find the best balance or the proper harmony among different choices and options.

One of the most interesting sources of competitive advantage is organizational culture. Let's take a look at the following case. The Mondragon Corporation[1] is a federation of worker cooperatives based in the Basque region of Spain. It is Spain's seventh-largest company in terms of asset turnover. At the end of 2012, it employed over 80,000 people in 289 companies in four areas of activity: finance, industry, retail and knowledge,

1 http://www.mondragon-corporation.com/eng/

with international sales of €4 billion. On October 2009, the United Steelworkers announced an agreement with Mondragon to create worker cooperatives in the United States. Mondragon cooperatives are united by a humanist concept of business, a philosophy of participation and solidarity, and a shared business culture, based on principles such as a democratic organization, the sovereignty of labor, participatory management, payment solidarity, social transformation, and ongoing education. Mondragon is well known for good wages it provides, for the empowerment of ordinary workers in decision making, and for equality for female workers. As such, it presents a strategic alternative to traditional corporations and paves one of the open roads to the more harmonious economic environment of the future.

Creating the future is the most important task of any leader. We must be interested in the future because the rest of our business, political and private lives will be spent there. Shouldn't we make it more harmonious and enjoyable?

4.2.4. Leaders Want It All, and Want It Now

Are you raising a child for a career in business? Here is an appropriate bedtime story. Once upon a time, a fellow named Ray Kroc entered a restaurant, owned by a family of Scottish descent, to eat some burgers. He liked their organization, the food, the table design, procedures for paying, in a word the whole business model. So he offered to buy the restaurant, all the technology and know-how. After they agreed on price and other terms, he promised that the restaurant would keep its original name.

Suppose that the McDonald family began as small entrepreneurs who built the first restaurant on a $20,000 bank loan. When the business took off, they increased the number of restaurants to three. There were ten tables at each location, and the family considered it the perfect size for their business, one they would be pleased with until retirement. But, like most entrepreneurs, they were risk-sensitive. If one day, for whatever reason, the demand for hamburgers dropped, the business could go bankrupt. So they decided to sell, for the right price.

Mr. Kroc was able to foresee the great potential of their business model. After the takeover, he turned it into a global franchise and it experienced rapid growth. Soon, there were 30,000 McDonald's restaurants worldwide, and the company developed one of the most valuable brands in history.

What is the point of that almost true fairytale? The same project may run high or low, depending on the vision and ambition of the person in charge. Obviously, ambitious leaders can extract much more from an idea than unambitious people, as shown by the McDonald's example.

Great leaders are known for their ability to think big. They are unsatisfied with average results, tiny projects or modest effects. Their expectations are great. They are pushed by a strong need to "shoot high" and hit the stars. It is important to know that ambition is closely related to the potential results of a system. Only ambitious leaders manage to extract as much from a product, political party, project or entrepreneurial initiative as possible, and more.

Most transitional countries are characterized by a business culture and environment lacking ambition. People are too frightened to think big and they quickly settle for modest goals. Of course, there are exceptions, but most businessmen decide to focus on the local market, hoping to get political support in creating a monopoly. Survival is their major concern. Staying alive is the name of the game — global ambitions are simply too much. Lacking self-confidence, courage and readiness to change, they don't dare to think big. Consequently, such an attitude prevents them from ever becoming a global success.

There is an old Croatian saying: *If you want to do something, you will find a way; if you don't, you will find an excuse!* "If you think you can do a thing or think you can't do a thing, you're right" is a saying attributed to Henry Ford. Shifting the blame is always easier than rolling up one's sleeves and getting the work done. Instead of facing a challenge, most people build piles of excuses, i.e., the judicial system is bad, and the market is too small, government is unreasonable and international support is just empty words...

Lack of belief in oneself, lack of ambition and low expectations are strong enemies of success in any business/political situation. The winners must be convinced they are the best; they should never cease to believe that. If we are the best, and we fail, it must be an exception. Next time we are going to win, as usual. What if it's the other way around? Losers face every situation with an inferiority complex, expecting things to go wrong. Aiming low, they are pleased with substandard performance. If we get something right, it must be an exception. The next time we are going to lose, as usual.

No one has yet calculated the economic value of optimism, self-confidence, ambition and winning spirit, as opposed to pessimism, inferiority complex, feelings of despair and a loser mentality. No doubt these emotions, as a result of self-perception, strongly influence the bottom line produced by business or political leaders and their organizations.

In order to win out there, you have to win in your mind first! If you feel like a winner and think like a winner, you become a winner! On the other hand, if you surrender before the game has started, your chances to succeed in business or politics are worth next to nothing.

Some people always win; others always lose. Why is that? The following ideas from a well-known book on leadership[1] describe the difference in

1   http://www.goodreads.com/book/show/815716.The_21_Irrefutable_Laws_

attitudes: After making a mistake a winner readily admits it by saying: "I was wrong." A loser tries to blame somebody else, saying "It wasn't my fault." A winner thanks his good luck for winning, even when luck had no part in the matter. Whenever he fails, a loser claims that he didn't have enough luck. A winner works smarter and manages time better. A loser is always busy, solving unimportant problems and spending time to analyze his failures. Winners study a problem in order to solve it. Losers try to ignore the problem, or save it for later. A winner says he is sorry and tries to correct what he did wrong. A loser says he is sorry, but does the same thing all over again. A winner knows when to fight and when to compromise. A loser makes unnecessary compromises, and fights for things that are not worth fighting for. A winner says: "I am good, but not as good as I should be." A loser says: "I am better than most people." A winner looks up, heading in that direction. A loser looks down on those who are below. A winner respects people who are better than him and tries to learn from them. A loser envies people who are better than him and jealously attempts to bring them down. A winner says: "There must be a better way to do this." A loser says: "It has always been done this way."

As a Visionary you must aim high and think big. You don't know what you can get away with until you try! Sun Tzu makes a great point by saying: "Your invincibility depends on you, while the enemy's vulnerability depends on him."

4.2.5. Leaders Trust their Guts

I like a joke about classifications. There are two types of people: those who agree there are two types of people, and those who disagree.

OK. Let's get serious. There are two types of leaders: the intuitive decision-makers and the rational decision-makers. Intuitive leaders base most decisions on their gut feeling. Setting aside facts and analysis, simulations, long-term discussions and hours of contemplation, they just go with the internal flow and do something because they feel like it. If you ask them why they made a particular decision, most often they would be unable to give you a clear answer.

Rational leaders make decisions after a thorough analysis. They tend to apply all available tools; they study facts, seek detailed information, consult databases, perform simulations, use computer models, do market research, and analyze customers. They decide only after all the facts and figures have been considered, and the decision seems logical and well thought-out.

During my seminars or workshops, I sometimes ask the participants whether they are rational or intuitive decision makers. As a rule, the majority claims to be rational; they base decisions on logical analysis, facts and objective reasoning. Then I offer a challenge: *Do you solve your private dilemmas in rational manner as well? Think about the five most important decisions you have made in your life; for example, what to study, who is going to be your best friend, the partner you want to your spend life with, the place where you'll live, the company to work for... How many of these decisions have you made rationally, i.e., after collecting all the available data, studying all the facts, developing optimization models, ranking the goals and constraints, extrapolating trends, devising plans, performing computer simulations, contracting experts for advisors ...*

After giving it a thought, most "rational" people admit that they make all the key decisions, not to mention the less important ones, in a "non-rational way." If that is the case, why are we so infatuated with rationality? Why do we keep unconditionally advocating logic, models, so-called objectivity and methods based on rigorous number-crunching analysis?

It's because we grew up this way. Throughout upbringing, education and training we have been exposed to logic, hard knowledge, methods, models and rational approach because all of that can be taught, explained and understood. It is far more difficult, at times impossible, to teach and train the ability to listen, develop and improve intuition, the capacity to trust the gut feeling, and the talent to make decisions based on a "sixth sense."

Unlike any rational decision-making tool, intuition cannot be learned; it can only be appreciated. It is deeply rooted in our personality as a part of our emotional, mental and spiritual inheritance. As such, intuition is a supplement, not a replacement for logical reasoning and good judgment.[1]

Successful people evaluate issues and make decisions using four sources of data and information: (1) what they know about a problem (facts and knowledge); (2) what they think about the problem (judgment and interpretation): (3) what they feel about the problem (emotions and feelings); and (4) what intuition tells them ("the gut").

Suppose you have to choose a supplier and there are five candidates. Your decision should take into account the rational (how the suppliers meet predetermined criteria such as price, quality, and delivery dates), the judgmental (what you can expect of the suppliers, based on past experience), the emotional (do you like, or dislike, some of the candidates) and the intuitive (the sense telling you which of the suppliers can be trusted).

Rational individuals appreciate logical explanations and information analysis. "Judgmental" people are in favor of empirical data and past experience. The emotional ones base their decisions on sympathy or antipathy. Intuitive types do what the gut feeling tells them to do. By

---

1 Laura Day, Practical Intuition, http://www.amazon.com/Practical-Intuition-Laura-Day/dp/0767900340

definition,[1] intuition is a non-empirical and non-rational process of acquiring information as an answer to (often not even openly expressed) questions or dilemmas.

Figure 5. Harmonious Decision Making

Many people distrust the relevance of the intuitive side and choose to ignore it. Intuitive information inflow is easily lost because it gets blurred by data coming from our experience, memory, the senses, and our logical reasoning.

In principle, it is wise to rely on intuition whenever there are no better sources of information. Also, intuition helps in filling the gaps between available data. Searching for harmony the leader will try to look at every problem through all the four information channels, not allowing any of them to prevail. Nevertheless, the best decisions concerning the future (in areas such as strategy, vision, innovation or business initiative) are almost always rooted in intuition. If you ask the most successful leaders in business or politics where their best decisions come from, they would, as a rule, mention chance and coincidence. Therefore, the sixth sense must be considered a valuable tool of the Visionary. Don't think that you are not equipped with it; rather, believe that you didn't wake it up yet!

Criminology research shows that many crime victims had a strong feeling that something would happen, but chose not to believe it. For example, a woman waiting for an elevator next to a stranger could receive an intuitive message: *Don't be left alone with this man*. As a rational person, she decides that the guy is not dangerous; he wears a business suit and acts like a gentleman. If she's "judgmental," she chooses to ignore the intuitive message because she never had any shocking elevator experience. If she's an emotional type, she would act depending on how much she liked, or disliked, the person in question.

Research has also indicated that most women who have actually been attacked in an elevator, and managed to survive, subsequently remembered the precognition which they did not want to believe. Studies indicate that intuitive information is always available, but we have difficulty to interpret

1 http://www.practicalintuition.com/

it in a reasonable way. Its symbolic language often makes no sense to us.

As a Visionary you are supposed to understand the dilemmas presented and learn how to use all four sources of information. If you are sure about a particular decision, don't evaluate the flow of intuitive messages. But if you are not, your intuition might be the best thing to lean on.

4.2.6. Leaders Dislike Bureaucracy

To most people bureaucracy looks like supreme harmony. Everything is perfectly organized; there are strict rules and precise regulations to avoid any surprise or unexpected situation. Everybody knows what he is supposed to do, there is a well elaborated control system to make sure all the goals are attained, all the worthy people are rewarded and all those responsible for failures are punished. Ideal bureaucracies are like perfect machines; each wheel contributes to the overall harmony by turning exactly as it is supposed to.

Now you wonder whether I am serious or ironic. Both, because we are surrounded by huge and powerful bureaucracies that make our business and private lives efficient and miserable at the same time. Why is that? First of all, human systems are not machines; the behavior of an individual resembles everything but a predictable wheel, always turning as expected and planned. Most of all because we are not run by orders and rules so as much as we are driven by values.

In every organization there is a value system designed to help people understand how they should (not) behave. Typically, the values are closely associated with mission and vision statements. But that is just a "philosophy." Its implementation is best seen through a set of rules, norms, standards, regulations and other elements of formal organization. It is the "paper" side of any system, a description of the life as it should be. On the other hand, there is the informal, "as is" side of the system, real life, including empirical rules, habits and practice in running the system on a daily basis.

Transitional countries have recently undergone drastic changes in political, business, judicial and value systems. To a certain extent the same is true for the recently united Europe. As for the USA, its systems are relatively stable and unchanged. Unlike the American business and political environment, which is in principle characterized by deregulation, the united Europe has adopted a system of elaborate and strict regulation. The cynics call it hyper regulation. Why? Take a look at the following numbers:[1] Pythagoras' theorem — 24 words; Lord's Prayer — 66 words; 10 Commandments — 179 words; US Declaration of Independence — 1,300 words; US Constitution

---

1 http://tomwinnifrith.com/articles/2332/eu-cabbages-why-this-insanity-must-cease-in-so-many-words

with all 27 Amendments — 7,818 words; EU regulations on the sale of cabbage — 26,911 words.

In Roman law there is an old saying: *Plurimae leges, minima iustitia* (The more laws, the less justice). A huge quantity and high complexity of legal norms create a regulatory forest in which particular trees become hard to notice. The tendency to regulate every aspect of life and work results in lack of freedom and initiative. Most people react like this: There are so many norms, too many to cope with; moreover, some are contradictory, others are stupid and ridiculous; this all gives me a moral right to disobey. This attitude is approaches the swine-fox morality described earlier. You stick to the rules you like, and you break the rules you don't like.

A wise leader knows that too many rules cause disorder and disharmony. However, in most cultures it is hard to implement extensive deregulation. As mentioned before, the European Union bureaucracy has spread its elaborated legal web covering all countries in the region. At the same time, the legal systems of the USA and most Asian countries have also reduced their tendency towards deregulation.

Hyper-regulation is based on mistrust; a huge legislative net is knitted to control all of economic, public and private life. Due to its complexity, it becomes inconsistent, lacks logic, and becomes hard to implement. In principle, it stems from the idea that everything is banned, if not specifically permitted. On the other hand, innovation and change require a formal organization with as few rules as possible, leaving enough room for initiative and freedom. The best formal organization is based on a small number of rules, which are willingly obeyed because they seem logical and acceptable.

Of course, there should be a balance between rules and free initiative. Deregulation leaves room for individual and collective initiative but strongly depends on shared values and norms. In principle, everything should be allowed, if there is no good reason to strictly forbid it. However, many political and business leaders, covertly or overtly, claim that people should not be given rights which could be misused.

A true Visionary must fight excessive paperwork whenever possible. He should prefer to lean on people who are moral, efficient and capable. Instead of building rigid bureaucracy, he should support and encourage self-organization. Instead of establishing numerous committees and task forces, he must try to let the problems be resolved by open communication, free initiative and a common search for win–win solutions. He should advocate a system which is based on a reasonable number of rules and norms that most people gladly follow and obey. Putting the bureaucratic approach aside, harmonious leader sends a clear message that he trusts his team, not the rules. He puts his faith in the trustworthy workers, their initiative and readiness to do their best. Instead of bureaucratic procedures, he relies on interpersonal relationships and communication. Instead of the artificial harmony of a hierarchic corporation (which is, as already observed, not a far cry from a concentration camp), he should engage in building genuinely harmonious human systems based on mutual trust.

Natural solutions are always best. Just look around, and you will quickly see that the Mother Nature's harmonious creations always win over human attempt to compete with its "self-organization." Therefore, one of the cornerstones of harmony-based leadership is the search for harmony in an organic way. The bureaucratic ideal is a robust, stable and invariable system on paper. Unfortunately, such a solution never works; real life situations ask for a flexible and dynamic system, able to adjust, grow and develop like an organism. A Visionary should always prefer a fair human system that works in a perfect machinelike bureaucracy which does not function.

4.2.7. Leaders Spend in Order to Earn

In spring 2000, I was appointed Head of the working group responsible for Croatia's ICT development strategy. As soon as the media learned about us, numerous ideas began to flow in via phone calls and e-mail messages. I particularly remember a man who phoned me and explained with a lot of emotion: *I want to help Croatia. I have a brilliant project with an annual profit of ten million Euros. Tell me which government office I should contact.*

I replied that, if I had a project like that, I would take a mortgage on everything I possess and try to implement the idea as soon as possible. That's the best way to help Croatia! Why do you need the government?

However, such an attitude is typical and widespread, especially in transitional economies. Most people would gladly invest other people's money, such as Ostap Bender[1] and his well-known motto: "Ideas are ours, but gasoline is yours." It is always sweet to avoid personal risk and feed on government funds. That poison, accumulated during the socialist period, has not fully evaporated. However, a Visionary must act like an entrepreneur, ready to take chances. In our example, it means to put one's head in the mortgage guillotine, and hope for the best.

We should spend money in order to earn it. He who doesn't plant the seed cannot reap the harvest. We are never going to profit if we don't invest. If we stingily weigh every nickel and dime we can hardly expect success. Wealth is generated by generosity and a readiness to put money, energy and effort in ideas, friendship, technology, people, knowledge and education.

As a consultant, I am often called for advice or help. Whenever my

---

1 The charming charlatan of Soviet fiction: http://en.wikipedia.org/wiki/Ostap_Bender

potential client maintains that his company would easily solve all its problems if they just had more money, I try to courteously back off. Not because I am afraid the person wouldn't be able to pay my fee, but because I don't like to work with people whose only problem is a lack of funds.

As proposed by an aphorism, money is the most important sideshow on earth. Of course, money is a necessary prerequisite, but it's not the only source of business or political success. Isn't it true that a fool and his money are soon parted? I hear you say: Come on, what do you mean, money is not important? Cynical people might add that cash is not everything. There is also something in real estate and something in stocks. But money alone will not do much. On the other hand, any meaningful proposal will find a sponsor. In today's world, there is an abundance of cash and a scarcity of ideas, projects and capable people likely to provide a return on investment. This is why I tend not to work with people who think that everything would be fine if they had more money. Instead, I gladly cooperate with everyone who claims that he lacks knowledge, ideas, time, and capable people. These are the true limitations of every project and business. Lack of finances is often just an excuse.

During my innovation management seminars, at home and abroad, I address this issue by asking: *What would you do tomorrow if you didn't have to worry about money, in other words if there were no financial limitations?* The reaction to this question by most managers reminds me of a Bosnian joke about Mujo and the goldfish. Having caught the proverbial fish, Mujo is granted three wishes. As he was thirsty, he asked for a barrel of whiskey. Then he looked into the stream, from which he caught the fish, and cast a second wish: Let this river flow with whiskey. He then decided to think deeply, in order to take full advantage of the final wish. After a while, the goldfish became impatient and stated: *Hurry, Mujo, I don't have the whole day. OK, then*, he replied, *give me another scotch on the rocks!*

Most people cannot put the limited budget idea aside and always expect to live and work within very strict financial constraints. As an outcome, they are unable to dream up big projects or rise above modest expectations. In response to the question above, for example, they come up with a list of tiny wishes: *If I had no financial limitations, I would like a better computer, still another assistant, larger office, and faster internet.*

If we are not able to put financial restraints out of the picture, we might never achieve great visions. Like Mujo, we are satisfied with just another drink, believing that there are no resources for something really huge. At the same time, we consider the lack of money as the major cause for not succeeding. Wrong! We should know that leaders with imagination can make even the impossible probable; and in the world of limitless financial resources the improbable becomes possible.

The word "impossible" does not belong to a dictionary of a leader. Especially not for lack of money! The city of Dubai is a great example. Fifty years ago, the whole place was practically nothing but sand and sea. There was no running water. Today 97% of the city's water supply comes from desalinization, and Dubai has become the second in the world (after Los Angeles) in water consumption per capita. Half a century ago, there was an airport the size of a gas station, today Dubai airport is one of the biggest, busiest and most beautiful in the world. Some say it is all because of their crude oil. However, today the contribution of petroleum production to the GDP of Dubai amounts to less than 5%. It took almost a decade to build the new, 541 meters high WTC tower in New York, the tallest building in the Western Hemisphere. The tallest building on earth, Burj Khalifa, which rises 828 meters above Dubai, was completed in less than six years. Even today, one third of the world's biggest construction cranes are proudly rising out of the desert in Dubai, making this former small harbor the world's largest construction site.

Only a Visionary, powered by great dreams, is able to fantasize huge projects and eventually becomes ready to make those dreams come true. Most people are doomed to stay forever locked in the constrained world of small projects. It is mostly because they run low on fantasy; they are grounded by lack of courage, fear of taking chances and inability to think big,

4.2.8. Leaders Are Generous

Mujo is not the only individual able to catch a goldfish. Once upon a time there was a farmer who also got lucky. As expected, the proverbial fish granted him three wishes, but advised him that his neighbor would always get double. Being a proud farmer, he wished for his corn to grow three meters high. However, his neighbor's cornfield grew twice as high.

Very displeased, he wished for a huge farmhouse, but his neighbor immediately got a house twice as large. Enraged, he turned to the fish with his final wish: *Pluck out my left eye!*

The let-the-neighbor's-cow-die mentality is a sure sign of destructive jealousy, leading to a dramatic lack of harmony. It's also a main cause of conflicts and poor interpersonal relationships in business, politics and everyday life. The phenomenon has been studied by many leadership authorities. One of them, Steven Covey, points at the sharp difference between a scarcity mentality and abundance mentality.[1] What is he actually talking about?

---

1 http://sanderssays.typepad.com/sanders_says/2012/07/an-ode-to-stephen-covey-sr-and-the-abundance-mentality.html

Have you ever watched a buffet table during a reception dinner? Suppose there is enough food for everybody and no dish ever runs out. How do people behave? Very politely! No one would push in line and the table would be surrounded by courtesy and generosity. The abundance mentality prevails, making us all look and behave at our best. Suppose, on the other hand, there is not enough food and all the people around the table are very hungry. A fearful race begins, with elbowing and unscrupulous snatching of a last piece of meat or a cookie. Whoever gets there first puts as much as he can on his plate. The scarcity mentality has taken over, bringing our worst to the surface. But, in principle, it is all in our heads. Our perception runs our behavior. When we think there is a shortage, we become aggressive; we attempt to grab as much as possible, even more than we are able to consume.

I have often witnessed similar behavior in both business and government. For example, when annual budgets are prepared and an overall cut is expected, everyone inflates the demands beyond any real need. On the other hand, if budget growth is expected, the general feeling of scarcity diminishes and most demands become realistic, even modest.

The Visionary should know that any balanced and long-term success depends on our ability to live in harmony with the logic of abundance. To have is not bad, to be able to share is better; to be able to give is the best! Great victories are based on a joint desire to succeed, produce results, and share all gains among members of the team. Business and political victories are long term only if they rely on generous partnership. Instead of fighting over a piece of the existing pie, we must organize to jointly make a larger pie.

The scarcity mentality to certain extent relates to a general level of prosperity. The affluent are less affected than the poor. A quick look at the world political and economic situation could shed light on the issue. Unscrupulous struggles for positions, influence and resources are less blatant in successful and rich countries and companies than in the poor and unfortunate ones. Most power shifts in developed countries or companies take place normally, according to a procedure, without fuss, fight or stress. On the contrary, people fight most severely over power, influence and resources in the least developed and backward environments where all these are worth little or nothing.

The political and business culture of most transitional countries is especially sensitive to this dilemma. The scarcity mentality makes people hate those who are rich, because they feel as though somebody took it from them. Those who have less keep talking about unequal distribution of power, about global exploitation, and world injustice. Most often it means: *I want more power, wealth, and influence.* In order to have it, I must take it from somebody else. Instead of getting organized to produce new wealth, let's fight to redistribute the existing wealth.

What happens in such a business or political environment? When someone gains control, the first thing he does is to take from those who have (influence, power, responsibility, in some instances even property) and give it to his followers. Instead of mobilizing all human and material resources to create more value, the leader engages in re-distribution and sets the stage for long-term conflicts.

The abundance mentality suggests that no one should be bothered by other people's property, under the assumption that it is acquired in a fair, legal manner. If the most deserving have more, it is better for all of us; they pay higher taxes, create new jobs, buy goods and services from us, and improve the conditions in which we all live and work.

In a short story by Mark Twain,[1] a poor boy, on a bet, temporarily finds himself with a million pound bank note in his pocket. Before, he had no money and everyone avoided him. Now, he has such a large bill that no one can break it into change. Anyway, everyone does him favors, showers him with goods and gifts, buys him things and pampers him, despite the fact that he is as poor as before, unable to pay anything back. His life slowly becomes a true illustration of abundance mentality.

Almost a century ago, Croatian politician Stjepan Radic referred to the issue by saying: *It is better to need less than to have a lot.*

Harmonious leaders must understand the abundance/scarcity mentality in order to take the opportunities, and avoid the threats which it brings along.

The scarcity mentality builds up conflicts. It makes us envious, stingy and aggressive, creating a poor environment for cooperation of any kind. On the other hand, the abundance mentality is harmonious and balanced. It leaves room for alliances and partnerships, increases motivation for common goals and provides the competitive environment with a touch of cooperation and friendship.

Good deeds are the best investment for the future. A generous leader is always liked, loved, even adored by his followers. As a harmony-based person, he can teach his teammates that success heavily depends on the unconditional and unanimous support of fellow-workers, based on the abundance mentality as well as on mental and physical generosity.

Throughout our business and private life we are surrounded with people and things. In principle, people are made to be loved, and things are made to be used. Maybe the world is heading towards a catastrophe because, more and more, we have a tendency to love things and use people.

---

1 http://en.wikipedia.org/wiki/The_Million_Pound_Bank_Note

4.2.9. Leaders Start Anew

Do you know the story of Dell Computers? It was founded in 1984 by Michael Dell, with start-up capital of only a thousand bucks. Believing in the originality of his business model, he started a company from his student dormitory room. Before he could even rent an office, he used to build tailor-made, personal computers from purchased components, to his customer's specifications. Thirty years later, as of 2012–2013, Dell Computers is the third largest PC vendor in the world (after Lenovo and HP) with annual sales greater than the GDP of a small European country like Slovenia, Croatia or Latvia.

We should be fascinated by the fact that such systems appear, develop and grow in a short time. What if Croatia or Slovenia had a guy like Michael, but did not build an infrastructure to support him and enable him to start his high-tech empire? If only one such start up had happened in Croatia thirty years ago, none of its 4.3 million residents would need to do anything and they would still produce the same GDP as now.

The Dell story is similar to those of Mark Zuckerberg (Facebook), Larry Page and Sergey Brin (Google), Bill Gates (Microsoft), Ray Kroc (McDonalds), Richard Branson (Virgin), Ted Turner (CNN), Larry Ellison (Oracle), Jeff Bezos (Amazon) and many other innovative leaders. They were ready to walk new paths, trusting one of my favorite sentences: no one can see any better if he keeps looking in the same direction.

A good leader should know when the regular course is to be followed and when it is better to steer in a new direction. He should make a choice when to engage in fixing, modifying, reorganizing or adjusting, and when it is better to start from scratch.

Starting anew, going back to the beginning, reinventing the job, and changing the approach are typical phrases associated with innovation, re-engineering, new business models and process redesign. For example, the twenty-year-old term *re-engineering* describes an activity to design a radically new process or develop a drastically new business model. It indicates big leaps and qualitative changes. Instead of mincing around with small, cosmetic and incremental shifts, people engaged in re-engineering try to see a problem differently, in search of new approaches. They are not interested in how something can be done a little better or more quickly or how a process could be slightly improved and the costs reduced a bit. The engineers dig deeper and ask fundamental questions, for example, why is something done in the first place, could it be skipped, ignored, or performed in a completely different way. Just like in the legend of the Gordian knot: instead of trying to disentangle the "impossible" knot, Alexander the Great simply cut it apart with his sword.

In the English language, there are 24 synonyms for the term *start anew*. It is interesting to analyze their particular meaning because they range from revive, pick up, overcome, return and rejuvenate to kick back, get better, get in shape, return to form and make a comeback.

Returning to the beginning and changing the system, instead of improving it, would seem to be an ideal cornerstone of visionary leadership in times of pending global crisis, or catastrophe. We need to search for a New Harmony in a world that has lost its balance and its values.

In times like these, a Visionary must think like a re-engineer, and behave like a child in the tale of the emperor's new clothes. It's time for more people to strip away the pretence that everything is normal and things are still going along just fine.

The task of a true leader is to show us that we are enslaved by our false perceptions and teach us to see the obvious. The Visionary should make us aware that we tend to be impressed by wrong ideas, stupid procedures, distorted values; he must help us understand that we get easily caught in a web of habits, lines of responsibility and formal organization rules. Such "blindness" can make our vision cloudy, and our future uncertain.

If we want to succeed, we must change. Contemporary business and public affairs, more than ever before, call for leaders who are agents of change and promoters of new ideas. Instead of efficient bureaucrats, masters of survival, tsars of routine and monotony, we need courageous innovators and visionaries ready to demolish the existing and build the new. Doing that, they must be able to change the rules rather than engage in their efficient implementation. More often than not, the established roads and trails are inefficient and lead nowhere. The search for new paths and visions calls for new leaders and new leadership models. Therefore, in business and politics alike, it is no longer wise to dance as your father did, because, as stressed by one Croatian poet, *change is the only permanent thing in the world*.

4.2.10. Leaders Are Enterprising

A few years ago, when Japanese consumers got fed up with pasta and demand for it fell dramatically, an entrepreneur named Shokukin thought of a clever way to survive. He invented the "new, genuine Italian" pasta. In his marketing campaign, he explained why his pasta was the best. While it is being produced and stored, throughout the factory, as well as in all warehouses, music by Vivaldi and Verdi is played around the clock. So, when you cook it, if you listen carefully, your pasta is likely to replay all these absorbed tunes and turn your meal into a genuine romantic Italian experience.

A New York cab driver, Frank, figured out how to receive the biggest tips ever recorded in his trade. He greets passengers in their native tongue (Google Translate helped him learn appropriate greetings in fifty languages). Then he offers them a newspaper, fruit or refreshment, plays their choice of music, provides accurate tourist and traffic information, and, if a client wants that service, he is a trained city tour guide.

Both examples indicate that there are endless ways to create value, and that it all depends on entrepreneurial spirit coupled with innovative thinking. However, most people think that it's easy for a small business to be entrepreneurial and creative, but that kind of spirit is hard to build in large companies.

Any analysis of contemporary business and political practice proves that there is no better mechanism to support innovation than an entrepreneurial mentality, just as there is no better way than the free market to make supply meet demand, nor is there a better way to rationally use resources than private ownership and competition, nor is there a better method of administering government than democracy.

As a rule, bureaucratic systems are inferior to enterprising environments. "Working hours are over," "We've just closed," "That is not my job," are typical reactions from a bureaucracy. They reflect the employees' disinterest and negligence, leading to customer dissatisfaction because the work is either poor quality, finished late, or not done at all. Bureaucrats are reactive and attempt only to survive, unlike the entrepreneurs who are proactive and development-oriented. Bureaucratic environments, build respect for rules and procedures, while entrepreneurs change the rules in order to achieve results. For breaking a rule you are punished by a bureaucrat but may be rewarded for innovation by an entrepreneur.

Bureaucracies are led by a strong authority aligned with a rigid organizational structure. Leaders-entrepreneurs are tolerant, democratic and flexible, ready to embrace changes whenever necessary. Bureaucratic decision making is based on outvoting, work is done by experience, and the formal hierarchy is fully respected. Entrepreneurial leaders search for consensus, appreciate innovation, reward initiative and support participation in decision-making.

Take a look at one example. W. L. Gore & Associates[1] is one of the 200 largest privately held companies in the United States with more than 50 facilities in East Asia, Australia, Europe and the Americas. It is best known for innovative products and a unique organizational culture. Instead of a formal management hierarchy, the company has a flat, lattice-like organizational structure and everyone shares the same title of *associate*. There are neither chains of command nor predetermined channels of

---

1 http://www.gore.com/en_xx/aboutus/

communication. Associates choose to follow leaders rather than have bosses assigned to them. The associates are encouraged to communicate directly with each other and are accountable to fellow members of their teams. Such teams are typically organized around opportunities, new product concepts, or businesses. As teams evolve, leaders emerge as they gain followers. This unusual organizational structure and culture is a significant contributor to overall company's success and associate satisfaction and retention. It has inspired the new management style called open allocation; the employees are given a high degree of freedom in choosing what projects to work on, and how to allocate their time.

In bureaucratic systems, you are good if the boss likes you; in entrepreneurial surroundings, if the customer likes you. In selecting and hiring employees, bureaucrats respect formal requirements while entrepreneurs prefer talent, ability and demonstrated skills. Trapped within a bureaucracy, capable individuals often have a feeling of lagging behind, while the entrepreneurial environment makes them bloom and grow.

Bureaucratic leaders seek dependent, obedient employees who think the same, act the same, and dress the same. Entrepreneurial leaders prefer independent, imaginative employees. In such systems young people advance quickly while most bureaucratic bosses try to make sure no one gets promoted before his time.

An entrepreneurial principle is to reward results and motivate people to work harder. Bureaucratic systems often reward working time, irrespective of results. Clients and customers are a nuisance for a bureaucratic system. Customer satisfaction is the paramount goal of true entrepreneurship.

Although most of the previously described differences may sound like exaggerated stereotypes, they are often proven by management research. It is important to note that either a culture is either enterprising or bureaucratic, irrespective of company size. For example, Google, Apple or Starbucks may be large systems built on entrepreneurial spirit. Also, a hairdressing salon and a car repair shop in my neighborhood can be sad examples of a small and rigid bureaucracy.

It is true that most large systems used to be small entrepreneurial initiatives. For example, Akio Morita and six young, curious college graduates established Sony in 1946. They started with 20 employees and a vision to build a company as a playground for engineers to develop innovative products. Sony of today is a company with annual sales higher than the GDP of a small European country; still, they are dominated by entrepreneurial spirit. Their famous products like Walkman, Discman and Playstation have all been outcomes of engineering playfulness. Morita has always been the first to play with various inventions at his office. He was especially fond of the telephones for two and helped establish the popularity of the walkie-talkie. He also used to send messages to his co-workers via remotely controlled flying balloons. His deputy was best known for a huge model of electrical railway installed in his office. He and Morita used to spend hours playing with it while discussing future products and services.

Coming from the top, playfulness and curiosity may become extremely contagious for all the employees, creating an environment of constant innovation. And, of course, ideas bring money!

Do you know how John D. Rockefeller Jr. became rich? He had an apple. Instead of eating it, he polished it and sold it for ten cents. With that money he bought three apples, "shined" them and sold them for thirty cents. Then he was able to buy nine apples, and then 27 apples... All week long he was doing it, day in and day out. Then his grandfather died, and he inherited $200 million.

Despite the joke, the entrepreneurial initiative is the main generator of personal and institutional wealth and success. Therefore, all harmony-based leaders must think and feel like entrepreneurs. Constantly working on themselves, as well as on their teams, the leaders-visionaries (we can also call them enterprising leaders) should continue to change our world and make it a better place to live and work.

4.3. The Mobilizer

> Vision without execution is hallucination.
>
> —Thomas Edison

4.3.1. Leaders Seek Initiative

In the times of Shoguns, a Japanese warrior, Nobunaga, decided to attack a powerful enemy army. He believed in his victory, but his soldiers were doubtful. So, before the battle, he took them to a Shinto temple. *After my prayers*, he shouted, *I am going to flip a coin. If it's heads, we win. If it's tails, we lose. Destiny holds us in its hand!* Nobunaga prayed in silence and then tossed the coin. It was heads. Seeing this, his warriors eagerly ran into the battlefield and defeated the enemy.

No one can change destiny, said Nobunaga's deputy, in the evening while they were celebrating the victory. *It's true*, said Nobunaga, showing the coin with the heads on both sides.

Successful leadership stems from initiatives coming from all the team members. A good leader must implant in his people a desire to fight, a winning spirit, a readiness to attack all problems as soon as they are spotted without seeking prior approval, support or permission. There is an old rule:

if you ask enough people for permission, you'll inevitably come up against someone who will say "no." Less effective people think: *If I haven't explicitly been told 'yes,' I can't do it*, whereas the most effective people share the belief: *If I haven't explicitly been told 'no,' I can.*

In 1995, the famous CNN reporter Christiane Amanpour came to Sarajevo to interview the leaders of the major political parties regarding the just-signed Dayton agreement. Among them was Zlatko Lagumdzija, a friend of mine, the wartime vice-president of Bosnian government and the head of the Social Democrats, also a professor of information technology management. He took her to the first floor of the Business School building and asked her kindly to wait for him a couple of minutes.

Being a perceptive journalist, Ms. Amanpour looked around in wonder. The floor was packed with computers, their screens throwing grayish light on a few dozen young, smart eyes, deeply immersed in work. The computers were top quality, more advanced than those in her CNN office. The scene surprised her. She knew that, until a few days ago, this building had thick concrete plates instead of windows, to protect the inside from sniper shots and mortar shells. Like all buildings in Sarajevo, the premises had no electricity for a full nine months. During that period, the price of fuel for an aggregate amounted to hundred dollars per gallon on the black market. How did this high-tech flower manage to blossom, surrounded by the atrocities of war?

Professor Lagumdzija explained that the whole floor is the MIS center (Management Information System), built with donation money. Instead of buying weapons, they invested in technology. It was an oasis for young, talented people, taking them from the deadly streets and providing them with modern hardware and software. Wars end sooner or later, and the country is best rebuilt with knowledge and technology.

The journalist smiled and said: *Forget about Dayton, which I originally wanted to discuss with you. Let's tell the story of the MIS center.* And she did. The three-minute report circled the world, depicting a fairytale of a technological oasis amidst the disasters of war. It provided a tiny shift in perception of Bosnian politicians, stressing their care for the future in the war-torn country. But there was a more substantial result; a new donation, used to rebuild and equip yet another floor of the school building which is now called the MIT center (Management of Information Technology).

Of course, the story may look a bit naïve. Christiane Amanpour is the wife of James Rubin, a distinguished US diplomat. Many people see her as a tool of her sponsors. If they want to make her viewers sympathetic to Bosnia, this is what she will do. Maybe so, but my point here is her freedom to go after a better story. If the journalist were from any of the local TV stations, she would have done it, as asked by the editor. No initiative would be appreciated by her boss. However, a globally successful network should allow freedom and creativity. If you come across a better story than the one you originally planned to do, then follow the better story. In the end, your mission is to do the best job possible, and not strictly obey the orders from the boss.

Any leader who seeks initiative could learn a lot from this example. Ideal networks are better off without a traditional editor, a powerful individual who approves all assignments. Rather, the reporters should be free to run after the stories they believe to be relevant. The journalist who constantly succeeds in tying up the pieces of his story into a valid product should eventually receive more time and get promoted as a headline news star. By analogy, a harmonious leader is supposed to create an atmosphere in which the best, smartest and most capable individuals can give everything they have. They must be recognized and promoted as quickly as possible. The task of a leader is to build an environment open for initiative and entrepreneurship. In order to do it, he must follow a simple rule: *Attract the best people, keep the best people, and never lose the best people!*

In creative environments permission should not be sought for everything. Each employee should presume that, whenever he wants to do something good for the system, his boss' confirmation is implicit.

As a supervisor to my students I am often asked how something should be done. How to compile a good seminar? What does a satisfactory dissertation look like? How many pages should a critical review consist of? What types of software should be used in team projects? How to prepare for the exam in order to earn the highest grade?

They expect answers narrowed down to "technicalities": e.g., the number of pages of a critical review should be between five and ten, the references should be quoted according to the Harvard System, the oral exam is based on this and that chapter from the textbook, projects should be prepared using the following software package...

Of course, the provided information helps the students understand what is good and what is bad, how things should, or shouldn't be done. I am ready to go into details, if necessary, but before that, I smile and say: *You know what I expect from you? Knock me off of my feet! Amaze me! Thrill me! Do something great and take my breath away!*

In fact, the message I want them to remember is that they have the initiative and can use it to the best of their knowledge and ability. I do not want to set formal boundaries of their creativity. Only the sky is the limit! By asking them to amaze me, I tell them that they are potential geniuses, able to knock me off my feet, should they invest enough energy, effort and time.

An employee who wants to "please" and "amaze" his boss will have to give it all. He should go beyond the expected. In order to succeed, he must show initiative because nothing great occurs by itself. He should be independent and eager to avoid the path already taken, because nobody is amazed by a routine solution. He should try harder, otherwise the outcome is a mediocrity. And, of course, his self-confidence grows because the boss expects him to do great, it means that he trusts his abilities.

Innovative leaders should practice the amaze-me approach. Every organization needs people who are ready to say "we can change things here, we can achieve awesome goals, and we can be the best!" A true Mobilizer keeps in mind that his employees are worth as much as the initiative and responsibility they are prepared to take.

As the Minister of Science, I had two senior advisor positions open. Whom should I promote? The standard practice suggested that I should look at those who were currently positioned immediately below in the hierarchy; in this case the regular advisors. Then, I should select the best among them. I did that, but I was not pleased with what I found at that level. A typical advisor has a dozen and more years of experience and is considered a solid expert, equipped with knowledge and skill. Also, he is an educated bureaucrat with the following attitude: *Every morning I come to work, drink coffee and read newspapers, waiting for my boss to call me and tell me what to do. If, for some reason, he forgets me, I can read newspapers and drink coffee all day long. If he assigns me a task, I complete it relatively efficiently. After I dump my product on his table, I go back to my office and the routine starts all over again: newspaper, coffee, gossip and waiting.*

This was not exactly what I wanted. I needed senior advisers with initiative, people who wouldn't sit calmly in their offices, reading newspapers and drinking coffee, waiting for me to invent a job for them. I wanted individuals who were ready to fight problems and come to me with proposals of actions to be taken. Instead of putting their work and problems on my desk (as most unproductive advisors do), I wanted them to take problems and issues off my table, hopefully before I even knew I had an issue or a problem. I needed independent people with initiative, able to think and work on their own.

After going through the list of all the people in my "pyramid" I decided to promote two former apprentices. One had three years of experience with the organization, the other only two. As soon as I declared my decision, there was a fierce reaction from the personnel department: That's impossible! It never happened before! However, there was no legislation standing in the way, so I did it. It was the first case of promotion based on capabilities, not results, usually personified by the years of bureaucratic experience.

There were two short-term impacts of my decision; on the positive side all the employees became more active and ready to take the initiative, in response to the signal my action sent. On the negative side, I was boycotted (though politely—they still fear the boss in government bureaucracy) by most of the advisors who were disappointed for not being promoted. Luckily, in the long run, my choice proved to be very good. Both newly appointed guys quickly became my most valuable associates, their work and attitude encouraged others to show more initiative and proactivity, and there was an overall rise in motivation, proactivity and entrepreneurial behavior.

The best lesson I learned from that episode was that a boss must work and think for all the obedient and initiativeless employees, while the proactive and enterprising employees work and think for him. And, of course, their dedicated effort contributes to the overall organizational harmony.

4.3.2. Leaders Delegate

As a consultant, I was working for a CEO of a hi-tech company with four hundred employees. One late Saturday afternoon, just after closing a two-day workshop on teamwork, I wished him a nice weekend, or, better said, what was left of it. He complained that he would be having no weekend at all. On Monday morning, he had a presentation for an important client and he would have to spend all Sunday preparing it. *I know*, he added. *This is not a director's job. But the person who was responsible handed me a presentation this morning, and it isn't exactly what I expected. That's why I have to prepare it myself. What would you do if you were in my shoes?*

OK, your Sunday is ruined, especially if you spend it working alone, I said. If I were you, I would call up the person and spend the day working on the presentation with him. In the evening you may have accomplished two things instead of one: the presentation will be to your liking and the assistant will understand what he did wrong and why. Next time you delegate a similar task to him, you can be sure there are no surprises.

Many leaders are hesitant to delegate work, mostly because they know that it's impossible to delegate responsibility. Whenever those reporting to you do something wrong (for example, put together a weak presentation for an important client), you are responsible. Therefore, you'd better do it yourself. This attitude is the main reason why so many bosses bust their fingers at work while some of their assistants just polish their nails.

Oftentimes, it's us, the bosses, who are blamed for not delegating with trust and confidence. We never gave our employees enough information, time or resources to do the job right. We explained what we wanted in a hurry and without being precise. Consequently, they make mistakes and do a bad job, and we end up considering them incompetent and untrustworthy.

Many bosses treat their assistants like an eagle would treat a small bird.

They swoop down, making great noise, they hurt and destroy, then vanish at the speed of sound and everything is back to normal. Except for the hurt feelings and the devastated working atmosphere!

Whenever a subordinate screws something up, a good leader tries to find out why. Maybe my employee made a mistake because he did not know how, and he didn't learn because I did not explain it well. Or he made a mistake and was unable to complete the task because I did not provide the necessary resources (time, money, equipment, or people)? Maybe he didn't tell me about a problem he was aware of, because I didn't ask? Maybe they never speak their mind because they are afraid of me? Do I listen to my assistants or just delegate without giving them a chance to provide feedback? Do I explain in detail, or do I just expect everybody to know exactly what I want?

Let's consider an apprentice at his first day at work. What kind of boss would he wish for? A democratic one who says: *Find your way around; you can do whatever you want?* I don't think so! Such a boss is like a parent who lets the newborn baby do whatever comes to his or her mind. *OK, stick your finger in the electric socket; if you survive, you'll learn it's dangerous. Alright, go ahead and crawl to the window sill; if you fall and survive, you'll know you shouldn't do it again.* That may be called learning by experience; you give the apprentice full freedom without supervision, and you hope for the best.

Of course, treating a clueless baby like this would be a crime. But is it not the same with the inexperienced trainee? We want to delegate with trust, but that trust must be earned. Delegation can significantly increase personal efficiency and save time. But, if not done properly, it can also cause more harm than good!

Leadership research, as well as my personal experience, can be summarized in a four-step delegating model, based on an analogy between apprentices and newborn babies.

The first step in the process takes place when a baby is born, or an apprentice hired. They are both new to their world and need orientation, help and full support. In other words, they are best served by a boss (a parent) who is autocratic. *I am not asking you anything, because you don't know anything. You are here to listen and learn. I'll take you by the hand and lead you through life, or the business process, taking care of your every step, teaching and explaining. You cannot do anything on your own, because you are not yet ready for independence.*

In the first stage, we are more rigid than flexible; we give orders, seek obedience, and insist on rules and regulations. The goal is to teach the novice (or a baby) discipline, develop his working (life) habits and prepare him to advance to higher stages.

The first phase is exhausting; the boss spends most of the working day with the apprentice (so do parents with babies) and doesn't have time to do much else. Therefore, it's important to move to the second stage as quickly as possible. In this phase, the boss, and the parent, start delegating simple tasks but maintain strong supervision. As soon as the rookie is able to do something on his own, you encourage him to do it. Your role is to be constantly by his side, supervising. Pushing the analogy, as soon as the baby is able to do something on her own, it makes sense to let her do it. It is easier to lead smart trainees (babies who are quick learners), because this leaves more time for yourself.

In this stage, many bosses (and parents) make a typical mistake; they continue to do the tasks for their assistants (babies) instead of gradually delegating the easy ones. For example, a little child knows how to tie shoelaces but does it slowly. You are in a rush to get to daycare so you tie her shoes on a daily basis. It seems to make sense because it takes her five minutes to do it with her uncoordinated fingers, while you can do it in a minute. However, by doing their jobs you slow people's progress and make it hard for them to grow. As a result, you end up with assistants (or children) who depend on you, who are unable to take care of themselves or solve problems without your help.

The continuous tendency to hand over to assistants (or kids) all they are able to handle leads you as a boss (or a parent) to the third stage, the one in which your role is to support. If, so far, you did a good job, your assistant should be able to work without close supervision and independently complete most of his daily tasks. But the former apprentice (an adolescent) still needs you occasionally, in case he faces a problem too big for him. In all such instances, you must be there for him, stepping in and offering necessary support; otherwise you may lose his trust. Bosses who are not there for their subordinates when needed are equal to the parents who neglect their teenage children, believing they are big enough to cope with all the challenges of life. A good boss (or parent) should never have "more important things to do," when asked by an assistant (or a child) for help. In dealing with the issues an apprentice (a kid) cannot solve on his own, we must always provide appropriate support. It makes the third stage crucial for building mutual respect, understanding and trust.

With time, the former trainee becomes an equal partner, the adolescent turns into a grown up. If we did our leader/parent job well, our partner/child now deserves full trust. In principle they know everything we know and they can do everything we can do. It's time to delegate with trust. Now you can, finally, become a democratic leader (parent). Instead of bossing around (strangling a child with advice), the moment has come to acknowledge her or his deserved independence.

In reality, such a nice and logical four-step model is rarely implemented.

There are numerous reasons for that. Most managers do not fully understand the process described. Many bosses view it as a way to produce competitors in hierarchy. If I teach the new guy all I know, he may soon take my place. There is a nice saying: *A man breaks through when he is young, and later takes care that the young will not break through.*

What should a leader do to benefit from such a model? First of all, the organizational rules must reward and stimulate the described four-step delegation development. Any tendencies to slow an assistant down, or prevent him from learning and growing, must be stopped.

Not all apprentices (not even all babies) are able to successfully pass through the four stages. Unfortunately, some lag behind or get stuck along the way. Occasionally, it's the boss who prevents his employees to fully develop because he likes to be irreplaceable (*I'm gone for a week, and the entire system collapses... If I'm not there, no one knows what to do*). The same thing could happen to parents. However, we must know that we are all better off if everybody reaches his full potential as quickly as possible.

Let me make another point here. First class people hire assistants who are better than they are. Only when surrounded by the best is a leader able to do his job brilliantly. Second class people search for third-rate assistants. Amongst them, the boss seems to be smarter and more capable, but in the end, he is going to achieve only mediocre results. And mediocrity is the main enemy of successful leadership.

The presented model draws a little on Ken Blanchard's ideas on situational leadership[1]. A good leader must be able to keep changing his approach in order to find the solutions that work best in a specific situation. Newcomers are fearful and inexperienced (like a child). They need autocratic leaders to teach them rules and discipline, to help them grow and develop. A good worker (a young man or woman) who can do almost anything seeks a leader to offer support when needed, and nothing else. If treated in an autocratic, rigid and inflexible way, such people would either back off or fight back. In both cases, their development may be jeopardized. A partner (or an adult) who has reached his level of competence and experience deserves a democratic boss (or a parent), ready to delegate with full confidence.

I hear some parents say: I have three kids. I brought them up the same way. The first is brilliant, with the second I had a few problems, but with the third I completely failed. How is it possible? The analogy between situational leadership and situational parenthood gives us a clue. We must be the parents each child needs and requires in any given situation. Since the kids are different, we must be different in order to find the best fit in any particular case. It is only natural that each child (like an assistant) calls

---

1 http://en.wikipedia.org/wiki/Situational_leadership_theory

for a different approach by the parent (or the boss) in various stages of his development.

The goal of every leader is to develop his team members to their full potential; only then he can delegate a good part of his work with trust. But our four-step model is not just aimed at delegating. It also describes the essence of coaching. Leaders are like coaches; their employees are like athletes, trained to win.

So, it is useful to know that, while developing your team members and making them ready to take over, you also develop your coaching skills and style. You must always keep in mind that it is the brilliant work of your employees that makes you a successful leader. Nevertheless, irrespective of your readiness to delegate, the most difficult decisions remain your personal responsibility.

4.3.3. Leaders Build Great Teams

In 1986, Jack Welch became the CEO of General Electric, one of the most successful global companies. The first thing he did was to reorganize their Institute for management development in Croton-on-Hudson, in New York. It was the place for young GE leaders to be taught and trained various topics, from teamwork and finances, to business strategy and time management. Also, they were supposed to spend a lot of time developing leadership skills, improving communication and building "human networks."

Welch imagined the GE Institute as a catalyst of change,[1] a stimulus of entrepreneurial spirit, a factory of leadership, a continuing team-building workshop, producing fresh ideas, innovative projects and programs, developing human resources and improving the organization. What methods did he use?

After some years of management experience, the newly fledged leaders would come to the GE Institute to attend a four-week seminar. The first week was spent in discussing the young managers' past experiences. The sources of success and failure were analyzed, focusing on the lessons learned.

This self-assessment session was followed by deployment into teams. The following week, all the teams would jointly engage in physical labor, for example to build rafts and race down the Hudson River. The races would last for several days and presented a real challenge. It takes a lot of skill and energy to organize a team to do something no one is familiar with. There were conflicts to be managed while the raft was built, or during the race. Also, they were supposed to find food, and deal with exhaustion, panic and injury. The race experience was supposed to help Welch recognize the best leadership talents in the company as well as to build the team spirit, based

---

1 http://www.slideshare.net/chci/leadership-development-at-ge

on initiative, entrepreneurship, and mutual responsibility.

After the race, they would spend another two weeks discussing critical GE problems and preparing projects to deal with them. The session would end with proposals of organizational or product innovation, presented to the GE executives. The team that managed to win the race down the river and/or the team that came up with best proposals would be put in charge of key development projects for the next budget year.

Such training is a good example of how leaders should emerge from self-development, as well as from successful team building. The race is a metaphor of an entrepreneurial project emerging within a competitive environment, designed to allow the fittest to win. They are given a chance to lead strategic projects, and sustain the competitive edge in one of the greatest global corporations.

My country went through a war twenty years ago, and it made us learn many lessons on leadership. For example, it takes 30 years for an officer to become a general in times of peace. But in times of war, it may take only a year. Why? Mostly because, in the first case, the promotion criteria are mainly bureaucratic, while in the "real situation" promotion is based on genuine natural selection. The expected and the real may differ dramatically. The Mobilizer must be well aware that organizational diagrams and formal titles are not worth much. They are just an infrastructure on paper, based on that-is-the-way-things-should-be principle describing the ideal world, impossible to create in business, economics or political practice. We should be aware that organizational rules are often ridiculous and make no sense. Most often, they serve no other purpose but to describe who should be reporting to whom. Formal authority in any innovative company is not a military rank designed to make organizational soldiers obedient, out of fear, and without resistance. True leadership authority should be fought for, not sought through the ranks and rules. Instead of being given, it must be deserved!

Self-developed harmony is always superior to any forced "harmonious solution." Imposed bosses never fully attain their commanding position if they don't deserve it as individuals. In the world ruled by knowledge, entrepreneurship and creativity, we need leaders who are trustworthy, whom we choose to follow and appreciate, regardless of their formal rank. The position is less important than the ability to influence and inspire. We all know that individuals who are respected by others represent the most valuable resource of any organization, regardless of their formal rank. These people are the best candidates to lead winning teams.

What is the difference between an average group and a winning team? What is the secret of teamwork success? Why are some teams superior to others?

The first cause of a success or failure lies in the very way the team is formed. In principle, there are three team-forming methods. In the first and the most common model, management decides on both the leader and the team members. For example, there is a boss above who says: you are going to be the head of the project team, consisting of these five guys. In the second case, the superiors appoint the leader and let him choose the members. For example, you are going to be the head of the team. Feel free to pick five people you want to work with. Finally, the third method implies that managers choose team members, and then ask them to select the leader among them.

Research proves that the first method is adopted in over 80% of real life situations. In the remaining 20% of cases, either the management picks the leader and he selects the team members, or the team is allowed to choose the leader. Research studies also show that, considering the quality of the team's output, the first method provides the worst results.

That conclusion should make us stop and think. Having three choices at our disposal, why do we, as a rule, pick the worst way to form a team? Are we stupid or something? But, first of all, why is it the worst way?

It is well known that people prefer a self-organized group to a concentration camp experience. Whenever top managers decide to exercise their power and authority and appoint the leader and the members of a team, they form a coercive, not a voluntary, organization. As soon as the first conflict, or the first failure, takes place, the leader is prone to come up with a simple excuse. He did not choose the guys he's working with. Emotionally excited, he would probably complain that no one could have possibly done better with the bunch of incompetents he was stuck with. By the same token, the team members would suggest that the failure should be attributed to poor leadership. Answering insult with insult, they would probably say that they did not select the leader. And, having such a jerk for a boss, no one could have achieved better results anyway. In principle, a team created by an outside force almost always lacks internal harmony. The group is not formed in a natural way; it did not grow spontaneously, like an organism. Instead of a marriage based on love, the bosses have created a shotgun marriage.

The ability to form and manage a winning team is an important skill of a successful leader. Its members should, above all, feel self-selected. The only way to succeed in doing that is to avoid any coercive team forming method. Therefore, to build a perfect team means to attract people who want to work together and who voluntarily accept the leadership authority. The best teams always represent a balance between individual and collective goals, desires, abilities and aspirations. We should keep in mind that voluntary harmony is far better that enforced and imposed discipline.

4.3.4. Leaders Love Consensus

One of my UCLA students told me about the event that made him rethink his decision-making philosophy. His company sent the head of sales to Tokyo to negotiate a business deal with a Japanese partner. After presenting his offer to the board members, he called his CEO. *How did we do*, asked the big boss. *Six of the Board members like our proposal, but the seventh one was not so enthusiastic about it. Well then, they must have accepted it*, said the CEO. *No, they rejected it because they couldn't reach consensus*, answered the head of sales.

Japanese business culture is founded on harmony and common agreement. It is not enough for a decision to be accepted by the majority. Everyone must accept it, or it is not going to be adopted. For Japanese business people, harmony is more important than speed or efficiency.

The Western business and political cultures are based on the 51:49 principle. If I am a majority shareholder I can run the company as I wish; I couldn't care less what the remaining 49% think. They must dance to the tune I play, because I have the majority to back me up. The same applies to politics. If my party holds a majority of the seats in Parliament, I have the power to crush the opposition and the right to ignore all their ideas, suggestions and proposals.

It seems so natural to make decisions by counting the votes. Hence, the 51:49 principle has become the accepted mental framework, allowing any majority to legally terrorize and oppress any minority. After getting approval by the half-plus-one, most business people and politicians choose to act as though the minority doesn't exist. Poor guys, they are below 50%. A bunch of losers! People in control of 51% of stock behave as though they own 100% of the shares. Parliamentary majorities often act as if 100% of the population voted for them.

However, to win by counting the votes does not mean you can make "the losers" change their mind. They still think the same, only now they are both outvoted and upset, because the majority decision has made their opinion unworthy. The effects of the majority voting are easily explained by elementary physics. We know that force has both magnitude and direction, making it a vector quantity. Suppose that 51% members of a group want to go left, and the remaining 49% prefer to go right. The situation is similar to two forces with almost the same magnitude, but with the opposing direction. The resultant vector equals their sum or $51 + (-49) = 2$. Therefore, the force available to push the whole group to the left equals to only 2%. The remaining "energy" is spent standing still, as in a tug of war game. We could say that 49% (out of 51%) of those who want to go left must pull the 49% who are "against," and want to go right. The outcome is an enormous waste of energy.

Let's imagine a company in which 51% employees support a new salary system, while the remaining 49% are against it. Suppose that the decision is made by majority vote. What happens next? Would you expect the minority to change their mind and join the majority in implementing the decision? Absolutely not! Those who voted against the new system are most likely to boycott its implementation, or at least slow it down. One cannot expect them to be fully committed to the solution they did not like in the first place. Rather, they are supposed to fight back, and do their best to prove that the majority was wrong. The example teaches us an important lesson. Even if we win, for example, by 80:20, it hardly deserves to be called victory. Remember the vectors? If four out of five wish something, and one out of five does not, the overall result is only 60%. This is the energy dedicated to action; the remaining 40% is spent standing on the site.

The 51:49 rule explains the absence of speed and efficiency whenever we act without reaching full agreement, be it a company or a parliament. Outvoting means quick decision making, but when it comes to implementation, actions are delayed or slowed down, and we get stuck in one place.

What is the moral of the story? The Mobilizer should always try to help his team reach consensus. To let any majority mechanically outvote the minority is always bad and should be avoided. Instead, a dialogue should be initiated, in an attempt to reach the common ground, harmony and full agreement. Consensus decision-making simply means that the group decision is based on a consent of all participants. In a nutshell, consensus is harmony, outvoting is conflict. Majority rule is quick and inefficient; consent is slow but highly effective.

Why do most leaders prefer majority and conflict to consensus and harmony? I guess it's a matter of habit; people are accustomed to traditional decision making values. Consensus means an open and lengthy discussion, a process of weighing all arguments and proposals, an attempt to take into account all available options. The standpoints of those who disagree must be seriously considered, and the final decision should be acceptable to all.

A friend of mine is one of seven shareholders in a very prosperous company. In his opinion, the key to their success is the way they make important decisions. Despite the fact that the ownership is not equally distributed among them, they have given everyone the power of veto. It provides a feeling of security and mutual trust. They openly discuss all important issues, convinced that no one would ever try to impose his ideas on others, counting on the majority vote. I teasingly call them the Japanese, because they have rejected the 51:49 culture and adopted the consensus approach. Consequently, they feel ownership as a search for harmony and a balance of interests.

Consensus is not easy to reach. Often, the interests are strong and the standpoints so different that any agreement seems impossible. Nevertheless, it is always important to give it a try. On the other hand, the practice of consensus should not be an excuse for abdicating. True leaders encourage the teammates to engage in participative management and bottom-up involvement, but ultimately, the essence of leadership is the readiness to make tough choices when necessary. As a rule, the Mobilizer should try to discuss and convince, and, if it doesn't work, he must step in and take full responsibility.

4.3.5. Leaders Believe, But Are Not Naive

During a visit to a famous distillery I learned an interesting fact from my host: 90% of all the beer produced gets consumed by 10% of customers, while the remaining 10% of beer ends up being consumed by the remaining 90% of customers. They explained that the same ratio applies to consumption of hard liquor such as French cognac, or gourmet food such as Russian caviar.

Obviously the 90:10 ratio seems to be applicable to many situations. Most people know from experience that 90% of the problems on their desk carry no more than 10% importance, while the remaining 10% represent more than 90% of what's import (Pareto's rule is 80:20; who cares?). Therefore, as pointed out in previous chapters, we must concentrate on a small number of relevant problems, while the rest should be neglected or delegated. Is it the same with the people, the members of our team?

For the argument's sake, let's assume that 90% of people are good and 10% are bad. If we agree on that, the ratio can be expected in every organization from an assembly line team to the board of directors. As a leader, you want everyone to work well, to meet the goals, to follow the rules and procedures, to be committed and responsible. But what should you do with the 10% bad ones? You can expect them to be irresponsible and late. Their work would stink, some of them would try to steal, cheat, lie, gossip and argue; others would do whatever is prohibited, unacceptable or wrong. Your task as a leader is to control them and stop them from doing the bad things. What should you do?

As a person you can have either a controller or an anti-controller mentality. What do I mean by that? The controllers know that some people are real bad. In order to catch them, they design control procedures aimed at monitoring everybody and everything, with no exception. The anti-controllers believe that some people are bad, but have faith in their team. They trust everyone and, in principle, they dislike control.

Let us simplify the issue to the bone. Suppose that you are a manager and your only task is to make your team members throw their garbage into a trash can. You know that, statistically, nine out of ten are good. If they had any garbage, they would walk over to the nearest trash can and toss it in. The remaining 10% are bad, and you can expect them to throw the garbage anywhere, messing up the working environment. Your goal is to make them all behave properly. As a controller, you tend to implement a strict supervision over all people. Most likely you choose to walk around and preach: *Throw your garbage into the bin, we are watching you!* Also, you decide to work out detailed control procedures, you hire additional controllers, to monitor, to analyze and inspect, treating everyone as a suspect. What is going to be the outcome?

Those who are accustomed to throw garbage all over the place become careful not to be caught in the act, but they don't change. Instead, some of them start searching for creative ways to outsmart the system. They do it for fun, as a habit, out of spite, or just because it's a challenge. Only the few who truly fear punishment might change their behavior and do the right thing.

How about the good ones? They throw garbage into the bins because that's the way they have been raised. But now, they must feel like idiots, thinking: *The boss has no faith in me; for him we are all the same!* The reaction might be a desire to trick the one who doesn't trust you; he deserves nothing better. So, when the boss is not watching, even a few responsible employees might be tempted to do the wrong thing, out of spite, or for fun; it's human nature. And what is the overall outcome? The controlled behavior hardly gets any better, there is a growing distrust within the team, and the high monitoring cost makes the system inefficient.

And what would the boss anti-controller boss do? He would probably close his eyes and ignore those who throw garbage around the bin, hoping that the situation gets better with time. However, he is totally wrong. The bad remain bad, but the no-control situation affects the good ones. They can hardly watch the bad guys throw garbage as they please and get away with it without consequences. It makes the good ones think: *Why am I the only idiot who takes waste to the bin?* Eventually, their self-control, or better said upbringing, based on a feeling what is bad, might give in. If there is no control, even good people turn sour. Opportunity can turn a decent person into a villain!

Can we solve the problem without making the controllers' or the anti-controllers' mistakes? Most managers think: *No, we can't! That's the way it is!* However, when facing an issue he cannot solve, an innovative leader tries to redefine the problem, see it with different eyes.

The 90:10 ratio provides a hint. Suppose the leader explains his control philosophy in such a way: I believe that 90% of all people are good, and 10% are bad. The good meet deadlines; they are committed to doing the job right, in a responsible and conscientious manner. They do not steal, cheat, lie or do anything wrong by our organizational standards. I trust each of you; I believe that you are all good. Therefore, I am not going to be going around checking up on anyone. However, I am not naïve. I know from experience that, in every organization, there are a few bad people. If they decide to break the rules, even without a control system, sooner or later we are going to find out. So, on behalf of all you good people, I promise to come down hard on those who break the rules. We don't want and we don't need any "bad apples."

This approach is based on some basic psychological principles: Those who believe in you deserve your trust. If a person doesn't trust you, by cheating on him, you lose nothing (you cannot lose the trust you don't have). On the other hand, you may lose everything if you try to fool a person who trusts you. When someone deserves a penalty, the leader should be consistent and hard, but objective. Let the punishment fit the crime, and not be voluntary. Even very strict rules are OK if announced properly, and explained in advance. People should be responsible for monitoring their own conduct as much as possible.

I have implemented this model several times and it works, under two assumptions: It must be applied consistently, and must be fully supported by top management. Critics usually have two objections. First, they point out that it is difficult to implement. It's true; some people don't take you seriously and try to test the limits of your patience. The second criticism comes from people who think that the 90:10 ratio is too optimistic. They claim that the portion of the bad individuals gets higher than that. In principle, that is not an issue; the model would work also in an 80:20 or 70:30 situation.

Speaking in terms of this book, the model is harmonious because it is based on trust and positive attitude. Also, it supports self-organization, relies on simple ethics and promotes a balanced approach to control systems development.

In conclusion, by implementing the model, the Mobilizer can get really nice results; above all, it reduces the costs of supervision, promotes self-management, and builds an organizational culture based on trust. But, if you don't like the model, skip it and move to the next chapter. We are never able to successfully implement the ideas that we don't fully trust.

4.3.6. Leaders Are Flexible

The previous model is based on still another important principle of harmony-based leadership: *A reward, not a punishment, is the best source of motivation!* Positive emotions strengthen team spirit, increase self-confidence, and improve efficiency.

In order to successfully manage their teams, leaders have at their disposal two powerful tools, a carrot and a stick. By offering the carrot (reward) they want to get the desired behavior, efficiency and proactive behavior. On the other hand, the stick (punishment) is used to bring people in line in case the carrot does not work. To illustrate the point, take a look at another Zen story.

A student was caught stealing and was reported to Benkei, his teacher. However, the teacher did not react. A few days later, the same student was caught stealing again, but Benkei again refrained from action. Other students were infuriated and the next morning, they approached the teacher with a signed petition. The thief has to be kicked out; otherwise the entire group would leave.

After reading the request, Benkei assembled them and declared: You may all go and study elsewhere, if you wish. You are wise; you know what is right and what is wrong. However, our poor brother is not aware of this yet. Who will teach him what is right and what is wrong, if we kick him out? Therefore, I intend to keep him here, even if it makes me lose all of you.

A rainstorm of tears, we are told in the story, started pouring down the face of the thief, and he never stole again. The reward, not the punishment, achieved the intended goal and provoked the desired behavior.

Do I hear you say that this story seems to contrast with my model in the previous chapter? If Benkei were to literally apply the 90:10 ratio, he would never invest energy in correcting the thief. He would rather get rid of the rotten apple. Yeah, you're right! In my defense, I can only say that no model, principle or concept should be taken for granted and applied without consideration. Managerial wisdom is not a recipe but is food for thought, to reflect upon and learn from. Mobilizers understand the space and time in which they work. They analyze and take into account the specifics of any situation. As stressed in the chapter on managerial mantras, no idea should be applied mechanically. What works perfectly within one set of circumstances might be of no value in another environment.

The Ancient Greek philosopher Heraclitus observed that you cannot enter the same river twice. Either the river is not the same, or you are not the same, or you have both changed. There are exceptions to every rule, every truth is relative, every magic sometimes works and sometimes doesn't. In a short film by the Oscar-winning team from Zagreb School of Cartoons, a young man gets a present from his professor. It is a book about the youngster's success in life. He opens his present only to find out that all the pages are empty. That's right, says the professor. It is you who must fill the pages with content, and not I or anybody else.

The Mobilizer must continually teach the members of his team but also learn from them. In writing his book of success, he should draw from all available knowledge, experiences and cases as if they were Lego blocks, ready to be played with. Each leader is different and so is his way of playing with leadership tools and toys. What works best for one, might not work for another! The finest tools and ideas are always those that you trust most, or those that you become emotionally attached to. There is no model of perfect leadership that can be copied and successfully pasted to all systems and conditions. Instead, there are Lego blocks of tools, ideas and models to play with and fail. And, if you do, start anew, in a search for a better combination. It should, eventually teach you to avoid mistakes and, with each new trial, get closer to winning. This leads us to the next chapter's title...

4.3.7. Leaders Want Everyone to Win

On his journey, the Little Prince from Antoine de Saint-Exupéry's novel[1] meets the king of a tiny planet, a ruler holding no tolerance for disobedience. But, as he is also a good man, he gives only reasonable orders. When he sees his guest barely suppress a yawn, he orders him to yawn. When the boy wants to say something, he orders him to ask a question. When the Prince complains of being tired, the king's order is to sit down immediately.

> "If I ordered a general to fly like a butterfly from flower to flower, or to write a tragedy, or to turn into a sea bird, and when the general was unable to obey, this would be my mistake, not his," explains the wise king. "You must not ask from a person more than he is capable of giving; authority rests, above all, on common sense."

The wise king is a perfect metaphor for the harmonious Mobilizer. Pursuing his goals and interests, he does not neglect the interests and needs of his teammates. Rather, he does his best to make sure that they all win. It is clear to him that the best and the worst of his subordinates will gladly do what is sought from them, if their own interest is appreciated.

In one of his lectures, Steven Covey[2] offered an interesting problem situation. There are two people with conflicting proposals. After a short argument, the first one says: *OK, we disagree, that's for sure. But, if you are ready to give up on your proposal, I will give up on my proposal; and then, could we, together, start searching for a solution that is better than both of our initial proposals?*

If accepted by both sides, the effect of such a simple idea may be magical. Whenever we disagree, and each of us wants to beat the other one, imagine that we both decide to abandon the options discussed because they don't offer common victory. Instead of insisting on the conflicting proposals, we decide seek a new solution fully acceptable to both parties. It means that

---

1 http://www.goodreads.com/work/quotes/2180358-le-petit-prince
2 https://www.stephencovey.com/7habits/7habits.php

we actually move from a situation with only one winner (Win/Lose) to a situation in which everybody wins (Win/Win).

This is one of the most important teamwork values. In order to succeed together, we must shift our attention away from the things that make us disagree and towards our common interest. Just by carefully listening to the other side and taking into consideration their arguments, we may get closer to a harmonious solution, one that could make us all win. If there is no such a solution, we can at least try to settle on one that is close enough. The aim of this process is to provide common benefit and ensure mutual victory.

Suppose it's Saturday night and my wife wants to go to the movies. I prefer dinner in a romantic restaurant. If we go to the movies, I might spoil her evening complaining about the film. If we go to a restaurant, my wife could spoil my evening by criticizing the food and service. What should we do? Search for a solution equally acceptable to both of us. After a short and friendly discussion, we might decide to spend the evening dancing.

The common optimum is often possible, but most of the time we don't search for it. Instead, we insist on our proposal and want our solution to be accepted no matter what. Such an attitude is deeply rooted in the common belief that "in order for one to win, the other must lose." The strong always beat the weak and manage to impose their will. The powerful crush the powerless; the rich exploit the poor. It's the natural state of affairs. It's a principle against which we cannot do anything. Or maybe we can?

There is another Zagreb School of Animated films[1] award-winning short film that I really adore. It lasts only two minutes, and the whole plot consists of two guys, a big one and a small one, running around. Actually, it is a ruthless race. The huge one keeps pursuing the tiny one, and, from time to time, manages to hit him with a hand, or a stick, or a hammer or whatever he grabs with his big hand. Then, after a minute of merciless violence, they suddenly stop. The small one asks in the six most common world languages: *Why are you hitting me?* The big one replies, again in all the six languages: *Because!* And the painful struggle for survival continues; the Big one keeps on pounding the Little one's head, until THE END fills the screen.

Yes, the big, the strong, the powerful, and the rich are supposed to win, and the small, the weak, the powerless and the poor are destined to lose. I am pretty sure that this very attitude prevents us from solving most of the political and economic problems in the present world. Whenever the powerful decide not to listen to the powerless, whenever the rich decide not to cooperate with the poor, whenever the polluters don't choose to speak a common language with those who care about the environment, whenever individual members of any group decide to win instead of searching for the

---

1 http://en.wikipedia.org/wiki/Zagreb_School_of_Animated_Films

common good, the global catastrophe is getting one step closer.

Can we do anything about it? I guess we can, if we try, even though it won't be easy. The Win-Win behavior is harmonious and ethical, but that's not the main reason why we should stick to it. In the long run a search for harmony reduces conflicts, increases a sense of unity, stops unreasonable competition, enables joint victories, eventually pays off and proves to be more efficient for all. Of course, it is easier said than done. Also, it is much simpler to do it within a finite team than on the global level.

Even though, in everyday business practice, there are situations in which it is difficult, at times impossible, to find common optimum, it is always useful to give it a try. The essence of the Win-Win approach is a voluntary search for solutions that make everybody happy.

The use of Win-Win logic in resolving conflict situations seems to be growing. The approach is successfully implemented in companies to resolve strategic discrepancies, or problems between departments. It is also applied in government-employers-trade union negotiations. It may be a basis for modern customer relationship systems, successful business partnerships and relations with the general public.

However, there are some among the rich, the powerful, and the strong who seem to have no interest in giving up. It will most likely remain so in the short run. But what happens when everyone's luck changes? Will the poor, the powerless and the weak be generous, once they get control over things? He who doesn't know how to handle defeat does not deserve a victory. That's why a harmonious leader, one who tries to make sure that everybody wins, eventually gets rewarded by a series of personal victories.

4.3.8. Leaders Prevent

A well-known American gangster, Al Capone, taken into custody because of a tax fraud, used to say that one accountant can steal more money with a touch of his pen that a hundred armed robbers. Such an authority should be trusted. An estimate of the USA economic loss due to theft, robbery and cheating amounts to a hundred billion dollars a year. That is the total value of what people employed by companies or the government walk off with, be it in raw material, products, components, or money. All kinds of frauds are also counted in.

Research indicates that almost half of employees have participated in theft, fraud and other criminal activities at least once. Most of this is really petty stuff; only five per cent of people are involved in large scale crime.

We have already discussed the philosophy of supervision, and the use of the 90:10 rule. In this chapter, I plan to go into details. The task of efficient control is to prevent abuses, if possible, and to remedy them whenever necessary. However, most control procedures deal with events that have already happened. Consider the managerial use of balance sheets, income statements, cash flow figures... In most cases the process being checked has already been completed. Only then are the results measured and compared with the targets. Such ex post control is the most common and the best known, despite the fact that it is of relatively little value. After we get wet from the rain, it is of no value to learn that it happened because we didn't carry an umbrella. After we have produced a giant loss, it is poor consolation to see a convincing explanation for it in the annual report. Experience is sometimes the thing we acquire only after we no longer need it.

A more useful form of supervision is based on the logic of "better-prevent-than-cure." The Marriott is one of the most prestigious hotel chains, with a yearly income amounting to $13 billion. Its 3,916 hotels are spread across 72 countries worldwide. The company is famous for its strict supervision, based on detailed procedures. For example, the room cleaning process consists of 66 steps. Preparation and serving of food is described by 6,000 recipes including such details as the exact position of horseradish in a mixed salad. In both cases, tests are performed at regular intervals to make sure that all the procedures are completed without mistakes.

The best control systems must affect the behavior of people and change it. When I was appointed director of the Croatian Informatics Institute, tardiness was pointed out as a problem impacting our reputation and efficiency. Most employees performed highly creative jobs, and any rigid control would be disastrous. I decided to act in a very unexpected way. Each afternoon I would send an email with the following sentence: *Please don't arrive at work after me, I may need you tomorrow morning!* Even though everybody knew it was a joke, people started to pay attention to their work presence. As they did not know exactly when I would show up, they decided to be in the office earlier than usual.

Rigid control is expected and accepted by people who perform simple tasks. Those with more creative and complicated jobs can only be managed using subtle methods. Strict control often does more harm than good. One of the most useful techniques is Management by Exception. A boss shouldn't be bothered with the processes and operations that are aligned with plans. He expects a report only in case the outcomes differ from expectations and call for corrective action. This allows the leader to focus on "exceptions," things out of balance that need to be taken care of. However, it's in the nature of every human to try to be an exception.

Most employees want to attract the leader's attention in order to inform him, present their results, and discuss issues. If a boss is not selective, he could spend most of his time meeting people, solving their problems and satisfying their need to be recognized. A huge number of minor issues could divert him from doing what is really critical. As an outcome, the priorities are neglected, the big issues not resolved, the real exceptions not dealt with. A leader who struggles with too many problems, trying to control everything, easily becomes a part of the problem and not a part of the solution. One of Murphy's Laws states that once the worms are let out of a can, they can only be caught in a bigger can.

It is always better to prevent a problem than to deal with it after the fact. In principle, any organizational crisis is a proof of poor leadership. We all know that big problems never become smaller. The Mobilizer must solve them while they are still in the cradle and not allow them to reach puberty. Many managers prefer to wait for a crisis to deepen and then introduce drastic and extreme measures. Isn't that exactly why they are appointed managers, to deal with tough issues? In a variation of the old saying, when the going gets tough, only the tough get going! However, that's a typical macho stereotype, and only careless people deal with forest fires—because they neglected a small flame.

Anyway, bad things happen. If we do not anticipate, we get caught by surprise. Managing crisis has always been an important leadership challenge. That's why successful bosses try to recognize important threats and prepare measures to counteract them. Most supervisory systems are set only to catch the individuals responsible and punish them. Instead of focusing on the causes, they take care of the effects. This leads us to the next role, that of the Mobilizer. He must manage conflicts.

4.3.9. Leaders Manage Conflicts

As long as any business or political system travels on peaceful waters, and there are no clouds on the horizon, it is almost irrelevant who holds the helm. However, as soon as a storm sets in, the captain's navigating skills become crucial. In stable conditions and a peaceful surrounding, leaders are barely needed. But in times of conflicts and crisis, the need for them grows sky high.

A conflict is a result of opposing interests or goals among people. It is a natural and common feature in any interpersonal relationship. As long as there are people, there are going to be conflicts. No company, political party, team or work group can escape from arguments and misunderstandings among its members. The conflicts emanate from the unsatisfactory distribution of power, from unjust distribution of resources, from differences in moral norms or from conflicting values.

A harmonious leader sees a conflict situation as an imbalance, or a state without harmony. We are not in tune with our goals, expectations, norms, and values, or we have not harmonized all the people inside our system, or we lack harmony with the people belonging to an outside system, or...

The conflicts themselves are neither good nor bad, but their outcomes may be great or damaging. Therefore, we can talk about constructive and destructive conflict. Suppose there are two employees competing for the title of Salesman of the Year. Their rivalry is constructive, because they make more sales for the company, develop new ideas and introduce marketing innovations. However, the same situation becomes very destructive if they set out to win at any cost, by cheating, manipulating their bosses or by faking the sales figures. Most conflict situations are both a danger and an opportunity.

At times, leaders, like good coaches, consciously provoke a conflict in order to get better results or to speed the development of individual capabilities. However, if such conflicts provoke employee resistance, boycotting, apathy or material damage, the leader must change course.

A boss who does not look ahead to anticipate problems but waits for them to erupt is not managing conflicts. He is being managed by them instead. A leader is expected to detect conflict triggers and make them work for him. However, even the best managers experience destructive crises from time to time.

There are a number of techniques for conflict resolution. Some are harmony-oriented, other are antagonistic. Let's take a quick look.

When a CEO tells the heads of both the marketing and production departments that their conflict over product design only helps their competitors, he uses the common enemy approach. He tries to manage the conflict by reminding them of the external threat. We all know that groups tend pull together if there is a common threat to their survival. This technique works well on a short-term basis. We always put our heads together to confront the common enemy. It may stabilize the system for a while, but the sources of conflict are not eliminated; and they could, eventually, reappear with a rejuvenated strength.

Can a wolf satisfy his hunger and a sheep stay alive? Leaders who prefer compromise as a conflict-solving technique believe they can. A compromise is the backbone of the political and economic culture in democratic societies. In order to reach common ground, the conflicting parties negotiate; each side gives in a little, until equilibrium is reached. Supporters of this approach claim that by reaching a compromise, everyone gains, while its opponents claim that everyone loses. Anyway, it takes a lot of time and energy to succeed, and the underlying cause of the conflict may not have been removed but only bypassed, for a while.

Many leaders believe in power as the best tool to end a conflict. Avoiding any discussion, they impose an unconditional truce, especially if there is no time to negotiate. In applying this technique most leaders rely on their formal authority, their position, and the available repressive mechanisms.

But even though exercising power seems to be the quickest method, its impact on organizational culture, team motivation and working environment can be extremely negative. The sources of the conflict are not removed and the use of coercion generates a desire for revenge, a sense of powerlessness, and mistrust.

Some managers believe in noninvolvement; organizational conflicts should simply dissipate after the clashing parties have huffed and puffed. The leaders try to minimize the effects by stressing how silly it is to argue by implying that the issue is insignificant in the grand scheme of things, or by convincing the competing parties to end their argument. However, this approach too only fails to eliminate the source of conflict; it's just a short-term truce. This technique makes the most sense when the leaders have to buy time (e.g., to complete an ongoing project) and no other solution seems feasible.

Another typical conflict resolution technique points out that, instead of arguing and focusing on the differences, the opposing sides could try to discover what keeps them together. The point is to persuade the conflicting parties that they have a common goal. People may decide to give up their ego-driven interests for the higher cause, but not for long. The technique appeals to the conscience of the people involved. Nevertheless, interests are usually much stronger than conscience or a sense of togetherness. The common goal method is likely to succeed only if there is a common threat.

These techniques deal with outcomes of a conflict, not with its roots. As such, they don't resolve the situation in a harmonious and balanced way. By contrast, a harmony-based approach would focus on the source of trouble, trying to remove the causes. Digging into the hard foundation of a conflict situation may be more difficult, but it's also more effective. It takes time, energy and readiness to go as deep as necessary.

We have already discussed consensus as a cooperative and balanced decision-making technique. It is contrasted to outvoting, and grants every stakeholder a right to veto any decision of vital importance. All participants in a conflict situation engage in open communication until they manage to reach full agreement. It means that all the interests, standpoints and arguments have been taken into account. Unlike other techniques that merely alleviate the outcomes of a conflict, consensus seeks to prevent later recurrences.

Successful leaders use more than one conflict-resolution technique. In principle, removing the cause is the best, and reaching consensus is the most effective approach. However, if appropriate, the Mobilizer may also make compromises, use power, try to water down tough issues, and search for a common 'enemy' and common goals. In any case, all the techniques should be supplemented by intuition and appreciation of interpersonal relationships within a team.

4.3.10. Leaders Deal with Chaos

Tough issues like conflicts deserve more than one chapter. Who is most responsible for them? Once upon a time a philosopher, a linguist, a theologian and a manager organized a meeting to discuss the importance of their professions and to decide which was the oldest. *First, there was a word; our profession is the oldest,* said a linguist. *Before the word, there was a thought,* added the philosopher. *Therefore, philosophy is the oldest. No, my friends,* stated the theologian, *God was there first, then his thought, and the word, from which the world came to be. Well,* asked the manager, *was there anything before the creation of the world? Yes, chaos,* they answered with one voice. *That chaos could have been created only by an executive,* answered the manager. *Therefore, we are the oldest profession!*

Chaos and conflict don't evolve out of nowhere. A number of situations serve as triggers. The conflict trigger is a set of events that increase the probability of an organizational conflict. One or more triggers may be involved in generating conflicts. The Mobilizers could benefit from understanding what the triggers are and how they work. Again, using the language of this book, the triggers are nothing but situations lacking organizational harmony, due to poor communication, unsatisfactory rules and regulations, inappropriate budget allocations, poor interpersonal relationships, promises not kept, etc.

One of the most typical sources of intra-organizational wars is the case of overlapped responsibility. Unclear boundaries between departments or tasks often create unhealthy competitive tensions. For example, there may be a fuzzy definition of responsibility for new product development. The same problem is shared by two departments, product development and marketing. In a best case scenario, their competition might provide better and more innovative solutions. More often, the overlapping responsibilities contribute to destructive intra-organizational struggles and should be avoided.

Limited resources also typically lead to organizational conflicts. Usually, a number of individuals, programs, projects and teams compete for budget money, for the best people, or for the sources of knowledge. The battle for limited resources is one of the most common conflict triggers.

In one company where I was a consultant, two great projects were submitted in an internal contest. Due to a lack of manpower and money, only one could be implemented. The people involved in the other project decided to leave the company and soon started working for the competition. In principle, limited resources create very destructive conflicts.

Within any organization, it is common to find people who just don't fit together. They constantly argue, fight, quarrel and disagree. Such personality clashes seldom do anything constructive. If there are two or more individuals who cannot work together, they must be separated or isolated in order to avoid the constant and fruitless arguing that might become contagious.

Information flow is the neural system of any company, responsible for successful work and decision making. Any communication channel blockage, preventing individuals and groups to learn what is going on in the system, might soon become a source of great conflicts. Information manipulation rarely contributes to anything constructive, and it must be prevented. The best way to overcome the communication barriers is to build an open, informal and efficient information system.

Nothing is as destructive as a failure. Whenever we fail, we lose emotional harmony. The greatest disappointment and hard feelings come from unrealized plans, unfulfilled expectations, unfinished projects, and broken promises. Conflicts evolving from unfulfilled expectations or unrealistic ambitions are extremely unpleasant. For example, suppose a person expects to get rewarded or promoted, and it does not happen. Or imagine the mood and the commitment of a team that has just successfully completed a project only to find that it is rejected by the market; or the enthusiasm of members of a political party who just lost an election. Defeats and disappointments are really hard to deal with; it can only be done through open communication between the leader and the teammates, based on honesty, self-criticism and integrity. In principle, Mobilizers shouldn't make promises that they cannot keep.

Time is money! No wonder time constraints put even more strain on individuals and teams than budget constraints. The key trigger of time-related conflicts is called the deadline. Many people cannot stand time pressure. They dislike running late and falling behind schedule. Working under the pressure of tight deadlines can, at times, be constructive if it builds up individual and group commitment. However, most individuals and teams are unable to handle the situation; as a result, there are conflicts, arguments, false pretenses and a shifting of blame.

The next in line are defects of the formal organization. They can trigger a lot of organizational conflicts. I am referring to poorly defined procedures, unsatisfactory standards, unjust and unpopular regulations, goals that are too high, etc. Such situations create a sense of internal conflict which is always destructive; harmonious leaders should avoid them by implementing a transparent system of commonly agreed organizational norms.

Constructive conflicts are like stormy weather. Before the storm, there is an unbearable feeling of heat, humidity, and pressure that builds up until one cannot stand it. After the storm, the air is cool, fresh and fragrant, you feel great, as if a heavy burden was lifted off your chest. A constructive conflict is healthy and necessary; it is a chance to solve accumulated problems, to clear up tough issues and to make everyone feel better.

On the other hand, destructive conflicts are more like a typhoon or a tornado. After such a storm, the dominant feeling is not relief; rather, we are faced with debris, flood and loss, and it's difficult to clean up. In dealing with destructive conflicts, leaders must act in a systematic and calculated way, first in order to head them off and, if that's not possible, at least to minimize the consequences.

Many bosses dislike conflicts and would much rather avoid dealing with them. But heroes are best recognized in times of trouble. There is not going to be harmony if we don't take care of the causes of disharmony. Managing organizational chaos is a true test of leadership.

4.3.11. Leaders Learn from Criticism

Remember the role of Evet-effendy at the Turkish court? His task was to suck up in order to teach inoculate his Sultan against the effects of flattery; in fact, to make him sick of it, as sycophants muddy a leader's thinking. People who constantly praise the leader and think (or act as though) he is always right are, in fact, no help at all.

The world of political and business leadership is full of inflated egos, and they demand unconditional loyalty, flattery, courting, and obedience. Such leaders, of course, end up surrounded by people who are pleasers and flatterers, lacking identity, integrity and opinions of their own. They believe that their task is to praise the great boss, cherish his person and celebrate his every act and deed. Yes, we all know that human vanity is in constant search of people who nod their heads in approval, who shower the leader with unconditional support as well as with unquestionable acceptance. Such adoration makes a boss feel greater, better and more successful. But it leads to disharmony in the long run.

In a harmonious culture of the Native Americans, the idea of erecting a statue of a leader, or carving the likeness of his face into the rock, or even naming the mountain after him would have been unthinkable. All these actions honor the ego of the leader, and true leaders should act in the spirit of humility. It is not their name that is important but the impact of their actions on the seventh generation.

After two years of seemingly excellent cooperation, Lee Iacocca shocked his management team with a decision to fire his vice-president. Dumbfounded and surprised, all of them commented: *The two of you have never had a single disagreement. The vice-president always stood behind all your ideas and actions. He was completely dedicated and fully committed to whatever you did. Why have you fired a man with whom you got along so well?* Iacocca responded: *My point exactly! Why should I pay a huge salary to a man who always has my opinion?* The founder and the legend of Xerox, Barry Rand, used to warn his managers: *If you have a yes-man working for you, one of you is redundant!*

A true leader must rise above the need to be admired, flattered and fully supported. True fellowship means that there are two independent individuals. Everything else is *"followship."* Quite true, being surrounded by think-alikes suits your ego and creates a climate of eternal partnership. However, such followship is fragile and unstable. Followers may be loyal to any leader and they might leave you as soon as you are no longer the boss.

That's why the Mobilizer must not let his ego get tied to his position. When the position is lost, the ego goes with it. He must not encourage a lack of criticism, sucking up and other bureaucratic inventions where position means everything and human integrity counts for nothing. Instead, a true leader must encourage an honest debate, exchange of views and open criticism. He must create a climate in which all ideas are analyzed by good judgment and common sense, regardless of who presented them.

The road to hell is paved with good intentions. Many mistakes leaders make are derived from good goals and honest intentions. Trying to create homogenous teams, many leaders believe it is best to think along the same lines, those of the boss. Such an attitude can be found even among people who otherwise believe in being open to a diversity of ideas and willing to hear everyone's opinion, including the critics. Here is a personal example. Like most bosses, I used to chair meetings in a traditional way. I would describe a problem, express my personal view, and then ask my teammates to make comments and suggestions. To my surprise, there was no criticism; almost everybody chose to agree with me. For a long time I was unaware that it was my fault; my own communication style was responsible for such feedback.

Namely, if I describe a problem, present my solution and then ask others for their points of view, I create two potential conflicts. Perhaps some teammates think that my definition of the problem is wrong, but I am the boss and I have already made my point. Perhaps some of them dislike the solution I propose, but again, I am the boss and it is not easy to confront me in public. Those who disagree with my problem definition, and the proposed course of action must stand up and openly challenge my proposals. In hierarchical organizations, this happens next to never. That's why those of my teammates who had different views than mine decided to remain silent, while those who participated in the discussion were either convinced by my arguments or accepted them out of the habit to please the boss.

Some leaders avoid giving too much discussion space to subordinates because they fear being perceived as weak and indecisive bosses. But we need to learn what the others think. A true leader would never let others decide, if he is personally responsible. But he should always use others to help him in making the best choice. One Dalmatian proverb says that a man and his donkey must know more than a man alone.

Some truths are self-evident, and others may require a lifetime to grasp. It took me decades to realize that a critic is a free consultant for me. Whenever someone criticizes me, has an opposing view, or does not agree with what I have said or done, I can learn something from him. Most people take criticism personally. Critics are bad people who hurt you, and you should defend yourself! Such an attitude is very unproductive. Instead of fighting back, you should ask yourself if there is anything you can learn from the criticism. Remember, the point is to improve, develop and grow. Seen from this angle, every criticism is a potential helping hand. Anything you do can be better. With a little help from your critics, or without! Isn't it ironic to try to turn the people who want to totally disharmonize you into unwilling builders of your internal harmony?

Of course, there are instances when your critics are genuinely malicious and ill-intentioned, and their arguments may be unreasonable. Even then, it is good to ask the same question: Is there anything I can learn from criticism that could help me become a better leader? And you know, there is always something; if you search for it, you will find it.

Many leaders pay consultants high fees in order to find out what is wrong with them, with their teams and their organizations, and what should be improved. Isn't it foolish then, to turn down free consulting and free consultants, regardless of their initial intentions? After all, it is completely up to you to decide whether criticism should make you angry and nervous or help you develop your full potential and enable you to grow into a great leader.

4.4. The Motivator

> There are two basic motivating forces: fear and love. When we are afraid, we pull back from life. When we are in love, we open to all that life has to offer with passion, excitement, and acceptance.
>
> —John Lennon

4.4.1. Leaders Motivate

Andrew Carnegie, the American king of the steel industry from the late 19th century, used to explain his vice-president's very high salary with the following words: *I pay him $50,000 a year for what he does at work, and another $50,000 for how he inspires others to work. He is a great demagogue!*

OK, inspiring subordinates is often a leader's most important task. However, "demagogue" is a word with negative connotations. We use it to describe politicians or managers who cheat and lie; who are ready to take us thirsty across the river (that's another Croatian proverb: a 'clever' man can get you straight across a river, no matter how thirsty you are). "Demagogue" originates from two Greek words: demos (people) and agein (lead). Originally, a demagogue meant a leader, a person who is able to activate people and make them do great things. In this sense, the Motivator must be a demagogue. His leadership style must make his team follow him voluntarily, even eagerly. In other words, a leader is someone who knows how to motivate.

In childhood, we are motivated by curiosity; later we are stimulated by the environment, our relatives, school, sport clubs, each group we join, political parties, the company we work for. As we become more mature, we recognize our needs and use our own willpower to self-motivate.

Self-motivation is an endless source of energy. Suppose you are reading a boring book. In ten minutes your eyes close and you are ready to sleep. Now suppose you are reading an interesting book. It captures your attention and imagination, and you read it until the next morning. Self-motivated people can accomplish great things only if they seem meaningful, and it pays off to invest time and effort. Motivation is related to the question "what's in it for me?" or "how do I see myself in this?" Whenever we wish to encourage our employees to do something, and to be fully committed, we must ask why they would want to do it. Most managers get only average results from their subordinates because they use coercion and orders instead of stimulation and encouragement. What is the secret of motivation?

Suppose that every individual is controllable by five switches. Each can be turned on and amplified, like the sound regulators on a stereo system. Motivation is similar to the sound quality, resulting from a leader's ability to perfectly set the five switches.

The first switch is the financial stimulation, or compensation. We work because we want to get paid. There are always those who say: Pay me more, and I will work harder! Offer me a raise, and I am ready to leave my current job this minute! But not everybody is like that. For each of us, there is a threshold, a salary that meets our financial needs; when it is reached, we are no longer motivated by money. This leads us to the second switch, the emotional side of our working environment.

Imagine a person saying: *The salary is not much, but I love my job and the people I work with. They like me, they respect me, and among them, I feel good. No financial offer from competitors would make me leave.* For that person the second switch is more important; it is activated by love, special attention and positive emotion.

There are also those who think: *My salary is not great, people around me don't turn me on, but I love this job because it is stable and secure. I would not trade it for a better salary or for love, if there is some risk involved.* Such people are most strongly motivated by the third switch, security and certainty about their future. For them, it is important to feel safe and to work without stress or risk until retirement.

The fourth switch is *responsibility*, rank and position. Some people are strongly motivated the prospect of advancement, by the possibility of being promoted, by the importance of their position and rank. They enjoy managerial responsibility and the respect that comes from power and status. *Forget about salary, love and security! Appoint me a president, a director or a boss, promote me, give me responsibility, and I will work harder...*

The fifth switch is the most unusual of all. It is activated by *challenge*. There are people who get a big kick out of something different from salary, love, security or responsibility. They need to do great and important things; they want to fight and win; they wish to leave a mark when they are gone, in the company, in society, on the market or in human history.

As a Motivator, you must learn to play with all the five switches. If you want them to work harder, the employees who are best motivated by money should get a somewhat larger paycheck. Those who fall for emotion should be showered with love and attention on a daily basis. The security-sensitive should be provided with a ten-year contract. Those who crave for position and rank should be promoted regularly. And those who are motivated by challenge must be put in charge of the most important projects and lead various "impossible missions."

Of course, the picture presented is a huge oversimplification. Clear types are rare; each and every one of us is turned on by all the switches, responding at least a little to each source of motivation. It means that we work better, longer and harder when the combination that suits us best has been reached. Experienced leaders know how difficult it is to get close to employees' hearts and minds; it is like opening a safe with the right combination of five switches. It is easy if we know the password, but almost impossible if we rely on sheer guessing.

Needless to say, it gets more complicated when we add two motivational tools, the stick (punishment) and the carrot (reward) to the picture. In principle, everybody wants to avoid pain and enjoy a gain. Motivation is a state of imbalance until we get the carrot and escape from the stick. In other words, we are set in motion by trying to get the things we want and elude the things we fear. What we want, or don't want, is a reflection of our needs, or the goals we wish to attain. We may call them positive and negative motives.

The positive motives are symbolized by the attractiveness of the goals we want to reach. These are, for example, satisfaction, happiness, peace, trust or security. Negative motives are associated with feelings like threat, fear, pain and discomfort.

Why do we do whatever we choose to do? For example, I am hungry, so I go out and buy some food. I am afraid of the dark, so I invent a light bulb. I am poor and ignorant, so I study all day and night... We are dissatisfied, either by the lack of a carrot or by the threat of a stick. Dissatisfaction is an incentive, setting us in motion. Our action leads to an outcome producing satisfaction. After we satisfy our need, we reach a temporary state of harmony. A need is satisfied, a goal is attained. But very soon, there is a new dissatisfaction; a new misbalance sets us in motion. We enter a new motivational cycle in which, again, our actions are triggered by the intensity of our unsatisfied needs.

Figure 6. Motivational Cycle

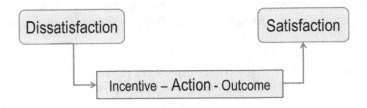

Parents often complain: I have given everything to my children. I provided them with the best toys, a computer, a car, fashionable clothing, books... Whatever they wanted, they got, even more than I can afford. In return, they have no ambition, no desire or will for anything, no goal to fight for. How is it possible?

The answer is provided by the motivational cycle. A person whose dissatisfaction is easily eliminated, without much effort or action on his part, gets used to it and loses motivation. By promising they'll achieve their goals and needs, a leader will always more easily motivate the dissatisfied. On the other hand, people who are already satisfied may have no goals and needs; therefore it is difficult to motivate them.

In his research, a friend of mine analyzed the success of pupils in elementary schools in Zagreb. The results indicated that the most excellent students was motivated by the following idea: *I don't want to live like my parents. Every evening, I hear them complaining about their salary, jobs, life and work. They would have had better lives if only they had continued with their education. I do not want their fate, so I study hard to avoid it.*

Success that comes out of handicap is not as rare as one would expect. The life journeys of many well-known politicians, business people, movie stars, top musicians, artists and scientists had a relatively bad start, their childhood was characterized by poverty, broken marriages, orphanage... They had to fight at least twice as hard, to earn their carrots and avoid an abundance of sticks along the way. Two of the best orators of the ancient Greece and Rome, Demosthenes and Cicero, are good examples. The first inherited a quiet voice and taught himself to speak louder by outshouting the noise of the sea. The second was born with a heavy speech impediment, and he decided to overcome his problem by tying sharp knives around his belt to stab him whenever he would shake from stuttering.

We know from experience that some people are easily motivated while others are almost impossible to move. The same can be said for different cultures and countries. Until twenty years ago the socialist regimes behind the Iron Curtain were examples of a massive lack of motivation. Most people enjoyed being given basic security and not having to compete with their brothers and neighbors, but they had no reason to put their heart into their work, either. The joke going around was, "*You can't under-pay me as much as I can under-perform!*

People change over time, and so do their needs. An apprentice is happy because he has a job and a regular paycheck. However, in a few years he expects a salary increase and promotion. After ten years he wants to run the most challenging projects and climb to the top of the organizational hierarchy. Towards the end of his career, maybe all he is looking for is security and respect.

Leaders motivate by setting a good example. Most people prefer bosses with integrity; they want to follow an individual with a strong personality. Each man's integrity is a result of his inner harmony, a balance between what he believes in and what he does. A leader with integrity always works in harmony with his words, practicing whatever he preaches. You cannot trust the boss who says: *I believe in law and order, but sometimes I cheat on my taxes; I believe in knowledge, but am not ready to study; I hate broken promises, but never keep those I make; I expect my employees to be cost conscious, but I spend extravagantly; I value punctuality but am often late.* Integrity means harmony and continuity. It motivates and builds confidence. On the other hand, conflicts and discontinuity are confusing and destructive. You can never be fully motivated by a boss whom you don't respect!

4.4.2. Leaders Care

I often ask participants at my workshops to comment the following story: Suppose there are two mental images that your collaborators rewind in their heads every morning on their way to work. The first looks like this: "Oh Gosh, one more day with the bunch of idiots I share the office with. One more day with the boss, a nervous jerk who doesn't recognize my potential. He is always angry and yells at us for nothing. Our office is poorly organized and my job is boring....I pray to God each morning to catch some contagious disease and stay home on sick leave..."

The second looks like this: "I can hardly wait to get to work and meet all those nice people from my team... They respect me, and the job is interesting and challenging. Besides, I have a great boss. He helps me develop and advance, praises me whenever I do something good... My job is like a hobby and the day at the office practically flies by...."

I ask them which story is closer to their daily routine. Nine out of ten choose the first one. To them the second story is idealized and looks more like a fairytale than real life. Namely, the business world is cruel, the competition is tough, work is not a hobby, and the office is a battlefield. Only the strong and the mean survive; an ideal working environment in which we would live happily ever after is not a real option.

Of course, we usually get what we expect to get. Our parents, educators, professors, bosses and other people who have influenced us, shaped us, and brought us up, they were all used to accepting the first story as inevitable. Even though, based on research, the second story lives in only one out of ten companies, I am sure it could exist in every company. Does it depend on a company's finances and the available budget? Not really; it is practically free, because it is nothing but a clear reflection of organizational culture and leadership style. Therefore, every leader is able to implement it on a daily basis.

Needless to say, the first story describes an environment characterized by permanent conflict and the second scenario is based on friendship and harmony. We all know that people who feel good, work better and produce more. People, who do not like their jobs, their bosses, and their co-workers lose energy from the beginning to the end of every working day. Lacking enthusiasm and aim, they can hardly wait to rush off to the peace of their home, to engage in hobbies, or, in the worst cases, to look to alcohol, drugs and similar forms of escape from others and self. Those who like their job, they treat work as a hobby. Filled with energy and good will, they may achieve awesome results.

The difference in productivity between the first and the second group can be dramatic. The latter are market leaders, and the former are candidates for bankruptcy. And it all depends on the attitude and values of the leader. He can freely choose how to relate to people, how to deal with work, how to manage problems and challenges. He is responsible for the organizational culture and the "mental image" with which his teammates start each and every working day.

In a Gallup Organization[1] poll carried out on a sample of more than 50,000 employees, the question was asked: *What do the most talented employees need from their workplace?*

The answer was astonishingly simple. In order to be successful at the workplace, all a young, talented and capable employee needs is a good manager. A boss who is able to recognize his talents, who supports him, helps him develop; enables him to do what he does best. A boss who provides him with challenge, a stimulating work environment, a set of clear and meaningful goals; who makes sure there are all the prerequisites for good work. Yes, we all know that, but too often we forget that the best boss is the one who cares for us and makes us care for him in return!

A harmonious leader who truly cares about his teammates spreads that principle throughout the organization. If the boss is a person who plants harmony, he will reap balanced and friendly workers; if he sows antagonism and carelessness, he is sure to harvest conflict and bad feelings. As Carl Jung, a Swiss psychiatrist, wrote in one of his essays, the meeting of two personalities is like the contact of two chemical substances: if there is any reaction, both are transformed.[2]

Caring leaders are the best motivators. Everyone does his best when his work is recognized and praised by the boss, when his effort and dedication are noticed. We expect from the leader to commend what we do well and to express his feelings about it. His task is to build us up and encourage us, as though he is our parent or a best friend. Such support brings out the best we have, and inspires us to excel.

For a leader who is just a good professional, I work OK, because my mind and brain say it's OK. But for a leader who is really dear to me, I work great because my heart and feelings make me do great. If I am appreciated by the boss as a person, not just as a worker, it builds my self-esteem and motivation, and I do my very best.

The employees are more successful and enthusiastic about their work if they are constantly stimulated. The fact that the boss keeps encouraging me, and shows that he cares about me, makes me want to give it back, so I work harder and become fully committed to the job. For the Motivator who knows how to inspire, I am ready to give all that I've got and to accomplish

---

1 Gallup Business Journal: http://businessjournal.gallup.com/content/1144/first-break-all-rules-book-center.aspx
2 http://en.wikiquote.org/wiki/Carl_Jung

even more than I believe I am capable of. Good leadership is the engine to power up everyone's evolution in the team.

4.4.3. Leaders Choose the Right People

In one of the most successful armies of all times, a very simple rule was used in personnel management. After the first month of training, the officers were asked to evaluate each recruit based on two criteria: is he stupid or smart, and is he hardworking or lazy.

Based on that, the recruits were divided into four groups: (1) smart and hard working; (2) smart and lazy; (3) stupid and lazy; (4) stupid and hard working. The taxonomy was used as the basis for career management decisions. Depending on the group they belonged to, the recruits were directed to different specializations. The smart and hardworking were advised to go into engineering; their ideal job would be to build new weapons and to work in army logistics. The smart and lazy were sent to best military schools to become strategists and leaders. The perfect professional challenge for the stupid and lazy was infantry; they were supposed to be trained and treated as "cannon fodder."

The reasoning behind all these ideas is relatively clear. Those who are blessed with brains and diligence are the ideal performers of complex and responsible tasks like weapon development, logistics and military infrastructure. They have the mentality of engineers and their abilities are best used in jobs like that. The smart but lazy are blessed with enough imagination and intellect to solve strategic issues, hence, it is only natural to destine them for headquarters and command posts. They should be kept apart from the operating environment because they are not hardworking, nor do they have the necessary motivation. The best place for the stupid and lazy is infantry where they perform routine military tasks and are dispensable. The generals of that army didn't have a problem with that particular group. Being neither smart nor diligent, they didn't deserve a better destiny.

How about the fourth category? What should be done with those who are stupid and hard working? The answer is rather drastic; they were forever banned from military service. And what was the explanation? Stupid people continuously do the wrong thing, and as they are diligent, they do a lot of it, and what is even worse, they do it with boundless energy and persistence. Therefore, the number of problems they generate is endless.

Frankly, my personal experience as a manager or consultant provides a lot of evidence to support that strange military policy. Whenever there is a huge problem caused by human error, it is always created by an individual from the fourth category. Members of that group are responsible for most everyday problems, making our work and our lives miserable. Wise leaders must be careful in dealing with the stupid and hardworking; they are the worst nightmare of any organization! (Of course, I am kidding. Or am I?)

As a consultant, I have often used a self-evaluation-based test of talents. Suppose you are asked to evaluate each of a hundred talents on the list, and you grade yourself from 1 (I am lousy) to 10 (I am great). On the list you can find your major strengths, the things that make you proud, but also the things you do poorly. Some of us are excellent speakers, and others tell good jokes. Some make easy contact with people they don't know. Others speak many languages fluently. Some are great dancers, while others paint and draw; still others are endlessly patient and know how to explain the most difficult concepts.

Now, suppose you make a list of your top ten personal talents, the things you do best. That's the set of your major qualities, your most developed capabilities. Then I ask you to look at it and sincerely answer the following question: *How many of these do I do at work each day?* If the answer is between eight and ten, everybody should envy you because you must be proud of yourself and happy with your job. Each day you do what you do best, and it must be fulfilling and satisfying. However, if the answer is under two, then everybody should feel sorry for you, because you have little reason to be pleased with your professional life. You may speak foreign languages, but never use them, or you may be a great Networker but your job requires that you spend the whole day in a cubicle, alone, or the like. Your greatest talents sleep, neglected, and your daily routine most likely bores you to death.

A leader-motivator must understand this problem, because it's really crucial for individual and team success as well as for the overall organizational harmony. What can be done about that?

Remember, every individual is a collection of knowledge, talents and skills. To complete any task, it takes certain capabilities. In practice, when deciding who is going to do what, most managers think: *I need the person with best knowledge, talent and skills!* Even though it looks quite natural, this idea is a sure source of trouble. First of all, the notion that there are good capabilities, talents, knowledge and skills is very vague. Any particular human ability is good only if it fits the need of the task that must be completed. For example, pedantry, diligence and discipline are brilliant virtues for a chief accounting officer. But would you appreciate a creative director of marketing with the same qualities?

Of course, we don't need the best people overall; we need the best candidate for a given job! That's why successful leadership heavily depends on the-right-man-in-the-right-place concept. Every person is capable of something and there are jobs he could do perfectly. When that happens, we have the winning combination. However, this is more often the exception rather than the rule. Why?

The problem lies in the very concept of the *workplace* and the associated *task/job description*. Being hired for a specific job, we do the things we know and can do well, but also the things we have neither will nor ability to do right. Suppose there are two salesmen; the first is great at selling but messes up all paper work. The second barely ever makes a sale, but his post-sale documentation deserves praise and respect. They are both hired for the same job and have identical task descriptions; each is supposed to sell as much as he can, and, after the deal is closed, he must fill out a huge pile of forms. At present, their boss spends most of the day criticizing the first for bad paperwork, and the second for poor sales. What would you do if you were in his shoes?

First of all, it would help to know why the good salesman keeps messing up the forms. Perhaps he wants to do it right but does not know how. The obvious solution is to teach him. But, my guess would be that he hates paperwork and has no talent for administration. Why don't we appoint the other person with a talent for administration as his assistant? Now, the first salesman can fully focus on sales (he is great at it), and his assistant does all the paperwork (he is gifted at that). Both are fully satisfied and highly efficient because now they do only what they are capable and motivated to do.

The idea is quite simple and obvious: do what you do best all the time, and your job becomes your hobby. It means that you can work long hours, be efficient, self-fulfilled and happy. But if your job requires that you do things you hate or dislike, you get tired quickly. Speaking in terms of this book, you and your job are not in tune. Day by day, you lose energy and enthusiasm, you get depressed, you go on sick leave, and you produce lousy work. A good leader doesn't want any of that to happen. He expects all members of his team to be in harmony with their jobs and do great. There are ways and means to find the dream job for each of them. Let's take a look at an illustrative example.

As a consultant, I have advised a high-tech company to solve this dilemma in the following way: whenever they hire a talented beginner, they give him a mentor and organize a two-week guided tour of the company. The novice and his mentor move from department to department, from office to office, from workplace to workplace, until they have been everywhere and seen everything. The tour helps the novice learn who does what, where and how, and he gets a perfect picture of what the company and its organizational units really do. After that, the apprentice and his mentor meet with the management board, and the novice is asked: *Where would you like to work in order to be most valuable for us?* In other words, we want you, and we give you the opportunity to pick the job, workplace or position where all your talents can be revealed. Of course, nobody could answer that question better than the novice himself. Hopefully, he knows what he does well and how all his talents, abilities and knowledge can best serve the needs of the company. Instead of hiring someone to do the predefined tasks which will, most likely, use only a portion of his talents, the person is given freedom to create his job in such a way to fully utilize his capabilities.

As an outcome, a few dozen gifted young people have been given the opportunity to select the work place. But, a few novices were unable to find the perfect job within the existing system. Eager to keep them, and interested in their abilities, the board members asked them to propose a job that would best suit their talents. There is no perfect workplace for a genius in your company? Let him invent one! Turn the disharmonious job bureaucracy into a harmonized environment in which each individual plays in tune with his talents and the organizational goals.

In my experience, most managers would reject such an approach as impractical or absolutely unfeasible. They rather stay surrounded with people whose talents keep being unused, because organizational rules and regulations don't provide a flexible, organic environment. Instead of forcing people to fit the boxes and pigeon holes of job descriptions and workplace requirements, why aren't they tempted to think different? My advice is simple: First give it a try, and then criticize! Remember, as a leader, you can achieve anything you wish! If you succeed, you'll be rewarded by unexpectedly high efficiency, because most of your teammates will start treating their job as a hobby.

Be that as it may, the right man in the right place is the only good and harmonious option. There are three poor choices: the right man in the wrong place, the wrong man in the right place and the wrong man in the wrong place.

4.4.4. Leaders Catch You in Doing Your Best

Harmonious leaders try to make sure that all the talent within their team is used to its full potential. Doing what they do best all the time makes people happy and efficient. But only if the boss keeps noticing, praising and rewarding their efforts and their results. Consequently, leaders should learn how to *catch people in what they do best*. It allows the Motivator to achieve all the positive goals listed in this book with less effort. The trouble is that very few organizational systems are designed to implement such an approach. Instead of the positive, they focus on the negative!

Suppose you are Jerry Seinfeld and you tell a joke to a group of people in a club. In response, they may either laugh or ignore you. If they burst out laughing, such feedback will inspire you to tell another joke and make it even better. If they ignore you, you could be the best standup comedian in the world but you are in big trouble. Running low on self-confidence, and high on jitters, you will hardly be able to tell another joke.

No office or factory floor is much different from that club stage. Whatever you do at work, the feedback from your teammates, and especially from your boss, can turn it into a wonderful experience or into a real nightmare. A positive reaction is a prerequisite of better performance and growing enthusiasm! A negative response will cut your wings in half!

There are different ways to provide feedback in different corporate organizational cultures. The boss and his teammates may be accustomed (or trained) to recognize and reward whatever someone does well, so that he can develop and improve. Or they may have a habit of bringing everybody down and systematically ignoring all the efforts and positive results. One of the key features of good leadership is the leader's ability to continuously encourage teammates to "laugh at good jokes" in order to make them even better next time. Such an attitude is powerful and motivating enough to turn us all into "world class stand up comedians."

The catch-them-in-what-they-do-best approach has other important advantages. For example, a typical boss spends a lot of time with the poor-performing employees, supervising them carefully, criticizing them and correcting their mistakes. As a result, he has no time for best employees. So, he misses the opportunity to learn from them, teach them, and listen to their problems. As a rule, those who are the best get buried by work the boss provides for them, while those who are the worst bury the boss with the work they impose on him. Is it logical?

My university regulations force me to spend a lot of time with the worst students. When they repeatedly fail, they are entitled to additional exams, extended deadlines, and supplementary consultations. There is a common and sad feeling that the system is designed for the bad students. They are always outspoken in "fighting for their rights." Not unlike the problematic employees who use all the legal options and "democratic means" to protect their rights and position.

Student organizations protect underachievers for the same reason why unions always fight for workers' rights for those who don't perform, or why government agencies, otherwise inefficient and disorganized, become very efficient in putting pressure on the bureaucracy to save them from bankruptcy?

The Motivator should always try to create rules to promote, protect, affirm and support all positive people and processes within the organization. Likewise, he should try to spend as much time as possible with the best employees. They are the ones he can learn most from, create the best results with, and lean on in challenging situations.

Spending time with the best makes you better. If I want to improve my tennis skills, I should choose a partner who is superior. Competing with him, and watching him, I can make my skills grow and improve. If I choose an inferior opponent, whom I can beat without difficulty, I may feel good, but my skills remain unchanged. A first class leader looks for people who are smarter than he is; and a second class leader surrounds himself with third-class people. This is because the former wishes to advance and do a great job while the latter just wants to outsmart his team.

Spending time with the best brings us to another leadership mantra, networking. It is good to be networked, to move in the right circles, to socialize with important people, and to have connections in the right places. It is always good to be well informed and to communicate with the most successful among your colleagues. For your career's sake, it is a smart more to mingle with top executives, and occasionally have dinner with respected journalists who deal with business, politics or the economy. It is of great importance to regularly meet authorities in the field like consultants or professors who are in touch with theory and research. It is vital to systematically contact people in government positions close to your line of work, as well as your suppliers and customers in order to learn what problems they are faced with.

Spending time with the best puts us on the edge. It enables us to deal with tough challenges; it sets our goals high, creates opportunities, and provides us with valuable information and encouraging experiences. Also, it sharpens our instincts. We always gain by networking with the best!

In practice that is often not what happens. The smart ones, people who are the best, whose intentions are good, who work long hours and do great things, often feel they don't need networking. Brought up and educated in the spirit of fair-play, they still believe in the American Western morality: the good cowboys wear white hats, the bad cowboys wear black hats, and the happy ending is guaranteed. Unfortunately, common morality is moving further and further from the ideal. And ironically the bad guys, those who share criminal interests, in conflict with the law and with good business practice, always make the effort to meet and communicate. Such networks are referred to as clans, cliques, gangs, the mob or mafia, and they are blooming.

Networking is one of the keys to success. It is also a harmonious way of bringing people together and allowing them to succeed more easily. On the outside, you should keep in touch with the best people in your professional environment! On the inside, you should keep in touch with the best members of your team! Therefore, it is an important and continuous challenge for every boss to assemble, recognize, reward and keep together the outstanding workers, catching them in what they do best and enabling them to tell, each day a new joke better than the day before.

4.4.5. Leaders Value Intellect

Are you tired of Sun Tzu's observations? If not, I have still another: "Those who send people to military operations without training destroy them. Look at your soldiers as if they were your children and they will gladly die for you." Do you think that soldiers or workers should be treated like your own children, beloved, most valuable? How much do we value people, our coworkers, employees, and partners? What is the value of human skills, attitudes, minds and knowledge?

During a management workshop for top executives in a large regional bank, we discussed the issue of intellectual capital. The bankers proudly stated: *Human capital is the greatest resource, and we use every opportunity to prove it's our number one priority!*

Trying to initiate creative discussion, I challenged them with the following question: Suppose a young, well-educated and very bright client applies for credit to start up a new business. Under what conditions would you approve his request? Would you, for example, give him money if the person had nothing to offer as collateral except his intellectual capital, or better said, his brilliant entrepreneurial mind? With ample laughter they answered that mortgages still require material guarantees and that collateral consists of some sort of physical assets. So, do the managers of that bank really value human capital highly?

Here is another example. Michael Warren, at that time a thirty-year-old head of jeans production at Levi's, in search of a new challenge, decided to apply for the job of quality control production line manager in the Toyota factory in Georgetown, Kentucky. He did not dream of spending a whole working week demonstrating his skills, capabilities, knowledge, and character to his future employer. It took him exactly 42 hours to fill out questionnaires, participate in various simulations, to complete all kinds of skill and problem-solving tests and to answer hundreds of questions in long interviews. Even the individuals who applied for jobs as assembly line workers were tested for 14 hours. Not only were their technical skills analyzed, but their overall literacy, state of health, and personal characteristics such as teamwork skills, communication style and ability to establish good interpersonal relationships.

Even though we consider people to be the most important business resource, such "input control" seems excessive. At the same time, we apply a zero-defect standard for testing raw materials and components which are far less important than people.

Good leaders know that everything depends on people. Hence, hiring, selection and training are the jobs of the utmost importance. In reality, hiring is still not taken seriously enough. In principle, human resource management is the job of all jobs. However, it is often treated as a low priority task or as just another technical issue. When searching a candidate for the CEO position, we may sometimes engage a head hunting agency, but the lower level hiring is still affected by nepotism, or the habit of giving preference to compatriots and friends and not to the most capable for the job.

For almost two decades, I have been engaged in various management development programs. I have worked with leading Croatian, Slovenian, American and multi-national companies. I have even lectured at an elite Chinese executive development institute. Often I was invited to run leadership or change management seminars and workshops for middle managers. My experience tells me that such training, proposed by the top management to be run for their subordinates, is most often a bad idea. How come? At the wrap-up and discussion session, at least one of the participants is likely to comment: *very nice, original and stimulating, but this is what my boss should have learned first, not me.*

Whenever they learn something new or special, most people want to be able to apply it as soon as possible. However, pretty quickly they become aware that the new idea cannot be implemented without executive support. A feeling that they have learned something valuable, or a belief that they can do better, but are not allowed to do so, creates a frustration, difficult to cope with.

So, if I am offered this type of cooperation, my suggestion is that we should start from the top; otherwise, I am not ready to accept the assignment. I try to convince them that any middle management training, skipping the top management level, is just a waste of time and money—at least as far as change management and leadership workshops are concerned. New ideas, concepts and tools dealing with leadership, change management and organizational culture can only be introduced from the top down.

According to legend, ancient Rome was first populated by men only. To grow, develop and succeed, they needed women. So Romulus, their leader, decided to solve the problem by kidnapping girls from the Sabine tribe that lived nearby. To placate the ladies in distress, they allowed each of them to choose which of the Roman warriors would be her marital partner. The first of the ladies wished for a guy who was desirable, gentle, muscular, courageous, humorous, humble, honest, hardworking, rich, strong and handsome. She was told she could only have one husband, not ten.

Many bosses often find themselves in a similar situation, especially if they are newly appointed to the job. It is hard to come across ideal people; we must learn to appreciate what is at hand. It is always a challenge to make the best out of the available human material. It pays off to put confidence in the people you are stuck with instead of using the poor quality of your human resources as an excuse for failure. It takes a good leader to make us a better team! It takes a bad leader to make us a lousy team!

4.4.6. Leaders Promote

Have you ever been promoted? Have you ever promoted somebody? The French emperor Louis XIV used to say: "After every promotion there are hundreds of unhappy people and one ungrateful." Another of Murphy's Laws teaches a leader that he must be courteous and fair to all the people he passes on his way up the corporate ladder, because he will have to pass them all again on his way down.

From the day we are hired to the day we retire, our daily commitment, energy and enthusiasm are fed by hope that we can advance, become more important and have a more responsible job, in a word, that we might get promoted. Climbing the organizational ladder is an interesting process and it should be well understood by the Motivator.

Have you heard of the Peter Principle?[1] Basically, it says that *Most managerial positions in large hierarchies are occupied by incompetent people.* The story usually goes like this: A person does a good job, and gets a promotion. Due to good results on the new job, he advances to a higher position. Again, based on his results, he may soon climb to an even higher rank. Finally, he is certain to climb to a position where he is no longer good. There, he stays until retirement, giving the superiors no reason for further promotion.

The Peter Principle suggests that, in hierarchical systems, people advance until they have reached the level of incompetence. As long as they work well, they climb up, when they no longer work well, they stay there until they retire.

The reason for such organizational shortcoming is a common practice, also a common misconception of all big systems: *People get promoted based on their results and not on their capabilities.* Being good and producing results at a given organizational level does not guarantee good results at higher levels. Suppose I am an exceptional designer, so I get promoted to head of the design department. A typical outcome is to lose a good designer and gain a lousy boss. As a designer, I was an expert with exceptional professional competence. As a manager, I am no longer doing stuff but running run people. I don't use my expertise anymore; instead, I need good leadership skills and

---

1 http://en.wikipedia.org/wiki/Peter_Principle

high emotional intelligence, because now my major task is to manage the design team.

Is there a medicine for this disease? Of course! Promotion should be based on competences and capabilities, rather than results. Someone's efficiency at lower levels of organizational hierarchy often has nothing to do with the efficiency at higher levels.

Such reasoning supports the trend to build flat hierarchies and appreciate lean management. Research has indicated that, in complex systems, there is an ever increasing number of people who coordinate, as opposed to a number of people who actually do something. Just by eliminating the work stations that don't produce value, the overall efficiency can be significantly improved.

That particular reason leads Tom Peters[1] to conclude that middle managers are *producers of negative value*. He claims their cost to be higher than their contribution. General Colin Powell[2] would definitely agree. He states that, "a leader must shift the power and the financial accountability to the folks who are bringing in the beans, not the ones who are counting or analyzing them."

The outcome of harmony-based leadership is a team of self-motivated and self-controlled individuals who deserve autonomy and need not be strictly supervised. In my experience, any organization based on trust is far more efficient than any hierarchy with multiple levels of coordination, supervision and control. Harmonious participation and mutual trust allow a leader to shift his attention to strategic issues, while most operational-level tasks get delegated. The participative decision making contributes significantly to the increased motivation and responsibility of all the "subordinates." By the way, that term becomes obsolete, because the teammates don't really feel "below" the boss but on an equal footing.

I was brought up in former Yugoslavia, a country that invented self-management, workers' participation in decision making and workers' councils as top management supplements. I could tell you a thousand stories about that experiment which was introduced in 1950 and lasted for four decades, with its ups and downs. On the positive side, from 1952 to 1960, Yugoslavia was the country with the highest annual GDP growth in the world. The practice of self-management[3] was not limited to the business environment. It equally penetrated federal and local government institutions as well as all public and social services, even art, culture and sports. As an outcome, the country's population and most workers developed a sense of ownership and responsibility concerning everything that was going on in their enterprises, local communities, schools, kindergartens, sport clubs,

1 http://www.tompeters.com/
2 http://www.blaisdell.com/powell/
3 http://en.wikipedia.org/wiki/Workers'_self-management#Europe

hospitals or theaters. Also, living in a country with a unique model of management, headed by a genuine World War II hero, Marshal Tito, a leader of the non-aligned movement, a person who managed to keep the country delicately poised between the capitalist West and the socialist East, the young population of Yugoslavia was overwhelmed with pride and a feeling of being special. This was reflected in the world-class results attained by individuals and groups in sports, science, medicine, and the arts.

On the negative side, behind the scenes the country was ruled by a one-party regime headed by one man, commonly called a (benevolent) dictator, although compared to others in the neighborhood Yugoslavia enjoyed a "socialist democracy" with consultative assemblies representing 6 republics and 2 autonomous provinces. A rather oversimplified and primitive method of self-management often enabled the incompetent majority to outvote the competent minority. To make a long story short, let me give you just one example. A plan to install a public water supply in a newly-built city district was presented to the citizens' council of my father's hometown. The residents were shown a detailed plan from which they learned that the water storage tank would be situated atop the local hill. They didn't like that, and asked why. An engineer explained that this was due to the law of gravity. After serious discussion, the "self-managers" decided to send a petition to the Federal Parliament and ask that the law of gravity be changed, because they wanted the water storage tank next to the river.

The idea of self-management died along with Yugoslavia, and the country was, in the early 90s, split into seven independent states. However, in the meantime, the concept of workers' and citizens' participation has gained a lot of support among both theoreticians and practitioners all over the world. It is mostly due to a shift in global economic, political, social and cultural values. Modern leaders no longer need obedient followers; instead they are in search of independent people ready for initiative, self-control, self-management, innovation and change. The key issue is not obedience to the boss, or how many hours someone worked, or how much he produced, but rather how the products or services did on the market. Instead of working to impress the boss, workers and employees should impress the customer. Client satisfaction is the only true measure of efficiency. External criteria are much more important than internal measures. The supervisors turn into coaches, the accountants become leaders. The key motivation tools are initiative and creativity. The most important question in performance evaluation is no longer "How well did you perform your job since the last time we met?" but, "How much did you change it?"

Accordingly, good leaders adhere to the following rule of thumb: There are two types of people who don't deserve promotion. The first are those who don't do what they are told; the second are those who don't do more than they are told.

4.4.7. Leaders Are Good at Meetings

I have a friend who, more than anything, despises meetings. He always describes them by the same comment: *Where was I? Nowhere! What was I doing? Nothing!*

On average, managers have up to ten shorter or longer appointments and meetings per day. Their goals vary from troubleshooting and problem solving, to exchange of information, from motivating the team at the start of a new project to team building and socializing. In any case, leaders spend more than half of their working time in meetings. Considering this, it is important to run them effectively; otherwise a lot of time, motivation and talent gets wasted. Can we turn that boring thing into something inspiring?

How should a business meeting be prepared, organized and headed? Here are a few hints and suggestions. Try to call the meeting only when necessary, meaning that the expected results cannot be obtained through personal contact, telephone calls or e-mail messages. Every gathering must be planned ahead of time and the information sent to participants in advance. The invitation should contain the detailed agenda, expected duration and clear purpose (i.e., exchange of information, counseling, proposal formulation, conflict resolution, brainstorming, decision making).

Who should be invited to attend? That issue must be given careful consideration. Inviting individuals who like to talk at length, or people who dislike one another and are sure to misuse the occasion to argue, all these might cause the meeting to fail miserably. A gathering should take place in comfortable surroundings, aligned with its purpose. One should definitely try to avoid any interruption or discomfort due to external causes (e.g., telephone calls, noise, heat, cold...).

All meetings should be well prepared, including a clear definition of goals to be reached. It is advisable to consider the issues that might arise during the meeting and prepare in advance to deal with them. It is recommended that the agenda be adhered to. The participants should not stray from the problem at hand, or talk for the sake of talking, giving no suggestions, proposals or arguments. The presiding style must be appropriate to the goal. If the purpose of the meeting is to exchange ideas and insights, the participants should be encouraged to share their points of view. If the aim is to brainstorm, any criticism or comment should be set aside in order not to limit the free flow of creative ideas. It is necessary to ensure participant equality during the meeting. Any who tend to monopolize the discussion or prevent others from sharing their views should be kept under control.

A good meeting must be concluded with action-oriented proposals. Nothing is more frustrating than a feeling of wasted time, or a conclusion that the discussion has no follow up. It is advisable to distribute well documented and KISS-based[1] minutes immediately after the meeting is adjourned. It may serve as a reminder of what was discussed but also as a list of conclusions, providing the meeting with sense, meaning and clear follow up.

Efficient meetings are very important tools in the hands of a good leader. Next to all the above mentioned, their goal is to build mutual trust and serve as a permanent team-harmony device.

A popular fable by ancient Greek author Aesop speaks of human vices and shortcomings. We carry the vices of others in a bag on our chest, so that we clearly and instantly see them. However, our own vices and shortcomings are carried in a bag behind our shoulders, and we don't see them at all. A leader must be aware of that. After making a proposal, he should allow the participants to openly question, criticize, and comment on whatever he said. In his search for harmony, the leader must learn to look at his own proposals and ideas as if he had an eye on his back in order to see what is wrong with them.

If the goal of a meeting is to introduce change, a leader must be very persuasive. Typically, routine approaches and traditional solutions get an easy pass in meetings. On the other hand, innovative ideas are almost always greeted with hostility. Managing change is a long-term process; the path is difficult, full of frustrations, disappointments and doubts. In order to succeed, the Mobilizer is supposed to run many meetings and use them to create a critical mass of supporters, enlightened with common trust, sense of direction, encouragement and motivation.

In one of my favorite films, "Dances with Wolves," every meeting run by the Indian chief, ends with his sentence: *That is all I am going to say about it, but we shall discuss it again.* In a harmonious culture of the American Indians a chief is not supposed to impose his will upon the people, but to listen respectfully to all and to summarize the discussion. The tribal culture was based on the idea that heading a meeting requires humility, ability to listen, and good oratory skills. Good oratory was expected to bring people together, not to separate, segregate, or alienate them. Leaders should choose their words carefully, as if they were living things that will continue to have an impact long after they are spoken. The focus of a good meeting should never be put on the leader, his ego, fame or personal goals, but on the common good and mutual trust.

Mutual trust is one of the key ingredients of good leadership, and successful meetings are very powerful trust builders. You could probably make a single deal without trusting your partner; however, any long-term

---

1 KISS – Keep It Simple and Short

cooperation becomes virtually impossible without emotional attachment. Remember Donald Trump and his TV show "Apprentice"[1]? Whenever he had to fire a candidate, Mr. Trump would sarcastically smile and say: *Nothing personal, it's just business!* As far as I am concerned, it's not really true. Today's business is completely and utterly personal, from the CRM (Customer-Relationship Management) software to the way meetings are run. If you don't trust the other side, there is no business, regardless of the amount of rationality involved. The world is personal, and all successful human relationships are based on interpersonal harmony! In other words, we choose the people we want to work with using our heart more than our mind.

Looking back, I am pretty sure that, in his TV show, Mr. Trump always fired the character who annoyed him most or who, for some reason, got on his nerves. Only afterwards, in justifying his decision, he would try to come up with more or less persuasive arguments and reasons.

4.4.8. Leaders Use Power

According to an old joke, there are four paths leading managers to destruction: women, gambling, technology and organization. Women are the most pleasurable, gambling is the quickest, technology the most complicated and organization the most certain.

Though we are surrounded with organizations, be it family, school, company, sport club, and local administration or the army, police and government bureaucracy, it is not easy to define what this term really means. Sociologists, psychologists, organizers and management scientists look at it from different perspectives. One of many definitions describes organization as an assembly of people who attempt to attain common goals through a coordinated effort, relying on organizational power, division of labor and management control. In principle, it is something opposite to anarchy. Namely, in an organization, there are managers, while the Greek origin of the word *anarchy* suggests that it is a state of a system "without managers."

Unlike self-managers and anarchists, our culture is based on a belief that organizations must be managed, and it is commonly agreed that the power to do that rests in the hands of the executives. That power is nothing but an assumed leader's right to steer the system and manage the work of the subordinates. They carry out orders because they accept and respect leadership authority. If they didn't, there would be no organization!

Organizational power is closely related to control. Leaders are responsible for goal attainment; they lead the subordinates in such a way as to ensure their coordinated effort. The need to control is reflected in the organizational structure, which means that the power and authority are

---

1 http://en.wikipedia.org/wiki/The_Apprentice_(U.S._TV_series)

distributed throughout the hierarchy. For example, a plant manager cannot watch every worker; he must delegate that job to line managers who keep an eye on the foremen, who, in turn, supervise the assembly line workers.

The concepts of power and control are very powerful. We strongly believe that leaders are necessary, without them, organizations would cease to exist, no job would be done efficiently, and no goal would ever be accomplished. If, one day, people decide they no longer need leaders, the world of organizations would still be there, but the organizational power would be administered in a different way.

Anyway, leaders must understand the concept of organizational power and learn how to use it effectively. The Ancient Greek philosopher Plato claimed that power has to do with intellect. The state must be managed by the most intelligent individuals; those with lower mental capabilities should be administrators, and those below them are fit to be soldiers. Plato's ideas, two millennia old, are still present in business and politics. Whenever we choose the most educated people for management positions, or apply ability tests to select candidates to for management school, or whenever we require certain professional qualifications and diplomas, we, in fact, accept the power distribution based on (formally approved) intellectual abilities.

There are three basic sources of organizational authority. They provide a leader with power to act in a chosen way and to manage his subordinates. These are: (1) tradition or status, verified through the behavior in the past; (2) laws, as a normative framework, ascribing power and authority, and (3) charisma or personality. Any organizational power is based on these sources of authority. It comes from tradition (power of priests, medicine-men, chiefs), from formal functions and legal positions (power of directors, ministers, generals, police officers); and from individuality and personal charm (power of prophets, charismatic leaders and wise men).

The task of a boss is to understand and control the complicated spectra of power that exist in every system. The creation of new sources of power or redistribution of the existing power is based on a (mis)balance between cooperation and competition among people and groups.

There are three forms of organizational power: (1) enforced power in hands of those who hold the "stick"; (2) power of interest held by those who control the "carrot"; and (3) moral power derived from the sense of duty, loyalty, and patriotism.

Nothing motivates like power. Therefore, the Motivator should master all shapes and forms of power and authority. The most efficient power source is the ability to reward and stimulate the subordinates, to help them satisfy their needs and interest. In case rewards don't work, the leaders use punishment or sanctions.

Organizational power has to do with position or function. One of its tools is called communication control or the *information monopoly*. A leader is like a gatekeeper who decides to whom a communication door is open and to whom it remains closed. In large hierarchies, the information monopoly has a huge impact on the overall distribution of power. It is not an exclusive leader's privilege. Secretaries who decide who can and who cannot communicate with a CEO, or chiefs of staff who decide who will get an appointment with a politician and who will not, are good examples of such "gate keepers."

Formal organizational arrangements, policy determination, strategy and decision making are usually determined by *power elites* which exist in every system. They take various forms, and have different names such as management boards, teams, and lobbies of interest, political parties, societies, associations, or informal organization. The elites always try to control resources, management roles and rewards. The actual distribution of power and authority in a large organization depends heavily on informal groups. They continuously compete, trying to promote their members and protect their interests; they also engage in lobbying, and constantly fight to defend their turf.

A true pluralism, an equal and fair distribution of power, does not exist. Not even in so called free societies with "democratic" power control. Instead, there are various forms of *poliarchy*. It's a name for the mighty elites that constantly compete for influence and power. Even within a seemingly democratic institution (i.e., management board, parliament, work group, project team,) all members are not equal. There are always some who are "more equal" than others. The distribution of authority is a result of the balance of power among groups, clans, political parties and similar organizations, based on common interest. A person who belongs to a superior group (e.g., the ruling political party or a business club) can count on a larger piece of the pie in terms of governance and power. An outsider has as much chance of enjoying power as a snowflake in hell.

Any business or government policy is dependent on the balance of power based on competition between groups whose interests and goals are in conflict. A leader must know that every time he makes a move, his decision and action have an effect on the balance of power. So, before making any important decision, it is good to evaluate its impact on the interests and goals of various groups. The best places to test the actual distribution of power are meetings dedicated to formulating (business or government) politics, or discussions concerning long-term plans and strategies.

Instead of fighting against individual and collective interests, harmonious leaders try to make them work for the common interest. There are many paradigmatic examples from Google to ABB group, from Kyocera to my home town agricultural cooperative named Progress. Here is just one. As the CEO of General Motors, Alfred Sloan[1] decided to change the way the automobile giant was organized, providing the small units with complete autonomy. He gave them freedom to use their capabilities and talents as they please. All the units were kept together by a powerful central team, which provided the company with general direction and leadership. As the head of that team, Sloan used moral authority; his workers and managers trusted him and respected him.

Concerning organizational power Sun Tzu advises us: "A good leader gives orders kindly, respecting people; he tries to unite his team with integrity and strictness. He may win if his goodness and strictness are fair and just." The Taoist way of facing competition is based on the following concept: "Those who manage well need not be armed, those who are well armed need not dig trenches in the battlefield, those who dig good trenches on the battlefield will not have to fight, those who fight well will not lose, and those who lose honorably will be spared."

These ideas are not far from contemporary concepts of a strong national economy, strong military, good business infrastructure, and well organized public administration as the best protective shields against the enemy. Internal harmony saves you from external threats. At the same time, uneven distribution of power and wealth around the globe is commonly perceived as injustice and eventually leads to terrorism, nationalism, separatism, a bloody redistribution of power and global catastrophe. In this sense, internal disharmony is a long-term problem, making the future of the system uncertain.

Our world is characterized by an unstable and a unbalanced value system, and it is more and more difficult to tell right from wrong. Modern leaders, working on self-development as well as trying to help their teams develop, are facing a spiritual challenge of the highest level. It makes them similar to the believers throughout the world. There are numerous gospels, prophecies, churches, and religious books, making it difficult to choose the true one. There are many theories, gurus, schools of thought and managerial bibles, and they teach modern leaders how to run organizations, countries, and people's lives. Despite the variety of approaches, there are no sure recipes how to use and control the sources of organizational power. This is why the best advice for a leader says: *First empower yourself, and only then put confidence in various sources of organizational power!* Fair and even power distribution serve as the best long-term protector of organizational harmony, success and stability.

---

1 http://www.economist.com/node/13047099

4.4.9. Leaders Love Ideas

The world of innovative leadership is the world of a million ideas. It rests on two things: huge amounts of money, and nice examples of creativity. As Nordstrom and Ridderstralle[1] point out, we should enjoy capitalism, because it *dances with the brainware*. We all know that ideas can save millions. Here are two examples.

While working on Wall Street, Jeff Bezos[2] studied the trends of the emerging internet economy. Being sure that he got the big picture, he went to Seattle to establish Amazon.com. Their marketing campaign of the century included the novelist John Updike, who wrote the first part of his story titled "Murder Keeps the Magazine Alive" and presented it on the Amazon web site. Readers were invited to continue the story by electronic mail. Every morning the best proposals were awarded a thousand dollars and added to the novel. Each day, eight thousand people would send their contributions, hoping to get the award and co-author with the famous Updike, because the book was planned to be published upon completion. The process of making the novel over the Internet had attracted media attention and intrigued the American public, increasing the web traffic. It was one of the best and the cheapest marketing campaigns ever.

Microsoft, the software giant globally known for the Windows operating system as well as for long litigation concerning its monopolistic behavior, has always used provocation and sensation as the means of advertising. For example, the company patented the binary codes 0 and 1, claiming intellectual ownership over anything coded in binary numbers. From then on, every author of a piece of software written in machine language would have to pay Microsoft a commission.

How do we manage creativity, innovation and production of ideas? There are two rules a leader of an innovative team must obey: (1) eliminate barriers to creativity; and (2) create a creativity-supportive environment.

Innovation is an outcome of ingenuity, a result of a creative process, based on individual and collective talent. Once an idea is born, it takes a lot of hard and responsible work of many people to turn it into reality. As German philosopher Arthur Schopenhauer pointed out, *between an idea and its application, there is an abyss which only a few ideas successfully cross.*

What is the mentioned abyss made of? What are the major barriers to innovation? Research focuses on the key enemies of creativity as follows: negativism, fear of mistakes, bureaucracy, limited resources and specialization.

It is in human nature to reject other people's ideas, to play devil's advocate

---

1 http://www.funkybusinessforever.com/
2 http://en.wikipedia.org/wiki/Jeff_Bezos

and to oppose to the proposals of others even before finding out what they're all about. The tendency is called *negativism*; it is often completely irrational, although at times it feeds on rational arguments. Typically, people resist change, in case their interests and status might be affected. An innovation could sometimes hurt somebody's feelings, cause a shift in power or threaten personal security. Changes are perceived as new responsibilities or new habits; therefore, it's always easier to say NO! It is much simpler to organize opponents than unite fighters for a new idea.

Innovation means uncertainty, most people fear and resist the unknown due to perceived risk and a prospect of possible failure. An American proverb points out that the devil you know is better than the devil you don't know.

A specific form of negativism is a desire to be prioritized. Other people's ideas are perceived as threats to one's own reputation, self-respect and personal integrity. However, we are ready to strongly support a borrowed idea, the one we would otherwise reject, if we are granted the honor of inventing it first.

The *fear of making mistakes* is another psychological fact of life. We have a strong need to be always right. In order to satisfy that need, we try to avoid mistakes. Because we hate to look stupid in front of other people, we always do our best to escape blame or responsibility. Mistake-avoiding mentality forces us to play safe and keep us out of trouble and uncertainty. On the other hand, creativity means risk-taking. It is based on trial and error; in most cases it takes many attempts and failures to succeed. No wonder innovative behavior is easily blocked by fear of punishment.

Innovation is always a kind of adventure. Therefore, in an innovative environment, a mistake is the key method of learning and creation. The right to make a creative failure is a catalyst for innovation. If a corporate culture defines errors and requests for help as weaknesses and faults, the employees engage in covering up their weaknesses and the team soon stops learning. A mistake made in an attempt to improve and advance should be rewarded, and any scapegoating should be replaced by analysis of the lessons learned.

If it isn't broken, don't fix it—that's a typical bureaucratic excuse for inaction. Bureaucracies are strong enemies of change, innovation, flexibility and disorder. Every creative individual perceives the rules and regulations as hurdles on the athletic trail. They are an additional challenge to deal with, but, at the same time, they slow you down and have a negative impact on your results.

Major *bureaucratic hurdles* include too much routine work, procedures with too many steps and an overall abundance of paperwork. Anti-innovative organizations are dedicated to very detailed planning and precise definition of all tasks. It's a mindset based on the assumption that today's realities should continue tomorrow in a tidy, linear and predictable fashion. In this sort of culture, people struggle with stacks of paper and bunches of procedures, and give up on inventing new ideas. Getting stuck with too much routine work doesn't allow you to stop and reflect upon what you do. It reminds me of a Croatian joke: a woodsman is cutting a log with a dull chainsaw and moans with the effort. A fellow worker brings him sharpener to help him fix the chainsaw. *I don't have the time*, says the woodman, *you see, it's going to take me all day to saw this darn tree.*

Usually, the best known barrier to innovation is called *insufficient resources*. For most people, money is the key to every door. If we had the right financial support, they say, we would be able to create miracles; however, without money we cannot be creative. I have already pointed out that the lack of funds is often just an excuse. There is enough capital available, but there are never enough smart people and profitable projects. Any brilliant idea should sooner or later meet its sponsor. The true limits of creativity are more often found in a lack of knowledge, skills, talent and time.

Narrow specialization is the last but not least on the list of barriers to innovation. A well-known German aphorism tells us that the only thing worse than a *fach-idiot*[1] is an idiot without a *fach* (trade). We live in a world of fach-idiots; as managers are fascinated by narrow specialization, more people are educated and trained to do a specific narrow task. By tradition, most companies seek, and the educational system provides, experts whose unidimensional background allow them to know "everything about nothing." Focused on a very narrow professional area, they lose ability to grasp what their coworkers do. Fach-idiots can hardly work in multidisciplinary teams with creative assignments. Typically, innovation comes from a team of people with various backgrounds, each contributing a little to the array of complementary skills. It's complementarity that counts, not similarity! The breadth of thinking brings more innovation than the depth!

If a leader wants his team to quickly agree, communicate and integrate, he should choose the members according to similarity; for example, a team of five individuals of the same gender, similar age, educated at the same school, and coming from the same department. They are most likely to do their job without conflicts, and with little struggle. However, none of them can learn much from the others because they are so similar. They reach agreements with no discussion; they lack self-criticism and are quickly self-satisfied, As a result, the outcome of their work is non-innovative and sub optimal. In monodisciplinary teams it is easy to reach agreement and even easier to make a mistake.

If a leader decides to choose the team members by complementarity,

---

1 Fach-idiot is a very narrowly specialized professional

i.e., people of different gender, age, education, and experience, it should take some time for them to find a common language. However, it provides them with an opportunity to learn from each other. Complementary means that everyone brings to the team something that others don't have. A group like this could reach consensus slowly, with a lot of difficulty, but they are creative and able to avoid mistakes. Multidisciplinary teams are slow, but their product is of high quality. Complementarity provides challenge, discussion and exchange of arguments; it opens the organizational space for creativity and innovation.

Old military wisdom tells us that the commander in the field is always right, and the rear echelon is wrong, unless proven otherwise. We must believe those who create results rather than those who write reports. Big central offices are often nothing but a huge bureaucracy, designed to prevent the true performers from communicating, cooperating and interacting. Based on that, Percy Barnevik of Asea Brown Boveri and Richard Branson of Virgin have kept their corporate staffs to a bare-bone minimum. In case of the ABB Group, it was less than 100 central corporate staffers for a global $30 billion-plus company. Let's cut out the middlemen. Within every hierarchy a leader must trust those from the bottom most, because they are deeply rooted in reality.

Along with other effects, the flat hierarchy increases the speed of reaction. The major problem in a large organization is the slow response. The time it takes for a signal from the top to reach the person at the bottom is enormous, not to mention the noise in the communication channel. Even the best ideas lose their value if not quickly implemented.

It is true that ideas change the world; hence, the most valuable resource of any organization is its people who are ready to innovate, initiate change, and make it happen. At the same time, they are the major builders of the long-term organizational harmony.

4.4.10. Leaders Are only Mortals

Many leaders believe to be most useful in a peaceful setting of their office. The higher they climb the company ladder, the less they wander around production facilities, the less time they spend with their workers, consumers and clients.

No wonder many of them lose touch with reality—they forget the warehouse smell after delivery, or the sparkle of sweat on the foreheads of the workers unloading trucks. They are no longer aware of what it looks like to get elbowed during the morning rush at the factory gate. They cannot recall the sweetness of a lunch break extended for an additional five minutes. Browsing through complicated reports, considering difficult problems and large investments, they easily forget that working life is composed of a number of small things and events happening to common people under their supervision, whose energy, enthusiasm, willpower and dedication are, in the end, responsible for the success of the guy at the top. Protected by thickly carpeted doors, long doorways with flowers and stubs, smiling secretaries, big agendas and appointment schedules, they become unreachable and distant, like the gods of the Mount Olympus.

During the triumphal marches organized to celebrate great victories, each emperor of ancient Rome had a servant whispering to his ear: *You are mortal, don't you ever forget that!*

Successful leaders should never lose touch with reality. There are various ways to make them learn that message. In Japanese companies, the people who reach the top are always well acquainted with the whole system. While very young, they began their career at the bottom and worked their way up, moving from one department to the next. As CEOs, they know their people, and they are familiar with all the processes and operations. It enables them to communicate with various levels of the system and grasp the problems that could never be seen from the heights of the headquarter office.

Such practice is described by Tom Peters as *management by wandering around*. From time to time, leaders should pay a visit to front offices, assembly lines, the market, and the customers; they should talk and listen, collect information and socialize with common folk. It is the best way to find out how various departments really work and how the customers perceive the quality of a company's products and services.

Any leader should know that the day when teammates stop seeing him regularly is the day he has stopped leading them. It can easily happen to any boss who isolates himself from his team, who builds too many barriers to upward communication, or a leader who creates the impression that seeking help is a sign of weakness.

Good leaders should not be difficult to reach; they must be available and ready to step in. They should always go where the action is and where the problems are. Jeff Bezos used to personally deliver products to customers or attend meetings unannounced, just to see what was going on.

During my four-year experience in government and one year as president of the Zagreb City Assembly, I have often managed by wandering around. Instead of staying in my office, distributing tasks and giving orders to my subordinates, I would walk through the office building and pop up at someone's door, almost like a client. Seeing me at their office doors, they would be immensely surprised. Presidents and ministers are expected to act differently. If I needed someone, I was supposed to call them through my secretary or chief of staff. I was expected to receive them in my huge office, sitting in the deep leather chair, in front of a large painting that covers half the wall, behind a stylish table made of rich wood, suggesting who the big boss is and who is there just to listen and obey. All my subordinates would prepare for such appointments, pull their best masks over their faces and learn by heart what they wanted to say. By no means would they allow themselves to be caught by surprise or show confusion. This is why I could not learn what they were really thinking, but rather what they thought I would like to hear.

However, if I just showed up, courteously knocking on the door, they would be totally unprepared for such a conversation. Their eyes would be wide open with an unspoken question: Why is the boss here? He needs something special and there must be some emergency! *I don't need anything special*, I would say, *I just wanted to see how you're doing. Is everything OK? Are there any problems, private or business matters that we haven't had time to discuss?*

Without any prepared answer, surprised by my interest, they would have no time for a masquerade. Instead, they would honestly say what was on their mind. If their concern was business related, I would try to deal with it at my first convenience. If they mentioned a private issue, I would write it down (because paper preserves while the mind forgets). The very next time I saw them, I would ask them about their parents' health, or about their only son's car accident, or anything else they had confessed to me when I came by.

During one of the walking-around visits, I found an advisor sleeping, his head resting on the desk. For a moment I wondered what to do, and then remembered an anecdote about Napoleon. One cloudy evening, the Emperor was making the rounds among the night guards at the front. Suddenly, he found an old soldier fast asleep in the guardhouse. He stood by his side for a while. In a few moments the guard woke up, only to see the face of the Commander-in-chief staring at him in concern. Scared out of his wits, he had just one thought in his mind: *I blew it, there goes my head!* However, Napoleon just gave him a kind look, patted him on the shoulder, and said: *This spot is very important. If the enemy breaks through, we are all dead. So I kept watch while you were sleeping. Now that you're awake, take over, I am moving on.*

From that day on, the old soldier was his boss's greatest admirer. He was spending his time walking around and praising the Emperor, wholeheartedly explaining to all who were willing to listen, that Napoleon was the greatest of all leaders. Also, from that day on, he declared that his life belonged to Napoleon and he would gladly die for him any moment. And, of course, he promised he would never again fall asleep on duty.

Most people righteously state that the Emperor's behavior was nothing but demagogy. I agree, in the positive sense of demagogy, the ability to move, mobilize and guide people. Therefore, every leader must develop his demagogic talent. Managing by wandering around sometimes requires from us to act and pretend, but we must do it in a natural and persuasive manner. Of course, if we truly cared about the system and the people we're in charge of, it would be a tremendous help. Good leaders do care! It's probably the most important of many facets of their inner and outer harmony.

After all, the ancient Romans were right; being a leader is far from being a god. Leaders must always keep in mind that immortality can only be reached by being a very good mortal.

Conclusion

As you see, we have reached the end and still haven't clearly answered the question how to avoid the global catastrophe. However, we have discussed the wisdom of harmonious leadership spread over 52 chapters. My approach was indirect. I tried to put things in their places, and hope they will put us all in our place.

Seth Godin wrote a book, *All Marketers Are Liars.*[1] When asked why the title is so drastic— after all, he is one of the people he calls liars—he laconically replied: *Mostly because no one would buy a book titled "All Marketers Are Storytellers."* To a certain degree my book mimics Godin's approach to titles. Maybe we cannot solve all the world's problems, but we can learn how to become better leaders and bring a touch of harmony into the world. In principle, I wanted to offer you an applicable, readable, enlightening and witty leadership model to help you manage yourself and your team in times of crisis. Even though it eclectically draws from many sources, approaches, ideas and experiences, it is my original look at the challenges of modern leadership, and it reflects my obsession with harmony.

The book is dedicated to managers, politicians, scientists, entrepreneurs, artists, students, and other change agents. The writing style stems from my desire to make the text easy to read at bedtime. I have tried to write it the way I would love to read it. If you like it, you can bet that our tastes don't differ much. As a methodology I have used mental models. Namely, I tried to break the complex concept of leadership into small chunks, integrated only by the overall harmony-based leadership idea. Otherwise, the chunks are just the food for thought, each chapter representing a small meal, or a snack. You were supposed to take them, plate by plate, according to your hunger and eating habits.

I wanted to write a book that is simple, blunt, humorous, wise and above all useful. I hope the text succeeds in revealing the key leadership truths, helping you become a more harmonious person and a more successful leader. Most of the ideas presented are clear, straightforward and simple. Just as

1 http://sethgodin.typepad.com/all_marketers_are_liars/

the sparks of Zen wisdom, or biblical lessons, the book has adopted an aphoristic common sense approach to leadership and life. Being brought up to think and act based on academic knowledge, we are often deprived of such views. To some people, I hope, the book occasionally provided a feeling of valuable discovery. I also hope that the meanderings of this text, illustrated by numerous anecdotes, stories, theories and experiences, did not mislead or hamper the reader in seeing the simplicity of the forest for too many trees.

Becoming a better leader means, as we already pointed out, to constantly search for a balance of the four H's — Hope, Head, Heart and Hand. They are integrated by the fifth H — Harmony. Our life is nothing else but a long and winding road taking us back and forth from what we hope for, to what we think, from what we feel to what we do. If all that is in tune, we deserve to be called harmony-based leaders.

Victor Hugo used to say that nothing is stronger than the idea whose time has come. Hopefully it applies to some concepts from this book. Its secret agenda is to serve as a tool to build a critical mass of harmonious leaders. Living in a world burdened with so many problems and issues, we need quite different men and women to change the status quo and lead us into a better future. Otherwise, we are not going to avoid the global catastrophe.

Wouldn't it be such a shame to live in the most knowledgeable and the best-informed society ever, and still, collectively, die of ignorance?

Bibliography

Albert M., "Parecon: Life After Capitalism," Verso, 2003.

Bennis W., "Becoming a Leader of Leaders," Macmillan, London, 1999.

Bennis W. (Editor), "The Future of Leadership," McGraw-Hill, 2003.

Blanchard K., "Leadership and a One Minute Manager: Increasing Effectiveness through Situational Leadership," Harper Collins, 2009.

Blanchard K., Peale N.V, "The Power of Ethical Management," Harper Collins, 2001.

Bloch A., "Murphy's Law," Penguin, 2003.

Bolman L. G., "Leading with Soul," University of Chicago Press, 2003.

Brandt R.L., "One Click: Jeff Bezos and the Rise of Amazon.com," Portfolio Trade, 2012.

Buckingham M, Clifton D., "Now, discover your strengths," The Free Press, New York, 2001.

Buckingham M., Coffman C., "First, break all the rules," Simon and Schuster, New York, 1999.

Burns J. M., "Leadership," Harper Collins, New York, 2004.

Buzan T., Keene R., "Buzan's Book of Genius," Stanley Paul, London, 1994.

Carper J., "Your Miracle Brain," Harper-Collins, New York, 2000.

Carson C. editor, "The Autobiography of Martin Luther King, Jr.," 1998.

Churchman C. W., "The Systems Approach," Delacorte Press, New York, 1968.

Covey S. R., "Seven Habits of Highly Effective People," Free Press, 2004.

Day L., "Practical Intuition," Broadway Books, 1997.

Dell M., "Strategies that Revolutionized an Industry," Harper-Collins, New York, 2000.

Denning S., "Become a Better Leader through Storytelling," McGraw-Hill, New York, 2002.

Deutschman A., "Change or Die: The Three Keys to Change at Work and in Life," Harper Business, 2007.

Drucker P., "Management Challenges for the 21. Century," Harper-Collins, New York, 1999.

Edvinson L., Malone M., "Intellectual Capital," Harper Business, New York, 1997.

Fairholm G. W., "Organizational Power Politics: Tactics in Organizational Leadership," Praeger, 2009.

Ferguson, N., "The Ascent of Money: A Financial History of the World," Penguin Press, 2008.

Galbraith J. K., "The New Industrial State," 1967.

George B., "Authentic Leadership," McGraw-Hill, New York, 2001.

Gibbs, A. M., "Bernard Shaw: A Life," Gainesville, Florida: University Press of Florida, 2005.

The Global Competitiveness Report, World Economic Forum, Davos, 2013.

Goleman D. et al., "Primal Leadership: Realizing the Power of Emotional Intelligence," Harvard Business School Press, 2002.

Gray J., "Men Are from Mars, Women Are from Venus," Harper Paperbacks, 2012.

Hammer M., Champy J., "Re-engineering the Corporation: A Manifesto for Business Revolution," HarperBusiness, 2006.

Handy C., "The Search for Meaning: Leader to Leader," Drucker Foundations, San Francisco, 1999.

Harari O., "The Leadership Secrets of Colin Powell," McGraw-Hill, 2003.

Hawley J., "Reawakening the Spirit in Work: The Power of Dharmic

Management," Berrett Coehler Publishers, 1993.

Hesse H., "Siddhartha," New Directions, 1955.

Hughes, E. J., "Proust, Class, and Nation," Oxford University Press, 2011.

Humes J., "The Wit and Wisdom of Winston Churchill," Harper Collins, 2004.

Ilf I., Petrov E., "The Twelve Chairs," Northwestern University Press, 1997.

Imai M., "Kaizen: The Key to Japan's Competitive Success," McGraw Hill, 1986.

Isaacsson W., "Steve Jobs: The Exclusive Biography," Little Brown, 2011.

Keynes J. M., "A Treatise on Money," Hartcourt, Brace, New York, 1930.

Khalsa M., "Let's get Real or let's not Play: The Demise of 20th Century Selling & the Advent of Helping Clients Succeed," Franklin Covey, 1999.

Kouzes J. M., Posner B. Z., "Credibility: How Leaders Gain and Lose It, Why People Demand It," Jossey-Bass, 2004.

Kouzes J. M., Posner B. Z., "The Leadership Challenge," Jossey-Bass, 2003.

Maxwell J., "The 21 Irrefutable Laws of Leadership: Follow Them and People Will Follow You," Thomas Neslon Publishers, 2007.

Mehring, F., "Karl Marx: The Story of His Life," Routledge, 2003.

Mintzberg H. et al., "Strategy Safari," The Free Press, New York, 1998.

Morita A., "Made in Japan," Dutton, New York, 1988.

Moxley R. S., "Leadership and Spirit," Jossey-Bass, 1999.

Naisbitt J. et al., "High Tech High Touch," Bantam Books, New York, 2001.

Nordstrom K., Ridderstrale J., "Funky Business Forever: How to enjoy capitalism," Pearson Education Canada, 2007.

Orwell, G., "Nineteen Eighty-Four," Secker and Warburg, London, 1949.

Pearce C. L., Conger J. A., "Shared Leadership: Reframing the Hows and Whys of Leadership," Dutton, New York, 2002.

Peter L. J., Hull R., "The Peter Principle: Why Things Always Go Wrong," HarperBusiness, 2011.

Peters T., "The Pursuit of Wow," Vintage Books, New York, 1995.

Peters T., "The Tom Peters Seminar: Crazy Times Call for Crazy

Organizations," Vintage Books, New York, 1994.

Peters T. "Talent," Tom Peters Essentials, Dorling Kindersley, 2005.

Peters T. "Leadership," Tom Peters Essentials, Dorling Kindersley, 2005.

Redstone S., Knobler P., "A Passion to Win," Simon and Schuster, New York, 2001.

Reich R., "The Future of Success," Knopf, New York, 2001.

Rodrik, D., "The Globalization Paradox," Norton & Company, Inc., 2011.

Saint-Exupéry A., "The Little Prince," Reynal & Hitchcock, 1943.

Schopenhauer A., "The World as Will and Representation," Dover Publishing Inc., 1969.

Senge P., "The Practice of Innovation," Drucker Foundations, San Francisco, 1999.

Sharma R., "The Monk Who Sold His Ferrari",Harper, San Francisco, 1999.

Sloan A., "My Years with General Motors," Crown Business, 1990.

Smith A., "The Wealth of Nations," Strachan & Cadell, London, 1776.

Srića V. "Social Intelligence and Project Leadership," the Global Management and IT Research Conference, New York, 2008.

Srića V. "A Few Comments on the Role of Social Intelligence and Leadership in Project Management," PMI Research Conference, Warsaw, 2008.

Steinbeck J., "America and Americans," Heineman, 1966.

Sun Tzu, "The Art of War ," Special Edition. El Paso Norte Press, 2005.

Thurow L., "Changing the Nature of Capitalism — Rethinking the Future," Nicolas Brealey, London, 1997.

Twain M., "The £ 1,000,000 bank note," Langenscheidt ELT, 1893.

Welch J., Byrhe J., "Straight from the Gut," Business Plus, 2003.

Welch J., Welch S., "Winning," Harper Business, 2005.

Wilde O., "The Picture of Dorian Gray," Ward, Lock & Co., London, 1891.

ABOUT THE AUTHOR

Velimir Srića BBA, MS, MBA, PhD is professor of management, University of Zagreb, former visiting professor at UCLA in Los Angeles and Renmin University in Beijing. He was a guest professor in Hungary, Slovenia, Bosnia Herzegovina, Dubai and Austria. As a Fulbright student, he earned MBA from Columbia University, New York, along with the best management science student award. He was CEO of Croatian Institute for Informatics, Minister of Science and a member of the Government of Croatia. Also, he was elected President of Zagreb City Assembly. As a scientist and politician, he met many leaders in Europe, Asia and the US, from Gerald Ford and George Bush sr. to Donald Rumsfeld, Sulejman Demirel, Recep Erdogan and Henry Kissinger. He was engaged in politics, first as an independent candidate, and later as the head of the Liberals in the Croatian capital. His independent list managed to win ten percent of the seats in the city council, and his party list made the best score the liberal option ever had in the capital. As a World Bank consultant, he helped a few regional high-science institutions transform into the seeds for startups. As a politician, he initiated and headed scientific and technological cooperation within Alps-Adriatic region. As a convinced cosmopolitan, he was a member of the Croatian Helsinki Committee for human rights, The Club of Rome, and The World Academy of Art and Science. As a consultant, he witnessed the birth and growth of many successful regional companies, including Coca Cola, Dukat, Fina, Gorenje, KD Group and Krka. He hosted Jack Welch, Tom Peters, Jonas Ridderstråle and Kjell Nordström on their tours of Croatia, and personally met Michael Porter, Garry Hamel and C. K. Prahalad. He is a coauthor of the International Encyclopedia of Business and Management, he earned Eisenhower fellowship, Golden Pen Award from Croatian Journalist Society and Strossmayer Award for Science. He was heading the project "Croatia — Regional Knowledge Society Leader" initiated by Croatian President and has found a place in "Who is Who in the World," "Who is Who in Finance and Industry," and "Living Legends" from the World Biographical Institute in Cambridge. He is the author of 64 books and more than 500 articles in scientific and popular magazines. Other publications include a collection of poetry (Various games), strategic monograph "Croatia 2020," a collection of political essays (From Crisis to Vision), picture book (The Small Globe's Big Journey) and a novel (Private investigations). Velimir is married to Ana, father to a daughter Lana and three sons Dario, Davor, and Luka.